ROAD BIKING ™

Michigan

Help Us Keep This Guide Up to Date

Every effort has been made by the author and editors to make this guide as accurate and useful as possible. However, many things can change after a guide is published—roads are closed, regulations change, techniques evolve, facilities come under new management, etc.

We would love to hear from you concerning your experiences with this guide and how you feel it could be improved and kept up to date. While we may not be able to respond to all comments and suggestions, we'll take them to heart and we'll also make certain to share them with the author. Please send your comments and suggestions to the following address:

The Globe Pequot Press
Reader Response/Editorial Department
P.O. Box 480
Guilford, CT 06437

Or you may e-mail us at:

editorial@GlobePequot.com

Thanks for your input, and happy travels!

A **FALCON** GUIDE®

Road Biking™ Series

ROAD BIKING™
Michigan

Cari Noga

GUILFORD, CONNECTICUT
HELENA, MONTANA
AN IMPRINT OF THE GLOBE PEQUOT PRESS

A FALCON GUIDE®

Photos by the author unless otherwise noted
Maps by Trailhead Graphics © Morris Book Publishing, LLC.

ISSN 1550-431X
ISBN 978-0-7627-2803-9

Manufactured in the United States of America
First Edition/Third Printing

To buy books in quantity for corporate use
or incentives, call **(800) 962–0973**
or e-mail **premiums@GlobePequot.com.**

To my dad, who believed I would write a book; to my husband Mike, who was there when I did; and to all who use it to explore and enjoy Michigan's beautiful outdoors.

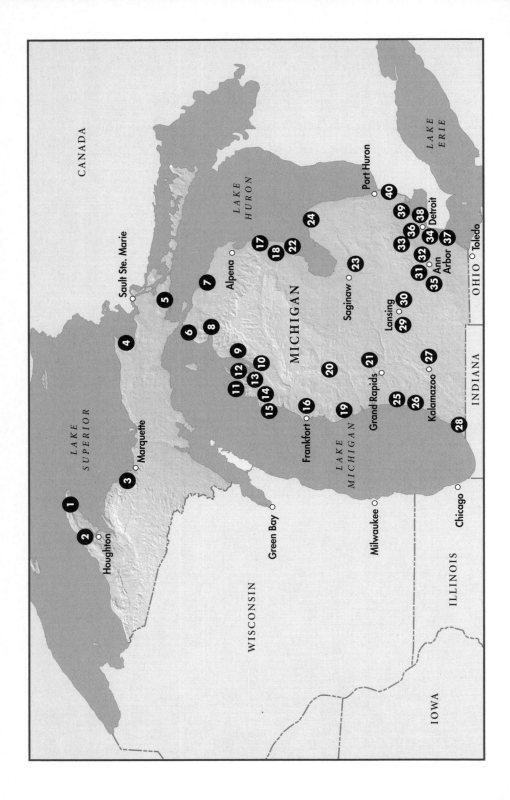

Contents

Preface

Michigan cyclists love their home state and are eager to share it. The willingness of dozens of Michigan cyclists to share their favorite ride recommendations was key to making this book a guide to truly the best of all that the Great Lakes State offers those who travel on two wheels.

In selecting the forty rides for this book, I relied on my five years as a tour leader for Michigan Bicycle Touring, as well as my membership in the Traverse City–based Cherry Capital Cycling Club. It was on MBT's trips, designed by owners Michael and Libby Robold, that I first pedaled much of the Upper Peninsula (U.P.) and Michigan's west "coast." As a member of the CCCC, which puts out a wonderful map of recommended routes in the bicycling nirvana that is northwest Michigan, I came to know the hills, lakes, and orchard land even better. However, when it came to the east side of the state, especially southeast Michigan, my bicycling experience was limited to the few teenage years I rode my ten-speed around Dearborn before succumbing to the lure of the car.

I began my research into unfamiliar territory with the League of Michigan Bicyclists' listserv. Members responded immediately to my request for ride submissions, sending suggestions, directions, and maps for routes all over the state. As a result, one of the things I'm most proud of is that this book does contain a good selection of rides in southeast Michigan. As a Traverse City resident, I relish my proximity to northern Michigan's beautiful, hilly terrain. But most Michigan residents have to take a weekend to make a trip up north worthwhile. With ten rides to choose from in the metro Detroit/Ann Arbor region, however, you can get in a good ride and still have some of your weekend left over.

Once I'd amassed a number of rides, it was time to pick and choose the best. Safety in terms of traffic and road conditions was a major factor in the choice of all the rides. Most are on two-lane roads, with and without shoulders. Scenery and routes that would take riders to points of interest including towns, historical sites, landmarks, wineries, parks, lakes, and waterfalls was the second factor. Third was the ride's location and what it added to the mix of routes and to the book as a whole. Rides needed to be convenient to where people lived and to represent a range of choices in terms of distance and terrain for various levels of ability.

Whether they know it or not, many people helped in the process and deserve thanks. The list starts with the League of Michigan Bicyclists, especially director Lucinda Means and former board member, friend, and fellow Cherry Capital club member Carol Danly, who turned me on to this project in the first place.

LMB was also invaluable for its bike club contacts and bicycle law information, all conveniently online at its Web site, www.lmb.org.

Special thanks also go to the following people throughout the state:

Southwest Michigan: Former fellow tour leader and friend Nancy Hulka submitted the Kent County, Big Rapids, and White Lake rides as well as photos. Kim Hayward suggested the Kalamazoo County route.

Southeast Michigan: Former Tour de France rider Frankie Andreu, a Dearborn native; Marcy Bauman (Ann Arbor); Fred Dore (Oakland Lakes Challenge); Bill Duemling (St. Clair River Cruise), who also maintains the Michbike listserv; Scott Lonoconus (Grosse Pointe); and James Partridge, a cyclist and attorney who shared his knowledge of Michigan's bicycling laws. The Ann Arbor Bicycle Touring Society, which puts many of its route maps online, also deserves thanks.

Lansing/Thumb area: Lynn Farabaugh, Brenda Cartwright, Carol Danly, and Martha Smith.

Northeast Michigan: Dave Smith, who suggested Ocqueoc Falls; and Rick and Susan Moorman and Denise Bazzett, who provided advance information on roads' pavement and shoulder status.

Northwest/U.P.: Carol Danly, Dennis Custer, and the Cherry Capital Cycling Club.

Finally, thanks again to Michael and Libby Robold, operators of MBT for twenty-five years, who have shared Michigan cycling with so many. My mom, Chris Noga, and my husband, Mike Henderson, provided companionship and a second opinion on several scouting rides. Mike also shot most of the photos. Cherry Capital Cycling Club members Dave Buck, Bruce Bodjack, and Sam Bodjack also provided photos as did Travel Michigan, the state tourism office.

Introduction

Si quaeris peninsulam amoenam, circumspice.

"If you seek a pleasant peninsula, look about you." That's Michigan's state motto, and there's no better vantage point than a bicycle seat.

By definition, a peninsula is surrounded by water on three sides. Literally, then, water is Michigan's defining characteristic. The distinctive mitten shape of the Lower Peninsula is due to the surrounding Great Lakes, and Michigan takes its name from the Indian word *michigame*, meaning "big water." More than 3,200 miles of Michigan shoreline wind along Lakes Superior, Michigan, Huron, and Erie. Alternately bordered by craggy rocks, sandy beaches, sheer cliffs, and dense forests and dotted with cities, Michigan's shoreline stretches longer than the entire eastern seaboard. In fact, it's the longest freshwater shoreline in the world.

Nearly 20 percent of the shoreline is in public ownership, managed by federal, state, or local authorities and open for you to enjoy. Inland, there are more

A tandem cruises along one of Michigan's roadways. Courtesy of Michael O. Henderson

Southwest Michigan has a thriving grape and wine industry. Courtesy of Michael O. Henderson

than 11,000 lakes dotting the state, and thousands of rivers crisscross Michigan. Wherever you're pedaling on Michigan's Upper and Lower Peninsulas, you're never far from water. Half the rides in this book feature Great Lakes shoreline, and only one, the East Lansing Cruise, is without some water view.

The retreating glaciers that carved these lakes thousands of years ago also sculpted hills and valleys, the most dramatic of which are concentrated in northern Michigan. You won't find mountains in Michigan, with their long, grinding, switchback climbs and blow-back-the-helmet descents. But in places you will find abundant hills that feature shorter, steeper, straight climbs and some respectably speedy descents. You'll also find rare freshwater sand dunes, waterfalls, wetlands, bike paths (nine rides use a portion of a bike path), small towns, and large cities.

Michigan offers a variety of terrain for all cycling abilities. Generally speaking, terrain is flatter in the south and east and hillier in the north and west. This is true of both the Lower and the Upper Peninsula. Hence the eastern U.P. is flatter than the west, with the most hills in the northwest (rides 1 and 2 in the Keweenaw Peninsula). Southeast Michigan is flatter than southwest, and northeast Michigan is flatter than northwest, where the state's hilliest terrain—ergo, some of the prettiest scenery—is found. A good rule of thumb, as you examine the statewide map of rides, is that shoreline riding is flat. Depending on your departure point, however, reaching that shoreline often involves a descent or a climb from or back to the inland terrain.

Michigan has four distinct seasons, but the extremes of temperature and snowfall vary considerably from north to south. I once made a New Year's resolution to bike every month and I did it—though the January, February, and March rides were pretty short! In southern Michigan, diehards will be out from April to November. In the U.P., however, a snowy Halloween isn't uncommon, nor is 50 degrees on the Fourth of July. Generally speaking, with a few basic clothing pieces (long tights, full-fingered gloves, a thin headband that fits under a helmet to cover the ears, a fleece vest, and a water-resistant jacket), you can ride fairly comfortably in most of Michigan from mid-May through mid-October. Located at the western edge of the Eastern time zone, Michigan enjoys long summer evenings. With the heat of the day past, evening is a lovely time to ride. Around the summer solstice in the U.P., you'll have daylight until 10:00 P.M.

ROAD AND TRAFFIC CONDITIONS

Within its borders, Michigan can claim both Hell (in Livingston County; see ride 31) and Paradise (in the U.P.; see ride 4). That range is also true when it comes to traffic.

Safety and vehicular traffic volume were major factors in the choice of the rides in this book, which are concentrated as much as possible on two-lane roads and/or roads with shoulders. Still, Michigan is a populous state and urban sprawl is well under way, particularly in southeast Michigan, where the metro Detroit area is growing out to meet Ann Arbor and Ann Arbor and the state capital of Lansing are growing out to meet each other. Hence, people and traffic are almost inescapable in the southern part of the state. Rides located here will all have more traffic. Specifics on traffic and hazards are discussed in each ride description.

Relatively speaking, traffic and congestion lessen as you head north, especially once you cross the Mackinac Bridge into the Upper Peninsula. Though it comprises a quarter of Michigan's land mass, the U.P. has fewer residents ("yoopers," as they're known, in contrast to the "trolls" who live below the bridge) than the metro Grand Rapids area. Northwest Lower Michigan is a very popular tourist destination, however, particularly in the summer and during fall color season from late September to mid-October. Weekend traffic in this region can be relatively heavy. September is an ideal month for cycling up north, as you'll miss the summer tourists and beat the fall color crowd. Temperatures are typically mild, with warmer days and cooler mornings and evenings.

Independent of traffic, Michigan's roads have their own quirks. As they say in many places, Michigan has two seasons: winter and road construction. Major construction doesn't usually happen on the roads used in this book, but seal-coating, a low-cost method of road upkeep, is a common summer event that can make for an unpleasant surprise on a ride. When a road is seal-coated, an emulsion of liquid asphalt and water is spread on the road and topped with a loose coat of crushed stone. Then it's left for vehicular traffic to work in and smooth out. You can imagine what it's like on a bike. Unpaved shoulders are usually sandy, especially in northern Michigan. If you go off the road, be prepared to come to an abrupt stop. Michigan also has a maneuver called a "Michigan left." More common at busy intersections in the south than in the north, it requires drivers (and thus cyclists) who want to turn left to instead turn right, move immediately into a left-turn lane, and execute what amounts to a U-turn, putting them back in the desired direction.

EQUIPMENT

Essential equipment for the rides in this book starts with a road bike purchased at a bike shop, not at a discount store, and a helmet. You can ride a hybrid, mountain, or recumbent bike, of course, but you'll ride most efficiently on a lighter bicycle with smooth, narrow tires, no more than 1¼ inch. Two frame-mounted water bottle cages and/or a Camelbak hydration system are another must, as is an under-the-seat tool pack with the essentials for fixing a flat and making other minor repairs or adjustments, like brakes. Be sure to squeeze a spare tube in there in addition to the patch kit, and a small snack for emergency energy. Fig Newton cookies are a cycling classic. Review the individual ride descriptions for details on restaurants and stores where you can purchase food. Most rides have at least one major break point, but depending on the length and location (like the U.P.), there can be long stretches in between, and it's a good idea to carry some food with you. You might also keep one water bottle filled with a sport drink, which can provide a quick kick if you're suddenly flagging, known as *bonking* in cycling parlance. If you've only got one, though, fill it with water.

Some extras to consider: If you're going to take on the challenges and classics, you might want to outfit your bike with a granny gear (third front chain ring) to help you up the hardest hills. Brake-mounted shifters, standard on most new road bikes, are a wonderful feature that allow you to change gears without taking your hands off the brakes. Clipless pedals are for my money the best equipment modification you can make to ride faster and more efficiently, since they provide resistance throughout your pedal revolution.

Beyond the bike itself, accessories I like include a rear rack with an expandable trunk pack to carry snacks (banana, bagel, trail mix, small candies), sunscreen, a camera, wallet/ID, extra clothing, and a pump. That's in addition to the under-the-seat tool pack. A front pack with a clear case for maps and directions is also helpful. If you choose this, it's a good idea to purchase this with your bike, so you can make sure it will attach without interfering with brake cables and levers.

Padded shorts are the first priority in your cycling wardrobe. Next come padded gloves, and then bike jerseys. Jerseys are nice—roomy rear pockets keep snacks, maps, and money handy, and their wicking fabric keeps you more comfortable, especially on hot rides—but they're not as essential as padded shorts and gloves. The layers I mentioned above for cold- and wet-weather riding are also good for extending your riding season. Finally, I wouldn't leave the house without a rearview mirror. I like the "third eye" kind that mounts to a pair of glasses. Models that mount to a helmet or to your handlebars are also available. Riding with a mirror does take some getting used to, however, so experiment on side streets or bike paths before heading out on the road with one.

One other thing to outfit yourself with for the rides in this book is an annual Michigan state parks pass. Prices in 2004 were $24.00 for the year for Michigan residents ($29.00 for non-residents). It pays for itself, since six routes start at state parks. You can pay $6.00 per park ($8.00 for non-residents) but the pass allows you to bypass the line at entrance booths.

BASIC SAFETY AND RULES OF THE ROAD

Cyclists can encounter three layers of laws in Michigan. First, there's the state Motor Vehicle Code (MVC), which applies to the whole state. Second is the Uniform Traffic Code (UTC), which municipalities including towns, cities, and villages can choose to adopt in its entirety or amend. These two policies

Cyclists enjoy the solitude of a Sunday morning ride through rural Ingham County.

occasionally contradict. The UTC, for instance, requires cyclists to use bike paths if they exist, whereas the MVC does not—unless there are local ordinances requiring it. These local ordinances that the thousands of jurisdictions may choose to create are the third layer.

Rather than wade into the sometimes contradictory legalese, here are four summary words of advice for safe road cycling in Michigan: Behave like a car. You're out there with cars, and in Michigan, you're subject to the same rights and responsibilities as cars. Act like one. You are part of the traffic flow, not an obstacle or impediment to it.

That said, there are a few footnotes. It is legal for cyclists to ride two abreast in Michigan. However, when cars come up behind you, use common sense and get in single file. Michigan law (the MVC) also states that "a person operating a bicycle upon a roadway shall ride as near to the right side of the roadway as *practicable*," an ambiguous term at best. Many cycling experts recommend riding in the middle of the lane if it's too narrow for a car to safely pass you. This "taking the lane" can also be important when you're going around a curve, enhancing your visibility to cars coming up behind you.

Visibility is a key part of safe road cycling. Like a car, your bike should be equipped with white lights in front and red rear lights if you'll be out in the early morning hours or at dusk. Wear light-colored, reflective clothing. Helmets go without saying.

Along with being visible, be predictable. Take responsibility for how you're perceived by motorists. Drivers get nervous around cyclists because they don't know what they're going to do. They've seen too many scofflaw cyclists blow through red lights and stop signs. Obey traffic signs and signals. Use hand signals to indicate turns. Show courtesy. If you're leading a group going around a curve, for instance, or up a hill, and you can see that it's clear for the car behind you to pass, wave it on by. The driver will appreciate the gesture with a return wave in the rearview mirror.

Finally, be confident on your bike. Know how fast you can accelerate. Practice using clipless pedals in the driveway before you get out on the road with them. Communicate with drivers by using eye contact. Make them aware that you're out there, and make them comfortable sharing the road.

HOW TO USE THIS BOOK

The forty routes in *Road Bicycling Michigan* are organized into four categories according to degree of difficulty. These classifications are subjective and take into account the combination of distance, terrain (i.e., hills vs. flat), and past biking experience necessary to ride the full route. Each route's name indicates its relative degree of difficulty.

♦ *Rambles* are the easiest and shortest rides in the book, accessible to almost all riders, and should be easily completed in one day. They are less than 35 miles in length and are generally on flat to slightly rolling terrain. Most rambles in this book are between 20 and 25 miles. Six are less than 20 miles or offer options that shorten them to that distance.

♦ *Cruises* are intermediate in difficulty and distance. They are generally 25 to 50 miles long and may include some moderate climbs. Cruises can generally be completed easily by an experienced rider in one day, but inexperienced or out-of-shape riders may want to take two days with an overnight stop.

♦ *Challenges* are difficult, designed for experienced riders in good condition. They are between 50 and 70 miles in length and may include steep climbs or more hilly terrain overall. They should be a challenge even for fairly fit riders to complete in one day. Less experienced or fit riders should expect to take two days. Challenge rides can also present more traffic and are intended for riders with more experience riding in traffic.

♦ *Classics* are long and hard. They are at least 60 miles and may be more than 100. They can include steep climbs and high-speed downhills. These rides are not recommended for less fit and experienced riders unless they are done in shorter stages. Classic rides also can present more traffic and are intended for riders with more experience riding in traffic.

Categorizing the rides was one of the hardest parts of writing the book, since degree of difficulty is relative to the individual rider. As you're choosing rides, remember that terrain is as much a factor as distance in determining degree of difficulty. The Pierce Stocking Cruise is only 6.9 miles, but due to the hills, it's a harder ride than the 33-mile Hines Drive Ramble. Eleven rides in the book have elevation profiles, which show how the elevation changes throughout the course of the rides. The remainder of the rides have elevation differentials of less than 250 feet, so profiles are not provided.

In my tour-leading days, I was inclined to make rides sound harder than perhaps they were, because I preferred hearing "That wasn't nearly as bad as I expected!" to "Why didn't you warn me?" Nowadays, though, I'm more inclined to want to give people the thrill of accomplishment, so I may have undersold the difficulty of some rides. Again, be aware of the regional differences in terrain. Someone who rides regularly in southeast Michigan and found the Frankenmuth Ramble easy may be surprised at the difficulty of the Leelanau South Ramble, in hillier northwest Michigan, though both are the same distance. If you're unsure about taking on a ride, note whether there are shorter options (the Oakland Lakes Challenge can be 46, 54, or 62 miles, for instance) or out-and-back portions, which allow you to customize the distance to your liking (the Tunnel of Trees Cruise can be any length from 38.2 to 52.6 miles). Most rides also have one major break point where you can find a hotel room.

The book is heavy on the shorter rides, with two-thirds under 50 miles; however, you can combine rides to create longer routes. Rides 6 and 8, for instance, can be combined for a 127.6-mile ride. Any two or all three of rides 11, 12, and 13 can be combined for a maximum distance of 85.8 miles. Rides 32 and 34 can be combined for a 95.1-mile ride. See the Rides at a Glance section for more information on combining rides.

As you read through the miles and directions and compare them to the maps, be advised that the miles and directions are based on actual field research conducted in 2003. *If the map and the miles and directions appear to conflict, follow the miles and directions.* Maps pick and choose what to label; available maps may also be dated and not reflective of current development, road name changes, etc. So follow the miles and directions, which are based on the physical road signs and conditions you will see while on the ride.

Finally, wherever you go and however far you travel on Michigan's peninsulas, ride safe, ride smart, and *circumspice.*

Map Legend

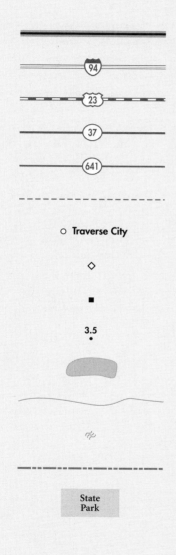

Featured Route

Interstate Highway

US Highway

State Highway

County or Local Road

Trail

City Center

Point of Interest

Structure

Mileage Point

Reservoir or Lake

River or Creek

Waterfall

State Line

Park

Copper Harbor Challenge

The Copper Harbor Challenge features the toughest climb in this book: Brockway Mountain Drive. A Midwestern version of the Appalachians' Skyline Drive, the peak rises some 735 feet above Lake Superior (1,330 feet above sea level) and the surrounding forests and is especially beautiful in fall, when the hardwoods put on their Joseph's coat of reds, yellows, and oranges. After descending, you'll ride undulating roads along the undisturbed shoreline of the world's largest freshwater lake. Nuggets of the Keweenaw's copper mining history, which earned Michigan an industrial reputation before a car was ever cranked out of Detroit, are also scattered along the ride. But it's the natural resources of woods and water that make cycling this area feel like a treasure today.

Located at the tip of Michigan's copper country, the stage for the Copper Harbor Challenge is set as you enter the community of Houghton, nearly 50 miles to the south. A small sculpture of a miner, adorned with the definitive miner's headlamp, strides through a flower bed as you approach downtown. Street signs have names like Agate, Ingot, and Mine. Crossing the lift bridge into Hancock and following US 41's steep course above the Portage Lake Channel, you pass the mining era's most well-preserved relic, the Quincy Mine Shaft overlooking the valley below. You'll pass mining ghost towns like Phoenix, Central, and Delaware before arriving at Fort Wilkins, built to protect the prospectors from the Indians back in 1844 and now a state park.

People left the Keweenaw Peninsula when the copper boom went bust more than a century ago. Today they return for other natural resources, like the

Start: Fort Wilkins State Park.

Length: 47.6-mile double loop.

Terrain: Rolling to hilly, including one very steep hill, Brockway Mountain Drive.

Traffic and hazards: The route goes up Brockway Mountain's east face, which is the steeper side and also features three switch-back turns. It is far safer to climb this side and descend the straighter, more gradual grade of the west face. Be alert for cars as you navigate occasional patches of poor pavement on both sides, sometimes necessarily riding in the center of the road.

Getting there: From Houghton/Hancock, cross the lift bridge and continue on U.S. Highway 41 for 47 miles to Copper Harbor. Follow the highway to its end and turn right into Fort Wilkins State Park. A $6.00 daily vehicle pass or $24.00 annual state park pass is required.

"purest, most vitalizing air on earth," Lake Superior, and the wooded, winding roads between the hamlets that somehow escaped ghost town fates.

From the state park you'll get a mile-and-a-half warm-up before hitting Brockway Mountain Drive. You are ascending the steep side, and the first half mile is probably the steepest section of the entire climb. There's a scenic outlook at the hairpin turn, and the road will then dip and plateau. There's another steep section at mile 2.6, followed by a mile of rollers, with periodic overlooks. You'll hit a couple more steep sections before the summit at 5.3 miles, 735 feet above Lake Superior and some 1,330 feet above sea level. At the summit there's a gift shop and restrooms and a 360-degree view.

The west face is much straighter and the grade is more gradual, making it far safer for descending. The pavement is patchy in places, usually closer to the road's edge than in the center. It's navigable, but keep alert for cars if you do veer away from the right side of the road.

Following the 5-mile descent, you'll turn left for a 4-mile stretch along Michigan Highway 26 toward Eagle Harbor. Silver River Falls, right after the turn, is a nice place to stop and rest. In Eagle Harbor you'll skirt the town to ride inland, toward the ghost town of Phoenix. You'll loop back through Eagle Harbor later. At the gas station in Phoenix, turn on MI 26 toward Eagle River, the Keweenaw County seat. (The Keweenaw Classic route also covers the 8 miles between Eagle River and Eagle Harbor.)

Judging from the sign at the turnoff from US 41, you'd think you were heading for at least a Copper Harbor–sized town. Eagle River amounts to one store with ice cream, hot dogs and the like, and the Eagle River Inn/Fitzgerald's Restaurant. Named for the *Edmund Fitzgerald*, the immortalized freighter that sank on Lake Superior in 1975, the restaurant is only open for dinner. If you're riding in midsummer, when the sun sets as late as 10:00 P.M., it might be doable

You'll see several of these signs going up Brockway Mountain Drive, over which you'll gain 735 feet.

if you arrive right when the doors open at 5:00 P.M. If not, do come back later. The menu and Lake Superior setting make for a most memorable meal.

Between Eagle River and Eagle Harbor, just past Jacobs Creek Falls, are a pair of unusual sights. First is the Jampot, a bakery and confectionary run by Catholic monks. Their jams, jellies, and fruitcakes are on the pricey side but make nice souvenirs. Just past the Jampot is the fruit of their labors: the monastery. Under construction when I visited in summer 2003, it was rising up on the lake, a modern-day version of the nineteenth-century copper barons' mansions.

After the Jampot the road gets hillier, and you'll be riding along open expanses of rugged Lake Superior shoreline. The overlook of Great Sand Bay at about mile 30 lists a litany of mind-boggling statistics about the world's largest freshwater lake. Use caution turning in and out of the overlook, as you'll be at the crest of a hill that is difficult to see over.

Highlights in Eagle Harbor, another 3 miles down MI 26, are the light-house, which has watched over the treacherous waters since 1871, and more restaurants. Leaving Eagle Harbor, you'll repeat the 4-mile stretch up to

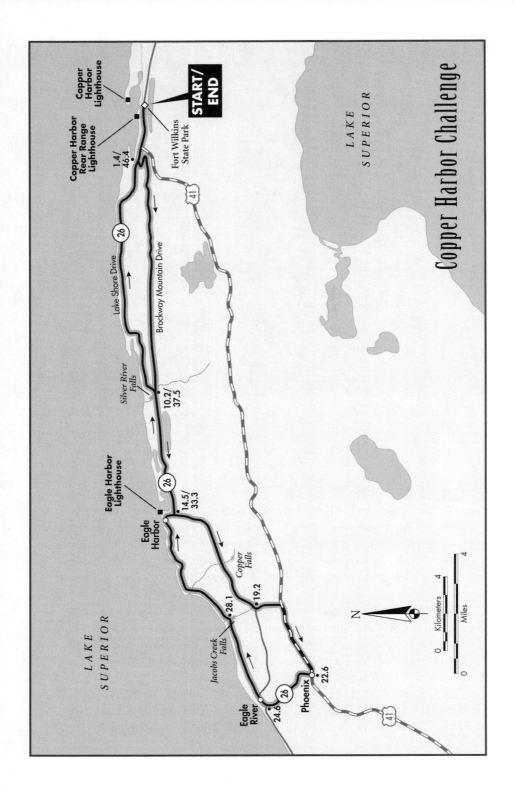

Copper Harbor Challenge

0.0 From Fort Wilkins State Park, turn left onto US 41. Lighthouse at 0.2.

1.0 Flashing light. US 41 turns left. Continue straight onto MI 26.

1.4 Turn left onto Brockway Mountain Drive.

2.0 Scenic lookout at hairpin turn.

5.3 Summit. 735 feet elevation at Skytop Inn. Restrooms.
Descent: From gift shop, turn left to go down the west face.

10.2 Stop sign. Left on MI 26 toward Eagle Harbor. Silver River Falls ahead.

14.5 Shoreline Resort. Turn left onto Eagle Harbor Road.

18.1 Copper Falls Park. Pit toilets.

19.2 Veer to left, staying on Eagle Harbor Road. Garden City Road goes to right.

20.0 Stop sign. Turn right on US 41.

22.6 Phoenix. Store on left. Turn right on MI 26 toward Eagle River.

24.6 Eagle River. Turn right at Douglas Houghton Memorial.

24.8 Turn left on East Main Street. Eagle River Store.

25.0 Road becomes Front. Eagle River Inn, Fitzgerald's Restaurant.

25.3 Stop sign. Eagle River Park/pit toilets on corner. Turn left on MI 26.

28.1 Jacobs Creek Falls/Jampot/monastery.

29.6 Great Sand Bay overlook.

32.4 Eagle Harbor.

32.7 Go straight to visit Eagle Harbor lighthouse.

32.8 Turn left at sign for lighthouse. Portable toilet. Return from lighthouse the way you came and turn left at stop sign (mile 33.1) back onto MI 26.

33.3 Shoreline Resort.

34.1 Stay to the right for Lakeshore Drive and Mountain Drive.

37.5 Silver River Falls. Veer to the left to stay on MI 26 instead of going up Brockway Mountain Drive.

38.3 Roadside park. Restrooms.

(continued)

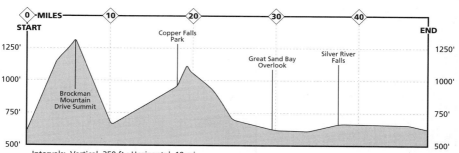

Intervals: Vertical, 250 ft.; Horizontal, 10 mi.

43.7 Roadside park. Pit toilets.
46.4 Brockway Mountain Drive intersects.
46.8 Flashing light for US 41. Continue straight.
47.6 Turn right into Fort Wilkins State Park.

Brockway Mountain Drive, passing Silver River Falls again. This time, stay to the left, along MI 26 and the Lake Superior shore, instead of heading back up Brockway. The best has been saved for last: the 11-mile stretch back into Copper Harbor is classic Lake Superior scenery. Large dark rocks break the lake's surface just off the shoreline, creating a craggy, stark look. In contrast, colorful wildflowers grow abundantly on the opposite side of the road.

Brockway Mountain Drive will re-intersect MI 26 just before the flashing light in Copper Harbor. Ride back through town to return to Fort Wilkins State Park. A turnoff to see the Copper Harbor lighthouse, located across the harbor, is the last stop.

LOCAL INFORMATION

♦ Keweenaw Tourism Council, Houghton; (906) 482–2388, www.keweenaw .org.
♦ Copper Harbor; www.copperharbor.org.

LOCAL EVENTS/ATTRACTIONS

♦ The Copper Harbor Fat Tire Festival features mountain bike races, food, and music. Early September. (906) 289–4303.

RESTAURANTS

♦ Keweenaw Mountain Lodge, on US 41 south of Copper Harbor; (906) 289–4403. Full-service restaurant and bar. Open seasonally.
♦ The Pines, US 41, Copper Harbor; (906) 289–4222. Awesome cinnamon rolls. Breakfast, lunch, and dinner. Open seasonally.
♦ The Mariner North, US 41, Copper Harbor; (906) 289–4637. Advertises "two-handed sandwiches." Lunch and dinner.

ACCOMMODATIONS

♦ Keweenaw Mountain Lodge, US 41 south of Copper Harbor; (906) 289–4403. Motel and cottages.

◆ King Copper Motel, 445 East Brockway Avenue, Copper Harbor; (906) 289–4214. On Lake Superior next to Isle Royale boat dock.
◆ Lake Fanny Hooe Resort, 505 Second Street, Copper Harbor; (906) 289–4451.

RESTROOMS

◆ Start/finish: Fort Wilkins State Park.
◆ Mile 5.3: summit of Brockway Mountain Drive.
◆ Mile 18.1: Copper Falls Park.
◆ Mile 25.3: Eagle River Park.
◆ Mile 32.8: Eagle Harbor Lighthouse.
◆ Mile 38.3: roadside park.
◆ Mile 43.7: roadside park.

Keweenaw Classic

L ocated at the very tip of the top of Michigan's Upper Peninsula, the Keweenaw is one of the most remote regions Michigan offers cyclists. Keweenaw County is home to about 2,200 people, or four people per square mile. Population increases during the summer tourism season, but the roads are still extremely lightly traveled, and the scenery, featuring miles of undeveloped, rugged Lake Superior shoreline, is superb. You'll also ride by remnants of the copper mining industry, which, though hard to imagine today, made the Keweenaw a hub of wealth and technology in the last half of the nineteenth century. The copper veins that once lured thousands of fortune-seekers are now history, but it is still well worth the effort to come to the Keweenaw.

From McLain State Park, you'll ride east up a gradual incline to Calumet. Once home to more millionaires per capita than any other city in Michigan, Calumet today is evidence of how a boom can go bust. The Calumet Theatre is still is decent repair, though it's hard to believe audiences of 1,200 once watched performers like John Philip Sousa, Douglas Fairbanks, and Jason Robards perform here. As you ride down Sixth Street onto the Sixth Street extension, which takes you past a Burger King, a grocery store and a strip mall, you'll see a somewhat jarring juxtaposition of nineteenth- and twenty-first-century lifestyles.

If you're hungry, Calumet and neighboring Laurium offer the best opportunity for food until Eagle Harbor in another 24 miles. There's one daytime eating option in Eagle River, but its hours are rather sporadic. At US 41 you'll turn north. At the flashing light in 0.2 mile, turn right to get an ice-cream cone or a pasty (pronounced "pah-STEE") in a couple blocks. Though they're sold all over the U.P., pasties really trace their history to the Keweenaw, where they were a main-stay in the miner diet. Essentially handheld potpies, pasties have a variety of fillings baked into a pastry crust, which keep them hot until lunchtime. You can pick one up for the bike bag and a picnic on Lake Superior.

Leaving Laurium (also the home of George Gipp), you'll ride north on US 41 for about 4 miles, until turning left toward Five Mile Point in Ahmeek. The road from here to Eagle River is beautiful, quiet, and well-paved. A roadside park over-looking Lake Superior at mile 22.5 is a good place to nibble on your pasty.

In another 2 miles is Eagle River, the Keweenaw County seat. The next 8 miles to Eagle Harbor are also

part of the Copper Harbor Challenge route. Back in 1855, Eagle River had two breweries, thirty-two saloons, and Michigan's most sophisticated hotel north of Detroit. Today it has one store with ice cream, hot dogs, and the like, and Fitzgerald's. Located at the Eagle River Inn, the latter is a worthy successor to the establishments of the copper era. It's only open for dinner, but if you're rid-ing in midsummer, when the sun sets as late as 10:00 P.M., it might be doable if you arrive right when the doors open at 5:00 P.M. Serving duck, swordfish, crab, and whitefish cakes and other out-of-the-ordinary dishes, its menu is all the more amazing considering the remote locale. You can dine alfresco overlook-ing Lake Superior.

If Fitzgerald's isn't open, the beach alongside the inn makes another good picnic spot.

Between Eagle River and Eagle Harbor are a trio of sights worth stopping for. First is Jacobs Creek Falls, right on Michigan Highway 26. Next comes the Jampot, a bakery and confectionary run by Catholic monks. Their jams, jellies, and fruitcakes are on the pricey side but make nice souvenirs. Just past the Jampot is one of the more unusual sights in the Keweenaw, the monks' monastery. Under construction when I visited in summer 2003, it was rising up

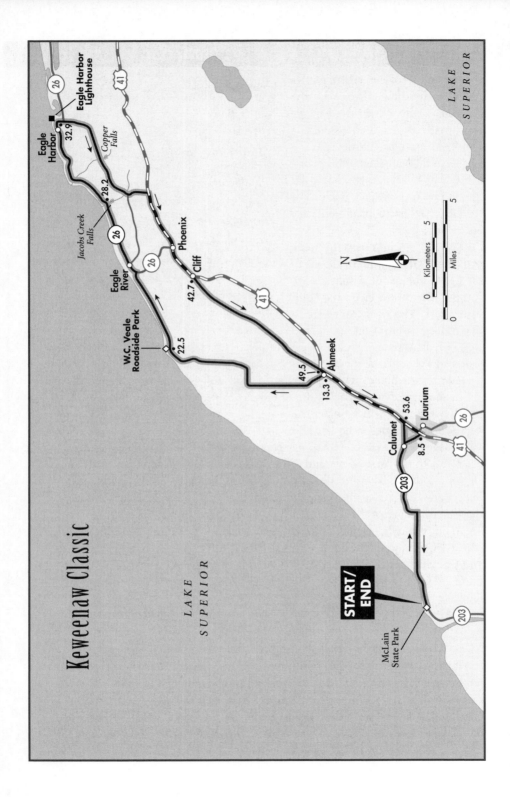

Keweenaw Classic

MILES AND DIRECTIONS

0.0 From McLain State Park, turn left onto MI 203.

7.6 Turn right on Sixth Street in Calumet.

8.5 Traffic light. Turn left on US 41. Restrooms at Keweenaw Information Center across the street.

8.7 Flashing light at MI 26. Continue straight or turn right to visit restaurants in Laurium in 0.4 mile: Toni's Country Kitchen Pasties, Honey Cone ice cream/Tina's Convenience Store. Return to US 41 and turn right.

13.3 Ahmeek. Turn left at Our Lady of Peace Catholic Church, following sign to Five Mile Point.

13.4 Stop sign. Turn left on Hubbell.

13.5 Turn right on Bollman in 2 blocks, following sign to Five Mile Point and Eagle River.

22.5 W. C. Veale Roadside Park. Pit toilets.

24.7 Stop sign. Turn left on Sand Dunes Drive.

24.8 Eagle River, falls and bridge.

24.9 Turn left on East Main Street. River store.

25.1 Road becomes Front. Eagle River Inn, Fitzgerald's Restaurant.

25.4 Stop sign. Turn left onto Sand Dunes Drive/MI 26. Eagle River Park/pit toilets on corner.

28.2 Jacobs Creek Falls/Jampot/monastery.

29.7 Great Sand Bay overlook.

32.5 Eagle Harbor.

32.8 Go straight to visit Eagle Harbor lighthouse.

32.9 Turn left at sign for lighthouse. Portable toilets. Return from lighthouse the way you came and turn left at stop sign (mile 33.3) back onto MI 26.

33.4 Shoreline Resort. Turn right onto Eagle Harbor Road.

36.9 Copper Falls Park. Pit toilets.

(continued)

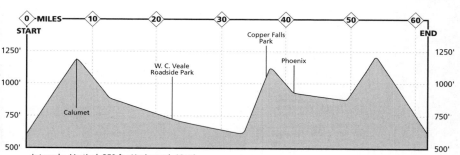

Intervals: Vertical, 250 ft.; Horizontal, 10 mi.

Jacobs Creek Falls is along MI 26 between Eagle River and Eagle Harbor.

37.9 Garden City Road intersects. Veer to left, staying on Eagle Harbor Road.

41.3 Phoenix. Store on left. Continue straight on US 41.

42.7 Turn right on Cliff Drive.

49.5 Stop sign. Turn right on US 41/MI 26. Use caution due to patchy pavement on shoulder.

53.6 Turn right at flashing light onto MI 203, after sign for McLain State Park.

54.0 Calumet village limits. Follow MI 203 (becomes Pine in town) to state park.

62.0 Turn right into McLain State Park.

on the lake like a present-day version of the nineteenth-century copper barons' mansions.

After the Jampot the road gets a little hillier, and you'll be riding along open expanses of rugged Lake Superior shoreline. The overlook of Great Sand Bay at about mile 30 lists a litany of mind-boggling statistics about the world's largest freshwater lake: area, 31,800 square miles; coastline, 1,500 miles; greatest depth, 1,333 feet. Use caution turning in and out of the overlook, as you'll be at the crest of a hill that is difficult to see over.

After the overlook it's another 3 miles into Eagle Harbor. You can tour the Eagle Harbor lighthouse, which has watched over the treacherous waters since 1871. Eagle Harbor also offers a couple restaurants, including the Shoreline Resort (serving till 2:00 P.M.) and Eagle Harbor Inn (lunch and dinner).

From Eagle Harbor the route turns back south and inland. You'll ride along wooded roads and, depending on the season, be able to pick strawberries (sunny areas along roadsides) raspberries (along logging roads and in small clearings), and especially thimbleberries, a U.P. delicacy found along roadsides and old railroad grades. Thimbleberry jam is one of the monks' specialties.

Eagle Harbor Road meets US 41. You'll be on the highway for a few miles, going through the ghost town of Phoenix, then turn onto Cliff Road, a quiet road with a hill or two and another former mine. You'll finish the ride on the same roads as the beginning of the ride: 4 miles on US 41 and then MI 203 (downhill this time) back to McLain State Park.

LOCAL INFORMATION

♦ Keweenaw Tourism Council, Houghton; (906) 482–2388; www.keweenaw .org.

LOCAL EVENTS/ATTRACTIONS

♦ BridgeFest marks the birthday of the Portage Lift Bridge connecting the Keweenaw with the rest of the U.P. Parade, arts and crafts, entertainment, dances. Keweenaw Chain Drive Mountain Bike Races held in conjunction. Held in Houghton/Hancock in mid-June. (906) 482–2388 (mountain bike race information only).

♦ Brockway Mountain Drive: If you don't care to pedal up it (see Copper Harbor Challenge for more information), drive on up to the top for spectacular views of Lake Superior and surrounding forests.

♦ The Delaware Mine, south of Copper Harbor (906–289–4688), and Quincy Mine, above Hancock (906–482–3101), both offer underground mine tours.

♦ Fort Wilkins State Park was built in 1844 to protect prospectors from Indians, and is the last remaining original wooden fort east of the Mississippi River. Costumed reenactors recreate fort life. Copper Harbor; (906) 289–4215.

RESTAURANTS

♦ Fitzgerald's Restaurant and Lounge, 2 blocks off MI 26, Eagle River; (906) 337–0666. Eclectic menu in spectacular setting. Located in the Eagle River Inn. Deck dining overlooking Lake Superior.

♦ Seasons at Lac La Belle, at Lac La Belle Lodge, Mohawk; (906) 289–4293. Italian all week, Friday fish fry, Saturday prime rib.

♦ The Gay Bar, Gay; (906) 296–0951. There really is a town called Gay, Michigan, and there really is a Gay Bar.

ACCOMMODATIONS

♦ AmericInn of Calumet, 56925 South Sixth Street, Calumet; (906) 337–6463. If you want the reassurance of national chain lodging, this is the only place to find it in the Keweenaw.

♦ Eagle River Inn, 2 blocks off MI 26, Eagle River; (906) 337–0666; www.eagleriverinn.com. "We're not easy to find . . . on purpose," say their brochures. Worth the hunt.

♦ B&Bs: Victorian Hall, 305 Tamarack Street, Laurium, (906) 337–5548; Laurium Manor Inn, 320 Tamarack Street, Laurium, (906) 337–2549. Sleep where a copper baron did.

RESTROOMS

♦ Start/finish: McLain State Park.
♦ Mile 8.5: Keweenaw Information Center.
♦ Mile 22.5: W. C. Veale Roadside Park.
♦ Mile 25.4: Eagle River Park.
♦ Mile 32.9: Eagle Harbor lighthouse.
♦ Mile 36.9: Copper Falls Park.

Marquette Ramble

Taking advantage of Marquette's beautiful location on Lake Superior, this ride utilizes the city's lakefront bike path. It also circles an island park and follows an out-and-back spur to a hiking trail that leads you to a bird's-eye view of the city and Lake Superior. Other highlights of this ride around the Upper Peninsula's largest city are Northern Michigan University and Marquette's historic, hilly downtown.

According to the local bike shops, road biking is making a resurgence in Marquette, which has been better known for its mountain biking. In 2001, in fact, *Bike Magazine* named it the No. 2 city for biking and living. Like many communities in the U.P., however, Marquette has a limited number of paved secondary roads outside of town. It also gets hilly. Consequently, to keep this ride at ramble level, the route stays mostly within city limits, with the exception of an 8.3-mile round-trip spur out to Sugarloaf Mountain.

The route starts at the lower harbor, below Marquette's historic downtown. Marquette was built on iron ore, discovered in the area in the mid-1800s. A can't-miss landmark is the 85-foot ore dock on Lake Superior. It's been unused since 1972, and the railroad trestle bridge over Front Street was torn down in 2000. However, there's a twin dock still in use on the north end of town where you might be able to catch a freighter loading or unloading iron ore pellets.

You'll ride for 4 miles along Lake Superior, passing the Ellwood Mattson Park, Marquette Maritime Museum, the beach, playgrounds, and the Lake Superior and Ishpeming Railroad Ore Dock before entering Presque Isle Park. A 2-mile one-way loop will take you around the perimeter of Presque Isle, which translates from French as "almost an island." You will be riding alongside Lake Superior.

Start: City parking lot at lower harbor, corner of Main Street and Lakeshore Boulevard. Look for the unused ore dock and the Quonset hut.

Length: 17.9-mile circuit.

Terrain: Flat to rolling. Some climbs around Presque Isle Park and around downtown Marquette. County Road 550 has a gradual incline out to Sugarloaf Mountain.

Traffic and hazards: Use caution on County Road 550 heading to Sugarloaf Mountain. The shoulder is good, but the traffic is extremely fast.

Getting there: From U.S. Highway 41/Michigan Highway 28, follow the signs to downtown Marquette, staying alongside Lake Superior instead of turning west. You'll be on Front Street. Turn right at Main Street, go down the steep hill, and park in the city parking lot by the ore dock and Quonset hut.

After Presque Isle Park you'll ride back south again for a mile before splitting off to the west. CR 550 heads north at the edge of town. It's 4 miles up a gradual incline to Sugarloaf Mountain, where two different hiking routes of varying difficulty take you to the top of the 315-foot granite cliff. There are staircases and the route is well marked. Atop it you'll have a 360-degree view of blue and green: Lake Superior, the city of Marquette, and the inland hills. It will take you about forty-five minutes to go up and down.

You'll coast much of the way back into Marquette after leaving Sugarloaf. In Marquette you'll return to the bike path for a short distance before returning to the streets as you ride through part of the Northern Michigan University campus. You'll pass the Superior Dome, where NMU's Division II football team plays. This is northern Michigan, however, and more fans flock to the Berry Events Center, which you'll glimpse just before turning. It's the home of the beloved Division I Wildcat hockey team as well as a U.S. Olympic short-track speed-skating training center.

You'll ride up a hill to return to downtown Marquette. At Arch Street, you might want to turn right and ride 2 blocks off the route for a hilltop view of St. Peter's Cathedral. At the intersection of Front and Main Streets downtown, you'll turn left and go down a steep hill to return to the harbor and parking lot.

LOCAL INFORMATION

♦ Marquette Country Convention and Visitors Bureau; (800) 544–4321; www.marquettecountry.org.

LOCAL EVENTS/ATTRACTIONS

♦ Art on the Rocks, a juried art show at Presque Isle Park, attracts more than 150 artists in all media. Held in July. (906) 288–4137.

♦ The Superior Bike Fest, in mid-June, includes both road racing and mountain bike racing. Course maps of the 25-, 55-, and 80-mile routes are available on the festival's Web site if you want a longer—and hillier—road route. www.superiorbikefest.com.

♦ Pictured Rocks Boat Cruises offers a three-hour cruise along Lake Superior's amazing sheer cliffs and rock formations in nearby Munising, about an hour east of Marquette. Signs along MI 28 direct you to Munising City Pier. (906) 387–2379; www.picturedrocks.com.

RESTAURANTS

♦ The Vierling, 119 South Front Street, Marquette; (906) 228–3533. Microbrewery and full-service restaurant in historic downtown building.

♦ Vango's Pizza and Lounge, 927 North Third Street, Marquette; (906) 228–7707. Near NMU. Greek food and pizza.

♦ Casa Calabria, 1106 North Third Street, Marquette; (906) 228–5012. The western U.P. has a strong Italian heritage. Enjoy it here.

♦ Third Street is a burgeoning dining/shopping district with many other establishments over several blocks. Check out Sweet Water Café, 517 North Third; Panini Grill, 1125 North Third; and the Pasta Shop, 824 North Third.

An ore boat bellies up to Marquette's docks on Lake Superior. Courtesy of Travel Michigan

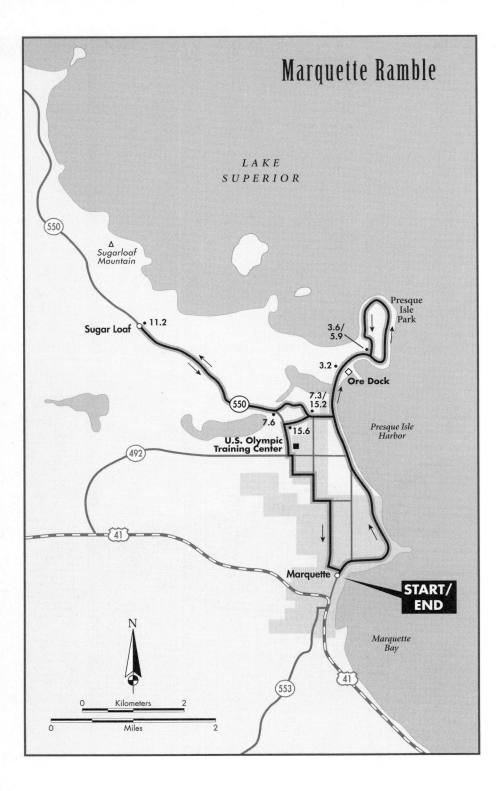

Marquette Ramble

LAKE
SUPERIOR

Presque
Isle
Park

3.6/
5.9

3.2 •

◇
Ore Dock

7.3/
15.2

• 11.2
Sugar Loaf ○

△
*Sugarloaf
Mountain*

550

7.6
•

•15.6

**U.S. Olympic
Training Center**
■

*Presque Isle
Harbor*

492

41

550

Marquette ○

**START/
END**

N

*Marquette
Bay*

553

41

| 0 | Kilometers | 2 |
| 0 | Miles | 2 |

0.0 At the corner of Main Street and Lakeshore Boulevard (under FRESH FISH sign), ride north onto the bike path paralleling the shoreline.

0.7 Veer to the right to stay on bike path. Marquette Maritime Museum on your left.

0.9 After crossing parking lot, take sharp turn to left. Restrooms.

1.5 Public beach. Restrooms.

1.6 Stop sign for beach entrance, followed by stop sign for vehicle traffic on Lakeshore. Stay on bike path.

2.8 Yield sign. Cross Hawley Road and continue on bike path.

3.2 LaBonte Park. Good view of ore docks.

3.6 Railroad tracks. Enter Presque Isle Park.

3.8 T intersection. Turn right to go around one-way path around Presque Isle Park.

5.9 Turn right just past snack bar to leave Presque Isle Park the way you entered.

6.1 Railroad tracks.

6.9 Yield sign. Turn right, following bike path alongside Hawley Road.

7.3 Turn right off bike trail onto Hawley Road, continuing west. Note: To eliminate the 8.3-mile trip to Sugarloaf Mountain, cross Hawley to stay on the bike trail, and then follow directions from mile 15.6 below.

7.6 Sugarloaf Highway intersects. Hawley merges into Sugarloaf/County Road 550. Shoulder begins just over hill.

8.4 Railroad tracks. Watch for logging trucks.

9.1 Phil's 550 Store.

11.2 Sugarloaf Mountain. Hiking trails to top.

14.1 Railroad tracks/truck entrance.

15.2 Turn right on bike path.

15.6 Turn left off bike path onto Sugarloaf Highway. NMU campus.

15.7 Turn left on Wright. Take an immediate right onto Schaefer at Northern Michigan University sign.

16.1 Stop sign. Turn left on Center.

16.5 Stop sign. Turn right on Presque Isle Avenue. Superior Dome on left.

16.7 Turn left on Fair. NMU Hockey arena ahead on left.

16.8 Turn right on Front. (To visit Third Street restaurants, turn one block after Fair, before Front. Third Street is busier, however.)

17.8 Turn left on Main Street. Steep downhill.

17.9 Cross Lakeshore Boulevard to return to parking lot.

ACCOMMODATIONS

♦ Landmark Inn, 230 North Front Street, Marquette; (888) 752–6362; www.thelandmarkinn.com. Restored historic hotel in downtown Marquette. Restaurants on premises.

♦ Big Bay Point Lighthouse, 3 Lighthouse Road/KCB, Big Bay; (906) 345–9957; www.bigbaylighthouse.com. B&B in historic lighthouse overlooking Lake Superior. 25 miles north of Marquette, in the town where the murder story told in *Anatomy of a Murder* (filmed in Marquette) actually happened.

♦ Ramada Inn, 412 West Washington Street, Marquette; (906) 228–6000. Just west of downtown.

RESTROOMS

♦ Mile 0.9: parking area.
♦ Mile 1.5: Marquette beach.
♦ Mile 5.9: Presque Isle Park.

4

Tahquamenon Falls Ramble

Yoopers (residents of the U.P.) and trolls (residents of the Lower Peninsula, who live below the Mackinac Bridge) alike often refer to the U.P. as God's country. Paradise goes so far as to claim title. Located on Lake Superior's Whitefish Bay, Paradise is the closest community to Tahquamenon Falls, one of the largest falls in the eastern United States. The ramble is an out-and-back ride from Paradise, with stops at the lower and then the more dramatic upper falls, which stretch more than 200 feet between riverbanks and cascade over a 50-foot drop.

There are more than 150 named waterfalls in Michigan's Upper Peninsula, but the upper and lower falls of the Tahquamenon River stand apart. They are mentioned in great literature; in *Song of Hiawatha*, Longfellow's hero builds his birch-bark canoe beside the rushing waters. The upper falls are especially spectacular in winter, when the churning amber water defies logic and resists freezing. Spray coats the trees and riverbanks with a thick layer of frost and ice formations.

It's a bit chilly for biking then, though, and the other seasons have their own appeal, too. Summer and fall are probably the best times for biking to the falls. You'll leave from Paradise, a community that sustains itself on the visitors who come for the falls, hunting, fishing, and snowmobiling. It's a pleasant 10-mile ride on a lightly traveled road to the lower falls, a series of five smaller falls that cascade around an island. You can walk around the falls basin to an observation deck or rent a rowboat ($2.00) to the island. The rowboat ride is a nice option, since it takes you closer to the falls and gives you a chance to exercise your arms. There are restrooms and a concession stand at the lower falls, too.

Start: Sawmill Creek Township Park, 0.1 mile north of traffic light in Paradise on the left.

Length: 30-mile out-and-back.

Terrain: Flat to rolling. A gradual downhill into the lower falls and uphill back out.

Traffic and hazards: The ride follows a two-lane state highway with light traffic, most of it going to the falls, too. There is a shoulder throughout the ride, and the road is in good condition.

Getting there: Paradise is located at the corner of the roughly triangle-shaped Michigan Highway 123, about 70 miles north of the Mackinac Bridge. From Interstate 75, get on MI 123 north at exit 352. In Paradise go through the traffic light where MI 123 turns left and continue north onto Whitefish Point Road. Sawmill Creek Township Park is 0.1 mile north of the intersection on the left.

Depending on whether you walk or row out to the falls, plan to spend between a half hour and an hour here.

Leaving the lower falls, you will have to climb up the hill you coasted down to enter. It's the only climb of any note, however. You'll turn left onto MI 123, continuing on a south-westward course toward the upper falls. These are the kind of falls most people think of when they imagine waterfalls. At peak flow more than 50,000 gallons of water per second can cascade over the falls. You'll be able to hear the roar as you start the walk down the trail (no bikes permitted) from the parking area. Two cleared observation areas above the falls allow you to peek before descending a long staircase to an observation platform positioned right at the plunge point. Expect to get a little damp from mist and spray.

One of the most interesting things about Tahquamenon is the amber color of the water, caused by tannin leached from the trees in the upstream swamps drained by the river. The foam along the riverbank is caused by the churning action and the soft water.

Plan to spend at least a half hour at the upper falls, longer if you decide to dine at the Tahquamenon Falls Brewery and Pub. Ice cream and snacks are also available here. On the way back to Paradise, keep your eyes out for wildlife. Moose, bald eagles, black bear, coyotes, otter, deer, fox, porcupine, beaver, mink, and many diverse birds all live in the state park area.

LOCAL INFORMATION

♦ Tahquamenon Falls State Park, 41382 MI 123 west, Paradise; (906) 492–3415; www.exploringthenorth.com/tahqua/tahqua.html.

♦ Paradise Chamber of Commerce; (906) 492–3219; www.paradisemichigan.org. Web site includes a helpful locator map of restaurants and motels.

♦ Paradise Area Tourism Council; (906) 492–3927.

Tahquamenon Falls, the second-largest waterfall east of the Mississippi, plunges 50 feet and churns up a lot of foam. Courtesy of Travel Michigan

LOCAL EVENTS/ATTRACTIONS

♦ The Wild Blueberry Festival includes an arts-and-crafts fair, entertainment, and food. Held in Paradise in mid-August. (906) 492–3219.

♦ The Great Lakes Shipwreck Museum is located at Whitefish Point, the critical turning point for ships traversing Lake Superior, 11 miles north of Paradise. Open from mid-May to mid-October. (906) 492–3747; www.shipwreck museum.com.

RESTAURANTS

♦ Tahquamenon Falls Brewery and Pub; (906) 492–3300. Microbrewery and restaurant located at the upper falls.

♦ Little Falls Inn, adjacent to Best Western, Paradise; (906) 492–3529. Specializing in whitefish and steaks.

♦ Yukon Inn, at the MI 123 corner; (906) 492–3264. Burgers and sandwiches.

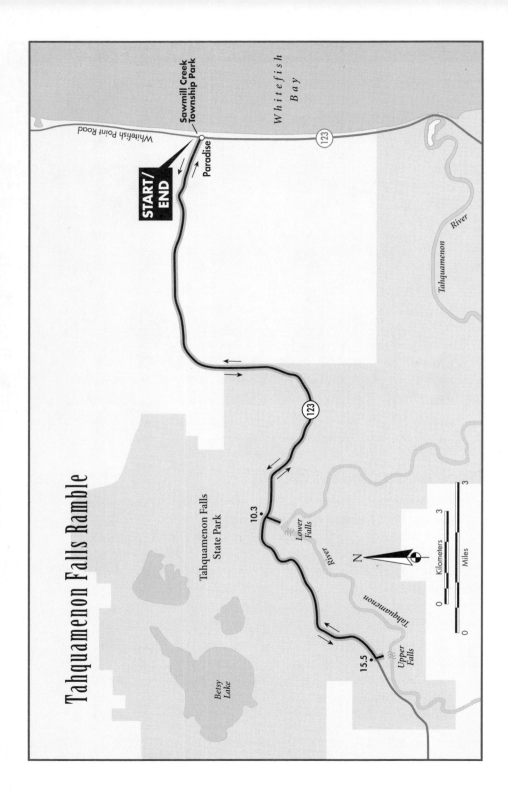

Tahquamenon Falls Ramble

MILES AND DIRECTIONS

0.0 Turn right out of Sawmill Creek Township Park onto Whitefish Point Road.

0.1 Turn right at traffic light onto MI 123 toward falls. (Sign saying 10 miles to falls is to lower falls; upper is another 3.5 miles.)

10.3 Entrance to lower falls. You'll go down a long hill (0.8 mile) to get to the parking area and trails.

12.0 From entrance to lower falls, turn left back onto MI 123 to visit upper falls.

15.5 Turn left onto Upper Falls Drive to see the upper falls.

16.0 Turn right at the stop sign onto Upper Falls Drive as you leave the parking area.

16.2 Turn right onto MI 123.

29.9 Turn left at traffic light in Paradise.

30.0 Turn left into Sawmill Creek Township Park.

ACCOMMODATIONS

♦ Best Western Lake Front Inn and Suites, 8112 North MI 123, Paradise; (906) 492–3770. On Lake Superior.

♦ Curley's Paradise Motel, at the MI 123 light; (906) 492–3445. On Lake Superior.

♦ Paradise Inn, on MI 123 at the light; (906) 492–3940.

RESTROOMS

♦ Start/finish: Sawmill Creek Township Park.

♦ Mile 11.1: lower falls.

♦ Mile 15.5: upper falls.

Eastern U.P. Cruise

Your destination for this ride is the village of DeTour. Upon arrival, it really will feel like you've detoured. Though only an hour away from Mackinaw City and Mackinac Island, the epicenter for summer crowds up north, fudge shop–free DeTour, whose chamber of commerce brochure notes the seasons for pike, walleye, bass, salmon, and perch fishing, feels completely different. To reach the hamlet at the extreme eastern end of the U.P., you'll ride along an excellent road paralleling Lake Huron and the Les Cheneaux Islands. You'll loop back inland after DeTour and then ride back along the Lake Huron stretch again.

More people must travel by water than by land in the eastern U.P., as light as the traffic is. That makes for wonderful biking, however, and you'll have a good view of the region's waterways from the bike seat, too. The ride starts in Cedarville, a small community that is the hub of the Les Cheneaux Islands. Meaning "the channels" in French, the Les Cheneaux Islands consist of thirty-six small islands scattered along 12 miles of Lake Huron coast.

Boaters love the shelter they afford. They make for nice scenery, too. For the first 8 miles of the ride, however, you'll get only occasional glimpses of the water through gaps in the trees that line the road. After about 10 miles come open swaths of beach with blue water sparkling beyond. If picnicking is your pleasure, pick out your favorite, since you'll pass some of these again on the way back.

The terrain also becomes more rolling at this point, and a hill brings you down into DeTour, situated on the easternmost end of the U.P. This village also owes its name to the French, who called it the "turning point" to the Straits of Mackinac. Today, instead of explorers and fur traders, pleasure crafts, fishing charters, and lake freighters ply the waters of the DeTour Passage at the mouth of the St. Mary's River, the funnel connecting Lake Superior with Lake Huron.

In DeTour you can grab a bite to eat at several restaurants; buy picnic supplies at Sune's DeTour Village IGA; check out the day's biggest catch, posted at North Country Sports; or take a ferry to Drummond Island. During peak season the ferry departs at least once an hour, but if traffic warrants, it will simply go back and forth as frequently as the ferry fills. You can

THE BASICS

Start: Les Cheneaux Community Schools.

Length: 49.4-mile lariat.

Terrain: Flat to gently rolling, a hill or two coming out of DeTour Village.

Traffic and hazards: This is a cyclist's dream, with extremely lightly traveled roads. Michigan Highway 134 has a good shoulder. Use caution at the limestone quarry at mile 3.9 and 45.4, where trucks are entering and exiting MI 134.

Getting there: After crossing the Mackinac Bridge, take exit 359 off Interstate 75 onto MI 134. Go east 17 miles, 0.2 mile past the flashing light to the Les Cheneaux Community Schools on the right.

After exploring the eastern U.P., enjoy a relaxing view of the Les Cheneaux Islands in Cedarville.

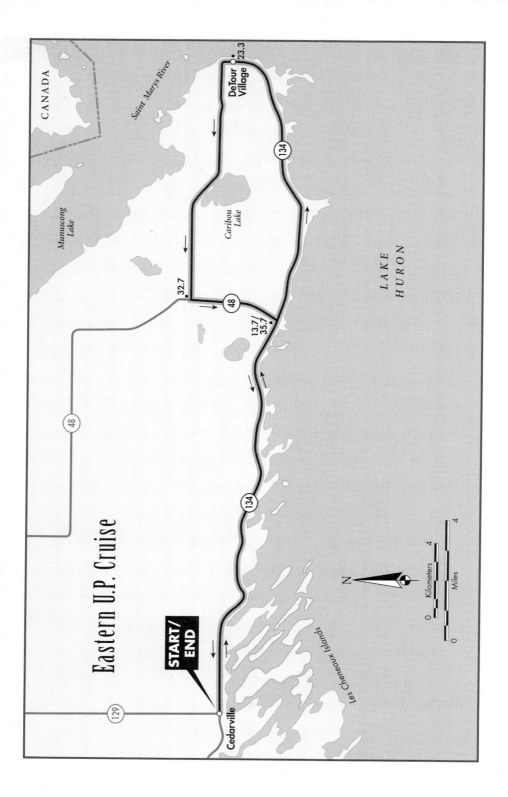

Eastern U.P. Cruise

CANADA

Munuscong Lake

Saint Marys River

Caribou Lake

DeTour Village ● 23.3

134

LAKE HURON

32.7

48

13.7/ 35.7

48

134

129

Cedarville

START/ END

Les Cheneaux Islands

N

0   Kilometers   4

0   Miles   4

MILES AND DIRECTIONS

0.0 From the school parking lot, turn right onto MI 134 east.

3.9 Michigan Limestone, Inc. Watch for trucks entering and exiting highway.

16.3 Roadside park. Restrooms.

23.3 Flashing light. Entering DeTour Village.

23.5 Flashing light. Turn right on Elizabeth Street, which dead-ends at dock for Drummond Island Ferry. Restrooms, Fogcutter Bar and Grille. Turn around on Elizabeth, return to the highway, which is Ontario Street in town, and turn right.

24.3 Road curves and goes uphill leaving town, becoming Democrat Road, then Caribou Lake Road.

32.7 Stop sign for MI 48. Turn left.

35.7 Stop sign. Turn right on MI 134 west.

45.4 Michigan Limestone, Inc. Watch for trucks.

49.4 Return to school. Turn left on Beach Street to visit Cedarville business district, then retrace route to school.

camp or stay in hotel accommodations on Drummond Island, which has both paved and unpaved roads.

You'll climb another hill leaving DeTour, heading inland. Midway along the 8-mile stretch of Caribou Lake Road is Caribou Lake. This is the hilliest part of the ride. At Michigan Highway 48 you'll turn back south for a short 3 miles before coming back to MI 134, which you'll take west back to Cedarville.

LOCAL INFORMATION

♦ Les Cheneaux Islands Area Tourist Association & Chamber of Commerce; (888) 364–7526 or (906) 484–3935; www.lescheneaux.org.

♦ DeTour Area Chamber of Commerce; (906) 297–5987; www.detourvillage .com.

♦ Drummond Island Tourism Association; (800) 737–8666; www.drummond islandchamber.com.

LOCAL EVENTS/ATTRACTIONS

♦ Les Cheneaux Historical Maritime Museum, corner of MI 134 and Lake Street, 4 blocks east of the intersection of Michigan Highways 129 and 134, Cedarville. Antique boats and motors, photos and other maritime memorabilia. (906) 484–3354.

♦ DeTour Passage Historical Museum, Elizabeth Street at the Drummond Island ferry dock, DeTour. Marine displays, including 1908 Fresnel lens from DeTour reef light, Native American and local arts.

◆ The Les Cheneaux Islands Antique Wooden Boat Show and festival of the arts is held on the second Sunday in August in Hessel, between Cedarville and DeTour. For more information see Les Cheneaux Islands Web site or call (906) 484–2821 for the boat show, (906) 484–2234 for the arts festival.

◆ The Soo Locks, between Sault Ste. Marie, Michigan, and Sault Ste. Marie, Ontario, are less than an hour from Cedarville. Boat tours take you through the locks, or just watch ships being raised to Lake Superior's levels or lowered to Lake Huron's. For boat tour reservations, call (800) 432–6301; www.soolocks .com.

RESTAURANTS

◆ Fogcutter Bar and Grille, Elizabeth Street at the Drummond Island ferry dock, DeTour Village; (906) 297–5999. Outdoor deck. Lunch and dinner. Walleye, steak, fresh whitefish every day.

◆ Dockside Cafe, Ontario Street/MI 134 at Elizabeth Street, DeTour Village; (906) 297–5165.

◆ Mainsail Restaurant Saloon, Ontario Street on the way out of DeTour Village. Whitefish, ribs, burgers, pizza.

◆ Cow Barn, on the corner curve out of DeTour Village. Ice cream, pizza, subs, burgers.

◆ Channel Marker Restaurant, 22 East Hodeck Road, Cedarville; (906) 484–2995. Sandwiches, salads, burgers, fish, pasta. Outdoor deck.

ACCOMMODATIONS

◆ DeTour Village Hotel, 100 Ontario Street, DeTour Village; (906) 297–5165.
◆ Cedarville Inn, 106 West MI 134, Cedarville; (800) 222–2949.
◆ Islands Inn Motel, 90 MI 134, Cedarville; (906) 484–2293.

RESTROOMS

◆ Mile 16.3: roadside park.
◆ Mile 23.6: DeTour restaurants.

Tip of the Mitt Classic

T he Straits of Mackinac, at the very tip of the mitten that is Michigan's Lower Peninsula, is the highlight of this coast-to-coast route. Here land and water meet, as Lake Huron and Lake Michigan flow into each other, while overhead, the Mackinac Bridge connects the Upper and Lower Peninsulas. You can visit a historic fort, take a ferry to Mackinac Island for some more biking, visit a museum on the construction of the world's longest suspension bridge, or blend with the "fudgies" in Mackinaw City. The northwest part of the ride follows roads popular with organized rides, so expect company.

As you ride along the tip of Michigan's mitten, you'll get a good sense of the diversity Michigan offers cyclists, from winding roads dusted with beach sand to a freeway overpass, from coastline to farmland to woods, from flat to not-so-flat.

The ride starts on one of the beach sand–dusted roads. As its name indicates, Wilderness State Park is situated on a rugged and beautiful stretch of northern Lake Michigan coastline. From the park, it's an easy 11 miles into Mackinaw City, whose history as a settlement dates back to 1671, when a mission was established here. Since then, many paths have crossed here. The French fort at Michilimackinac, below where the Mackinac Bridge now arcs across the Straits, was established in 1715. The English took it over in 1761, fleeing to Mackinac Island in 1781 during the American Revolution.

You'll skirt most of the Mackinaw City traffic by turning left just before the Interstate 75 overpass. The main drag starts on the opposite side. You'll pass under the approach to the bridge, riding past Fort Michilimackinac and Old

Cyclists circle the 8-mile perimeter of carless Mackinac Island, an optimal extra on the Tip of the Mitt Classic. Courtesy of Tom Buchkoe

Mackinac Point Lighthouse. Stop somewhere here to take a closer look at the 5-mile-long suspension bridge that connects the Upper Peninsula—which by geographic logic should belong to Wisconsin—to the Lower. Completed in 1957, it sits 295 feet above the Straits at its highest point and contains 42,000 miles of wire in its 2-foot-thick main cables. There's a bridge museum above Mama Mia's restaurant in Mackinaw City where you can learn many more facts about the "Mighty Mac."

The bridge is open to bikes on only a few occasions per year, as part of organized group rides (Big Mac Shoreline tours, one-day loop rides held in mid-June and mid-September, contact the Mackinac Chamber of Commerce at 888–455–8100, and DALMAC, a Lansing-to-Mackinac linear tour sponsored by the Tri-County Bicycle Association, held just before Labor Day, call 517–882–3700, ext. 2, or visit www.dalmac.org). That's a unique experience that should go on the to-ride list of all Michigan cyclists. The rest of the year, if you need to get over to the U.P., the bridge authority will haul you and your bike across for a couple bucks.

After the bridge, you'll turn south, now following Lake Huron shoreline, to ride through Mackinaw City. If you choose to take a side trip to Mackinac Island, the carless island famous for its fudge and the Grand Hotel, there are three ferry lines to choose from, departing every fifteen minutes during the height of summer.

The ferry trip itself is one of the highlights of a trip to Mackinac Island. Once there, most people spend their time on the main drag at the island's southern end. There's an 8-mile loop around the perimeter that's also quite popular with both bicyclists and the horse-drawn carriages. Less popular are the roads in the island's interior. You'll climb steep hills to get there but be rewarded with shady roads, great lake views, and near-privacy at some of the historic landmarks.

Back on the mainland, continue riding south through Mackinaw City and turn left on US 23, keeping Lake Huron on your left. There's a wide shoulder on this two-lane highway. US 23 will take you into Cheboygan at mile 27, the best option for food before the nearly 30-mile stretch back west toward Lake Michigan. You'll see the Cheboygan Opera House on your left as you leave town.

Stay on Levering Road for this entire leg of the trip. The shoulder is intermittent along Levering in both Cheboygan and Emmet Counties, though it seems a little better in Emmet, which you'll enter west of Interstate 75. Use caution at mile 34.8, on the I–75 overpass, and at mile 42.1, where Levering jogs briefly north along US 31 (also a two-lane highway) before continuing west. The road gets a little more rolling after I–75, and after US 31 you'll hit the hills on the ride.

Levering Road takes you into Cross Village, a destination mostly for patrons of Legs Inn. Also mentioned on ride 8, the Tunnel of Trees Cruise, Legs Inn specializes in Polish food, which is a little heavy for some riders. At this point on this ride, however, with 55 miles behind you and only 20 to go, it's probably fine to pile the pierogies on your plate. For those with lighter fare in mind, there's the Village Cafe.

THE BASICS

Start: Wilderness State Park.

Length: 75.4-mile lariat.

Terrain: Flat to rolling, with some bigger hills toward the end of the ride, in Emmet County west of U.S. Highway 31.

Traffic and hazards: Watch for pedestrian and vehicle traffic in Mackinaw City. Stay on the wide shoulder on U.S. Highway 23 south of Mackinaw City to Cheboygan. The shoulder is intermittent on Levering Road. Avoid riding this stretch in the late afternoon or evening as it is due west and the sun can blind drivers.

Getting there: Wildnerness State Park is located 11 miles west of Mackinaw City. From Interstate 75, take exit 338 and follow County Road 81 to the B&L Camp Store. Continue straight to the park. As you approach the main intersection, you will buy your permit ($6.00 for a day pass, $24.00 for an annual) at the station on the right and then turn left into the Pines Campground. Follow the sign to the day parking area. From US 31, exit at Carp Lake. Go west on Gill Road and north on Cecil Bay Avenue, then turn left at the camp store.

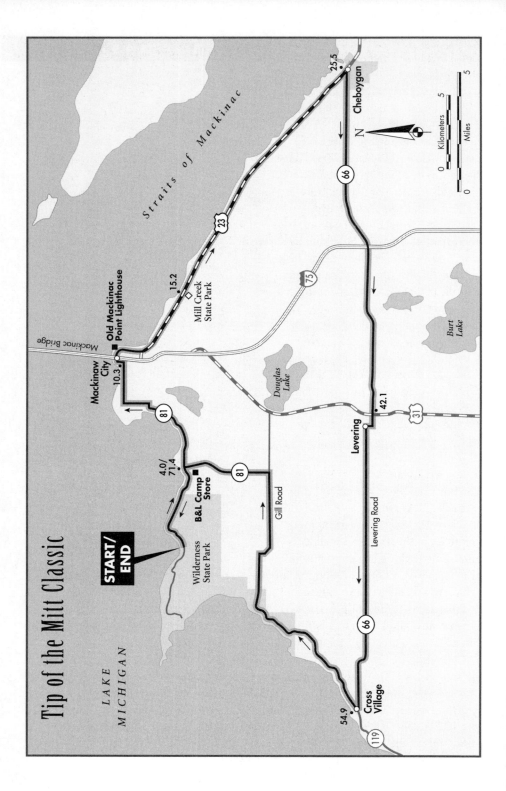

Tip of the Mitt Classic

LAKE MICHIGAN

START/END

Wilderness State Park

B&L Camp Store

4.0/71.4

81

Mackinaw City

10.3

Mackinac Bridge

Old Mackinac Point Lighthouse

15.2

Mill Creek State Park

Straits of Mackinac

23

25.5

Cheboygan

66

75

Burt Lake

Douglas Lake

42.1

Levering

31

Gill Road

Levering Road

66

Cross Village

54.9

119

N

0 Kilometers 5

0 Miles 5

MILES AND DIRECTIONS

0.0 From Wilderness State Park Pines Campground, turn right onto Wilderness Park Drive.

0.4 Picnic area and restrooms.

4.0 B&L Camp Store. Continue straight.

7.5 Road curves to left. Stay on CR 81.

8.5 Yield sign. Turn right onto Central Avenue.

9.9 Village of Mackinaw City recreation complex. Restrooms.

10.3 Turn left on Louvigny, before going under I–75.

10.5 Enter Colonial Michilimackinac. Follow road around to right, passing Fort Restaurant on corner and going under approach to Mackinac Bridge. Road becomes Huron.

10.7 Stop sign for Nicolet. Continue straight. Restrooms at Old Mackinac Point Lighthouse park area ahead on left.

11.1 Turn right on Langlade Street at the Church of the Straits.

11.3 Stop sign for Central Avenue. Cross and continue onto South Huron Avenue. Note: To go to Mackinac Island, turn left into Shepler's Ferry docks or at the docks for the Arnold and Star ferry lines, coming up in the next 0.8 mile.

12.1 Turn left on US 23, riding on the shoulder.

15.2 Historic Mill Creek State Park.

19.1 Roadside park. Restrooms.

25.5 Cheboygan city limits.

27.0 Turn right onto Main Street. At the light in less than 0.1 mile, go straight to visit downtown shops and restaurants. Turn right to continue on ride, heading west on State Street, which becomes Levering Road.

34.8 Gas station on left. Use caution on overpass over I–75.

39.7 Enter Emmet County.

42.1 Stop sign/flashing light. O'Leary's Pub, Levering Café. Turn right onto US 31/County Road 66.

(continued)

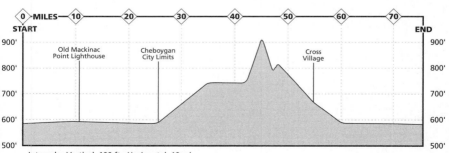

Intervals: Vertical, 100 ft.; Horizontal, 10 mi.

42.4 Turn left on Levering Road.

54.8 Turn right on State Road. Gas station.

54.9 Turn right on Lakeshore Drive into Cross Village.

55.0 Legs Inn.

59.6 Turn left at T intersection (Sturgeon Bay Trail intersects from right), staying on Lakeshore.

67.8 Turn left, staying on CR 81, following signs to Wilderness State Park, B&L Camp Store, golf course, and Carp Lake general store.

71.4 T intersection. B&L Camp Store on left. Turn left onto Wilderness Park Drive.

75.4 Wilderness State Park main intersection. Turn left to return to Pines Campground and day parking.

You'll ride north out of Cross Village on Lakeshore Drive, another beach sand–dusted two-lane road. Lake Michigan appears again after the 60-mile point. You'll turn back inland and then north again. At the intersection with Wilderness Park Drive and the B&L Camp Store, turn left to repeat the 4 miles back to the parking lot. Congratulations on completing a coast-to-coast ride.

LOCAL INFORMATION

♦ Wilderness State Park, 903 Wilderness Park Drive, Carp Lake; (231) 436–5381.

♦ Mackinac Bridge Authority (to arrange for transportation for you and your bike over the bridge); (906) 643–7600; www.mackinacbridge.org.

♦ Mackinaw Area Visitors Bureau; (800) 666–0160; www.mackinawcity.com.

♦ Cheboygan Area Chamber of Commerce; (800) 968–3302; www.cheboygan .com.

LOCAL EVENTS/ATTRACTIONS

♦ Labor Day Bridge Walk: Mackinac Bridge is closed to vehicle traffic for Labor Day morning, and thousands of pedestrians, usually led by the governor, walk the 5-mile span, starting on the St. Ignace (U.P.) side and going south to Mackinaw City. Buses load in Mackinaw City starting at 5:30 A.M., and the walk begins at 7:00 A.M. Shuttles also take St. Ignace starters back across.

♦ The first fudge shop opened in Mackinaw City in 1889. Now there are more than a dozen, with a similar number on Mackinac Island. Who knows why, but to paraphrase, when in Rome, indulge your sweet tooth. Tourists who flock to the area in the summer are nicknamed "fudgies."

- Mackinac state historic parks: Colonial Michilimackinac, where life in a fortified fur-trading village/military outpost is reenacted, and historic Mill Creek, a sawmill and nature park, are right on the route. Fort Mackinac, to which the British fled from Michilimackinac during the American Revolution, is on Mackinac Island. (231) 436–4100; www.mackinacparks.com.

RESTAURANTS

- Mama Mia's, 231 East Central Avenue, Mackinaw City; (231) 436–5534. Great pizza. While away the wait at the Mackinac Bridge Museum above the restaurant. Everything from a video on the construction to hard hats worn by workers. Kitschy, but informative.
- Scalawag's, 226 East Central Avenue, Mackinaw City; (231) 436–7777; www.scalawagswhitefish.com. Specializes in whitefish and chips.
- Legs Inn, Michigan Highway 119, Cross Village; (231) 526–2281; www.legsinn.com. Polish and American food. Must-see decor.

ACCOMMODATIONS

- Budget Host, 517 North Huron Avenue, Mackinaw City; (877) 864–3227. View of the bridge, walking distance to downtown.
- Brigadoon Bed and Breakfast, 207 Langlade Street, Mackinaw City; (231) 436–5543. Victorian home just 2 blocks from heart of Mackinaw City.
- Best Western River Terrace, 847 South Main Street, Cheboygan; (877) 627–9552.
- LeDuc's Creekside Motel, 1380 Mackinaw Avenue/US 23, Cheboygan; (231) 627–4696.

RESTROOMS

- Start/finish: Wilderness State Park.
- Mile 0.4: park picnic area.
- Mile 9.9: Mackinaw City Recreation Area.
- Mile 11.0: establishments in Mackinaw City.
- Mile 19.1: roadside park.
- Mile 27.0: establishments in Cheboygan.
- Mile 34.8: gas station.
- Mile 55.0: establishments in Cross Village.

Ocqueoc Falls Cruise

A waterfall and a lighthouse familiar to locals but well off the beaten tourist path highlight this ride through northeast Michigan's Presque Isle County. Ocqueoc Falls, the largest waterfall in the Lower Peninsula, is a popular local picnic and swimming destination. A trail alongside the Ocqueoc River below the falls allows you a little more solitude. 40 Mile Point Lighthouse, a pretty brick lighthouse with a somewhat unusual square lighthouse tower, is one of those lighthouses that looks like it actually might have been a comfortable home, in contrast to many others. Open stretches of Lake Huron and lightly traveled roads are other highlights.

Given its location on Lake Huron, the only port along the 80 miles of shoreline between Cheboygan and Alpena, Rogers City has a long nautical history. Along Huron Avenue the Avenue of Flags pays tribute to the merchant marine industry and the sailors who work in it. In Lakeside Park, a fitting place to start, a giant ship propeller and anchor are a memorial to sailors who lost their lives on the *Carl D. Bradley* and *Str. Cedarville*, ships based out of Rogers City that sank on the Great Lakes.

From Lakeside Park the route first heads inland, however, to Ocqueoc Falls. You'll ride along a shoulder for the 12 rolling, sometimes hilly miles to the falls, passing farms and slough areas. Consisting of an upper and lower falls, Ocqueoc (meaning "sacred") Falls is the largest waterfall in the Lower Peninsula. If you're here on a hot summer day, Ocqueoc Falls is likely to be filled with local picnickers and swimmers and might not feel too sacred. If you walk to the river's edge, there's a narrow trail you can take down from the falls for a bit of solitude.

Turn right out of the falls and then right again in about another mile and a half on Ocqueoc Road, heading north. There are more hills along this 6-mile stretch. From Ocqueoc Road you'll turn back east toward Rogers City. You'll be riding along US 23. Although it's a highway, there's an extra-wide shoulder and the road is smooth and in great condition. It's relatively lightly traveled, though what traffic there is moves at highway speeds. In about 5 miles you'll turn off the highway onto Tucker/County Road 646, another road in great condition, with some fun curves and rollers. When it intersects US 23, you'll turn back for a 0.7-mile spur to 40 Mile Point Lighthouse, named for the spot it occupies on Lake Huron, 40 miles southeast of Old Mackinac

Point and 40 miles northwest of Thunder Bay. It's now a museum, open weekends from noon to 4:00 P.M. Memorial Day through mid-October.

Returning to US 23, there's a pit stop at P. H. Hoeft State Park. (You can enter state parks for free on a bike.) Those with an interest in Indian history will want to take the 10-minute walk on the beach north of the park to Sacred Rock. Measuring 20 by 8 by 6 feet, this rock was the Anishinabe nation's sacrificial and council meeting site. Legend has it that ages ago the point where the rock now stands was the dividing line between the hunting grounds of two tribes. To the rear of the rock is a cliff about 80 feet high composed of clay and sand. Numerous springs rise out of the banks, causing the soil to constantly shift so that it looks as if the banks are moving into the lake; thus, these are called the Sliding Banks.

Less than a mile after the state park, you'll turn off US 23 for good onto Birchwood Road. You'll ride the last 5 miles on local roads and take a bike path the final mile and a half back into Lakeside Park.

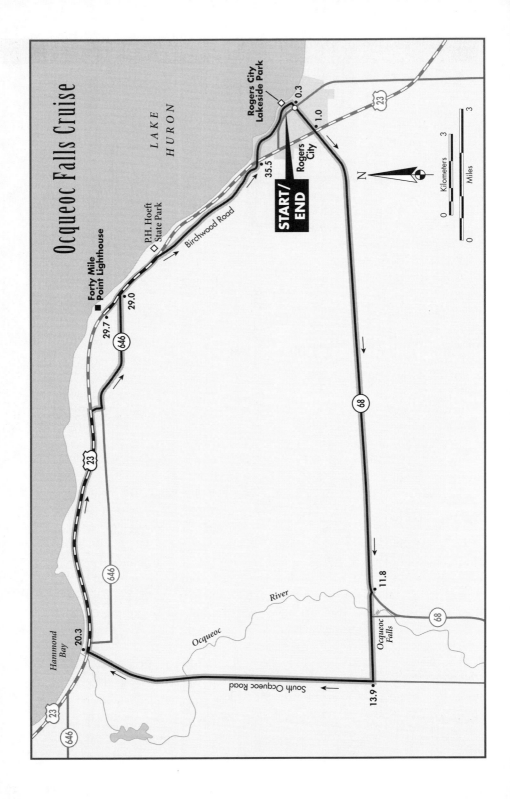

Ocqueoc Falls Cruise

LAKE HURON

Forty Mile Point Lighthouse

P.H. Hoeft State Park

Rogers City Lakeside Park

0.3

1.0

Rogers City

START/END

35.5

Birchwood Road

29.7

29.0

646

23

646

Hammond Bay

20.3

Ocqueoc River

South Ocqueoc Road

13.9

Ocqueoc Falls

11.8

68

68

23

23

646

N

Kilometers

Miles

0   3

0   3

0.0 From Rogers City Lakeside Park, ride out the way you entered, turning left onto Lake Street at the basketball courts.

0.2 Turn right on Erie Street, and go straight through town.

1.0 Traffic light. Cross US 23 and ride west on MI 68.

11.8 Right on Ocqueoc Falls Road.

12.2 Turn right into park entrance to visit falls. Restrooms. After visiting falls, turn right out of park to continue west on Ocqueoc Falls Road.

13.9 Turn right on South Ocqueoc Road.

20.3 Turn right on US 23.

25.6 Turn right on Tucker.

25.8 Stop sign. Turn left at T intersection onto CR 646.

29.0 Intersection with US 23. Turn left and go 0.7 mile to visit 40 Mile Point Lighthouse. Retrace route to intersection and continue south on US 23. (Mileage now 30.4.)

31.9 P. H. Hoeft State Park. Restrooms.

32.7 Turn right on Birchwood Road.

35.5 Stop sign. Cross US 23 and turn left onto Forest, then take an immediate right onto Huron Sunrise Trail.

37.0 Stop sign. Turn left from path onto First Street.

37.2 Stop sign. Turn left onto Huron Avenue. Turn right immediately on Lake Street, which then turns left into the parking lot.

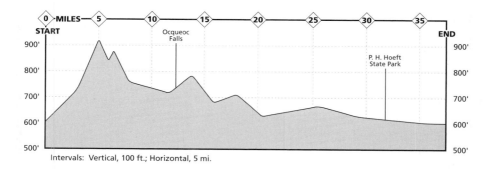

Intervals: Vertical, 100 ft.; Horizontal, 5 mi.

LOCAL INFORMATION

♦ Presque Isle Tourism Council; (989) 734–4722; www.presqueislemi.com.

♦ Rogers City Travelers and Visitors Bureau; (877) 230–2840.

Ocqueoc Falls is the largest waterfall in the Lower Peninsula. Courtesy of Michael M. Smith

LOCAL EVENTS/ATTRACTIONS

♦ The Nautical Festival includes a parade, carnival, entertainment, and arts-and-crafts fair. Held on the first weekend of August at Rogers City's Lakeside Park. (989) 734–4722.

♦ At the Salmon Tournament in Rogers City, anglers vie for the biggest catch in August and again in September. (989) 734–4722.

♦ A farmers' market convenes at Lake Street and Huron Avenue in Rogers City on Saturdays from 8:00 A.M. to noon May to October. (989) 734–4722.

RESTAURANTS

♦ Kelly's Venture Inn, 3090 US 23 south (toward Posen), Rogers City; (989) 734–2865. Pizza.

♦ Karsten's Restaurant and Ice Cream Parlour, 1072 West Third Street, Rogers City; (989) 734–2050. Diner menu and ice cream. Recommended sundaes.

♦ Water's Edge, 530 North Third Street, Rogers City; (989) 734–4747. You'll see it from the bike path. Outdoor deck.

◆ The Gaslight Restaurant, 351 North Bradley Highway/US 23, Rogers City; (989) 734–4531. Recommended at the local bike shop.

ACCOMMODATIONS

◆ Driftwood Motel, 540 West Third Street, Rogers City; (989) 734–4777. On Lake Huron, next to Water's Edge restaurant.
◆ Presque Isle Lodge Bed & Breakfast, in Presque Isle, about twenty minutes south of Rogers City; (989) 595–6970.
◆ Manitou Shores Resort, 7995 US 23 north, Rogers City; (989) 734–7233. Cabins and motel on Lake Huron.

RESTROOMS

◆ Start/finish: Lakeside Park.
◆ Mile 12.2: Ocqueoc Falls.
◆ Mile 31.9: P. H. Hoeft State Park.

Tunnel of Trees Cruise

The Tunnel of Trees is an 18-mile stretch of blufftop state highway overlooking Lake Michigan. This section of Michigan Highway 119, as it is more practically known, is designated as a state Heritage Route for its scenic beauty. In terms of biking, it is one of Michigan's and the Midwest's best-known rides. The ride begins just south of Harbor Springs, a town whose huge summer "cottages" in the exclusive associations along Little Traverse Bay are a Midwestern version of Newport, Rhode Island. Once out of Harbor Springs, however, you'll be in rural territory. There's a 4-mile stretch of hills midride, between Harbor Springs and the Tunnel of Trees. As the route is out and back once it reaches the Tunnel, riders can choose to increase or decrease the distance. Riding at least to Good Hart is recommended.

Starting in the state park allows you a few miles to warm up on flat roads before hitting the hills just outside Harbor Springs. Parking hassles in Harbor Springs are also avoided. From the parking lot, ride back out to MI 119 and turn left on the trail that parallels the highway. When the trail dead-ends, turn left onto Beach Road. After meandering a few miles through a densely wooded residential section, you'll get a beautiful view of Little Traverse Bay. Upcoming are the Wequetonsing association "cottages," a collection of private summer residences founded in 1880. It's easy to see why many of the original family owners have hung onto the homes through the years.

Locals call Harbor Springs simply "Harbor." If you listen closely, you might detect an East Coast–accented pronunciation, i.e., "Haaah-bor." It's not just coincidence. Harbor Springs is reminiscent of upscale East Coast resort communities. You'll pass by the marina, where public restrooms are available, and the Little Traverse Bay Yacht Club.

On the return trip through town, it's worth a moment to stroll the docks. Sailing is particularly popular on Little Traverse Bay, and the boats match the homes in terms of size and extravagance. Downtown Harbor Springs also has plenty of tempting shops and restaurants, but I advise riding first and relaxing afterward.

The hilly 4-mile section lies ahead, followed by the official start of the Tunnel of Trees between Middle and Stutsmanville Roads. Hardwoods dominate, primarily beech, maple, and oak, as well as aspen, birch, hemlock, and a few varieties of pine. There is almost no commercial development along the Tunnel, save the Good Hart General Store and Legs Inn (see "restaurants" for more information). Residential development, however, has boomed over the past thirty years. Vacation-home owners seeking to capture a bit of the view have driven growth in the townships along the Tunnel above even the healthy 25 percent increase Emmet County overall experienced between 1990 and 2000. The development, along steep slopes with unstable soil conditions, often accompanied by tree cutting to clear a building site, concerns many in the area. The Heritage Route designation may prove to be a saving grace, as it makes MI 119 eligible for federal funding for maintenance and preservation, including acquisition of scenic parcels.

Just past Robinson Road on MI 119 you'll come to the Good Hart General Store. Equipped with picnic tables and a pit toilet outside, and serving deli and bakery fare inside, it is a perfect place for lunch.

After Good Hart either turn back south toward Harbor Springs or continue north on MI 119. In another 7 miles you'll come to Cross Village and Legs Inn, a

THE BASICS

Start: Petoskey State Park, in between Petoskey and Harbor Springs.

Length: 38.2-mile circuit with an optional 14-mile sidetrip to Cross Village.

Terrain: Flat to start. Four-mile section of hills outside Harbor Springs. One of the tougher cruises in this book. Small rollers on the Tunnel of Trees.

Traffic and hazards: Motorists like the Tunnel of Trees as much as bicyclists do. Traffic can be heavy on the Tunnel, which while considered a two-lane road sometimes seems more like one and a half. The winding road does keep car speeds down, and many drivers are also sightseers and not in a hurry. Still, a rearview mirror is strongly advised on this ride.

Getting there: From Petoskey, take U.S. Highway 31 north. Turn left onto MI 119 (not the Tunnel of Trees at this point). In about 1 mile, turn left into Petoskey State Park. A $6.00 day pass is required to park at the beach/picnic area.

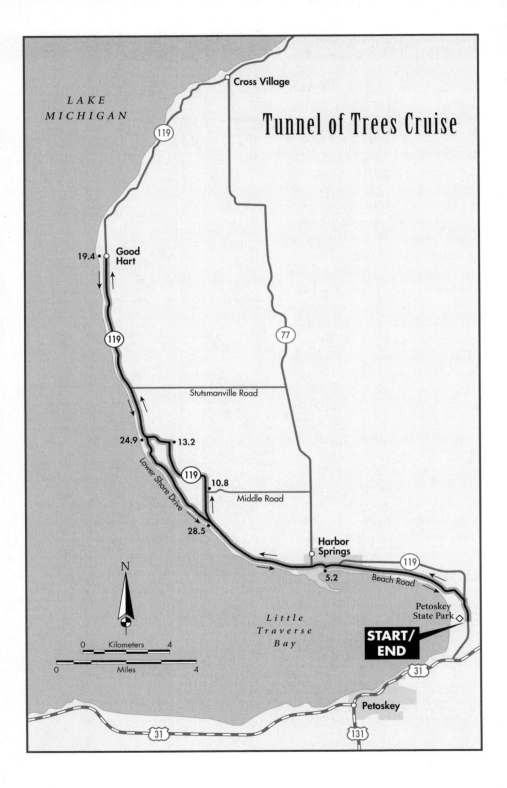

LAKE
MICHIGAN

Cross Village

Tunnel of Trees Cruise

119

19.4 • Good
Hart

119

77

Stutsmanville Road

24.9 • • 13.2

Lower Shore Drive

119

10.8

Middle Road

28.5 •

Harbor
Springs

119

5.2

Beach Road

Petoskey
State Park

START/
END

31

N

0   Kilometers   4

0   Miles   4

Little
Traverse
Bay

Petoskey

31

131

0.0 From the parking lot at the beach/picnic area, leave the park the way you came in.

0.5 Turn left onto bike path where park entrance road T's into MI 119.

1.1 Turn left onto Beach Road.

3.6 Follow curve to left, away from Bridge Street.

3.8 Turn right onto Pennsylvania.

4.0 Turn left at stop sign onto unmarked road. Follow it around the quick curve to the right, riding along Little Traverse Bay.

4.5 Stop sign. Continue straight on Beach Drive.

5.2 Zoll Street Park. Follow road as it curves to the right.

5.3 Turn left onto Bay Street. Drinking fountain across intersection.

5.8 City of Harbor Springs marina. Public restrooms.

5.9 Turn right onto State Street. Sign says TO M–119 SCENIC ROUTE.

6.0 Stop sign. Cross East Main Street and continue straight. At next block, turn left on Third Street.

6.1 Turn right onto Church Street, which immediately curves to left and becomes Fourth Street.

6.4 Rough, bumpy pavement for next 0.2 miles.

6.8 Turn left onto MI 119.

10.8 Use caution crossing intersection with Middle Road as you come down a hill.

13.2 Follow MI 119 around to the left. Official beginning of the Tunnel of Trees State Heritage Route. Fast, curving downhill ahead.

19.4 Good Hart. Picnic fare inside Good Hart General Store. Pit toilet outside.

Sidetrip: Continue north on MI 119 for 7 miles to Cross Village and Legs Inn, adding 14 miles total to the trip. Turn around to retrace your route to Good Hart.

(continued)

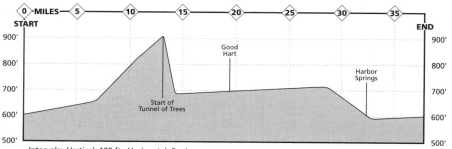

Intervals: Vertical, 100 ft.; Horizontal, 5 mi.

24.9 Turn right on Lower Shore Road. Watch for easy-to-miss turn, just before yellow arrow sign indicating curving uphill ahead.

28.0 Thorne Swift Nature Preserve.

28.5 Turn right onto MI 119.

32.1 Use caution on downhill coming into downtown Harbor Springs.

32.3 Turn left at stop sign onto Main Street. Many shops, restaurants, coffee, fudge, ice cream, and cookies all available.

32.4 Turn right on Spring Street if you need to visit restrooms at marina again. Otherwise, continue straight.

32.6 Turn right onto Judd, then turn left at the stop sign onto Bay Street.

32.9 Turn right at stop sign onto Zoll Street. Follow the curve around to the left onto Beach Drive.

34.1 Turn right at stop sign onto unmarked road.

34.4 Turn right at stop sign onto Fern Street.

35.0 Follow curve to left, and turn right at yield sign onto Beach Road.

37.2 Turn right onto bike path.

37.7 Turn right into Petoskey State Park, follow drive 0.5 mile to return to parking lot.

restaurant unlikely in both décor and menu. It's worth a peek inside, but, specializing in Polish food, it makes a better postride than midride meal. At this point the Tunnel of Trees will have thinned noticeably, and you'll be riding in sun.

Returning south along MI 119, you'll retrace your route until turning right on Lower Shore Road, which enables you to avoid climbing the downhill you enjoyed on the way out. Lower Shore Road meets MI 119 again in about 4 miles—use caution riding back into Harbor Springs. Now's your chance to browse the shops, sample ice cream, and walk the docks of the yacht club. If you're here on a summer weekend, downtown will be bustling. It's hard to believe, but Harbor Springs has a tradition of bowling on Main Street in early April, when the town clears out for spring break. You'll leave town riding alongside the bay, retracing your way back to the bike path and the state park.

LOCAL INFORMATION

♦ Petoskey–Harbor Springs–Boyne Country Visitors Bureau; (800) 845–2828; www.boynecountry.com.

♦ Harbor Springs Chamber of Commerce; (231) 526–7999; www.harbor springschamber.com.

♦ Petoskey Regional Chamber of Commerce; (231) 347–4150; www.petoskey .com.

LOCAL EVENTS/ATTRACTIONS

♦ The Little Traverse Bay Regatta is run the end of July. Little Traverse Bay Yacht Club; (231) 526–7919.

♦ At the Annual Bliss Fest Music Festival in mid-July, camp overnight a la Woodstock or come for a day of folk music. (231) 348–2815.

♦ Petoskey's Festival on the Bay, held in mid-August, was inaugurated in 2003. Sunset celebration with jazz, arts and crafts. (231) 347–4150; www.petoskey .com.

♦ A year-round local activity is petoskey-stone hunting. The shores of Little Traverse Bay are rife with petoskeys, Michigan's state stone. Really fossilized coral, petoskey stones feature a pattern of hexagons, each with a dark center. Both the state park and Magnus Park, at the end of Lake Street in Petoskey, are fertile hunting grounds. The pattern is most obvious when the stones are wet.

RESTAURANTS

♦ City Park Grill, 432 East Lake Street, Petoskey; (231) 347–0101. Trendy but casual. Live entertainment on weekends.

Located midway on the Tunnel of Trees ride, the Good Hart General Store is a great picnic stop.

♦ Stafford's Perry Inn, corner of Bay and Lewis Streets, Petoskey; (231) 347–2516. Pricey, but great view of sunsets over Little Traverse Bay from dining room inside. Outdoor veranda. Regional menu.

♦ Legs Inn, MI 119, Cross Village; (231) 526–2281; www.legsinn.com.

♦ The Pier, 102 Bay Street, Harbor Springs; (231) 526–6201. Overlooks Harbor Springs Marina. Menu runs casual to prime rib.

ACCOMMODATIONS

♦ Terrace Inn, 1549 Glendale (off US 31), P.O. Box 266, Petoskey 49770; (800) 530–9898 or (231) 347–2410. Authentic Victorian decor in the heart of historic Bay View, between Petoskey and Harbor Springs. Dining with outdoor veranda.

♦ Stafford's Perry Hotel, Bay and Lewis Streets, Petoskey; (800) 737–1899 or (231) 347–4000. Centennial hotel overlooking Little Traverse Bay in Petoskey's Gaslight Shopping District. Upscale dining and casual pub.

♦ Best Western Inn of Petoskey, 1300 Spring Street/U.S. Highway 131 south, Petoskey; (888) PETOSKEY (738–6753) or (231) 347–3925.

♦ Best Western of Harbor Springs, 8514 MI 119, Harbor Springs; (231) 347–9050 or (800) 528–1234 (worldwide reservations).

RESTROOMS

♦ Start/finish: Petoskey State Park.

♦ Mile 5.8: city marina on Bay Street in Harbor Springs.

♦ Mile 19.4: Good Hart General Store.

Torch Lake Challenge

Every July the Traverse City–based Cherry Capital Cycling Club hosts the Ride Around Torch, or RAT. Cyclists from around the state come for the gorgeous scenery, especially for Torch's clear waters that range from light green and turquoise to deep blue. This route is based on one of the options offered on that tour. It's a shorter, flatter route that hugs the shoreline of one of Michigan's largest inland lakes and avoids the inland hills to the east. The route includes one stretch of heavier-trafficked highway and scattered more difficult climbs. There are great local dining options to choose from postride.

National Geographic once named Torch Lake the third most beautiful lake in the world. This tidbit is often cited by local tourism folks and real estate agents, and it's become more lore than fact. Some fudge it, saying only that the magazine deemed it "one of" the world's most beautiful. But don't waste your time looking it up. Instead, look at the lake. Its clarity and changing colors, from green to turquoise to deep blue, will likely convince you that Torch Lake will make for a beautiful ride.

The ride starts in the town of Elk Rapids. You'll cruise through town for 5 miles, riding past Elk Lake, until coasting down to West Torch Lake Drive, where you'll take a sharp left. The road is shady and relatively flat here, and you can glimpse the lake now and again, though most of the homes have long driveways with woods in between them and the road.

After 6 miles you'll turn left on Barnes Road and encounter the first significant climb, a two-hump hill that gives you a bit of respite in between. At the

THE BASICS

Start: Parking lot of Elk Rapids High School.

Length: 52.7-mile lariat.

Terrain: Mix of flat and rolling hills. Most climbs are short and gradual.

Traffic and hazards: One 5-mile stretch along U.S. Highway 31 is heavily trafficked in summer. Try to arrange your ride so as to pass this stretch early in the day. Watch for sand on roads and a dropoff edge on the shoulder, especially riding out of and into Elk Rapids.

Getting there: From Traverse City, take US 31 north through Acme. It is 10 miles from the light at Michigan Highway 72 to the traffic light in Elk Rapids. At the light, after crossing the bridge, turn right onto Ames Street. In 0.6 mile turn right on Henry Street (orange sign for Elk Rapids Schools), then left on Buckley Street, a quick right on Park Street, and left on Third Street to enter the Elk Rapids High School parking lot.

top of the hill, you'll turn right onto US 31. Stay on the shoulder and watch for traffic. The "town" of Torch Lake—really a spot on the road with a name—is along the highway. Pick up a snack at Sonny's Torch Lake Market, which has something to tempt every appetite, and take it down to the Township Park, where you can admire the lake from a short pier.

Torch Lake received its name from Native Americans, who used torches to fish from their canoes at night. My explanation is that the water is so incredibly clear that it appears to be illuminated from below, perhaps by torches.

While Antrim County residents no longer literally depend on the water for food, it remains the bread and butter of the region. The beauty of the lake is a beacon to summer residents and retirees. As the biggest of the county's "chain o' lakes" that lead to Lake Michigan, Torch Lake creates a tourist economy driven by boaters, anglers, and water-loving vacationers in general.

Leaving the park, you'll soon round the north tip of Torch Lake and leave the highway behind. As you begin your ride down the east side, you'll notice lots more open water views. The road separates many of the homes on this side from the shore, affording you a better view from the saddle.

After a dozen or so relatively flat miles, you'll come to the Clam River and the Dockside, one of northern Michigan's favorite summertime restaurants. It's basic burgers and sandwiches, but, when eaten on the big deck in view of the lake, they can't be beat. Even if you're not hungry, take a stroll out to the end of dock and read the names of the families who've bought a board. Leave the restaurant by turning right again onto East Torch Lake Drive.

The community of Alden is next, a clump of shops plus a bar and an ice-cream shop. You're now at Torch Lake's southern end. You'll round that tip and pass through Torch River before heading north for the closest shoreline riding and the greatest concentration of hills, to work off the burger and the ice

The deck at the Dockside is a good place to refuel for the hills on the last 20 miles of the Torch Lake Challenge.

cream. You'll have room for a Cajun dinner at Pearl's or a snack at one of the River Street cafes by the time you get back to Elk Rapids.

LOCAL INFORMATION

♦ Elk Rapids Area Chamber of Commerce; (231) 264-8202; www.elkrapids chamber.org.
♦ Traverse City Convention and Visitors Bureau; (800) TRAVERS; www.my traversecity.com.

LOCAL EVENTS/ATTRACTIONS

♦ The annual Harbor Days summer festival is held in Elk Rapids at the end of July/beginning of August. (231) 264–8202.
♦ Alden's annual Strawberry Fest takes place in mid-June at Alden Depot Park and Museum. (231) 331–6811.
♦ The National Cherry Festival is held around the first week in July, usually including the Fourth. Music, cherry food, an air show, and fireworks, centered

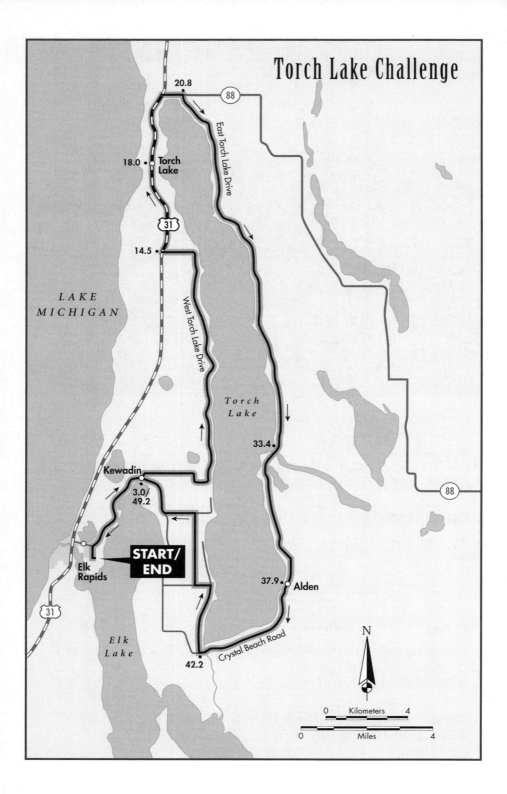

Torch Lake Challenge

20.8

88

East Torch Lake Drive

18.0 • Torch
Lake

31

14.5 •

LAKE
MICHIGAN

West Torch Lake Drive

Torch
Lake

33.4 •

Kewadin
3.0/
49.2

Elk
Rapids

START/
END

37.9 • Alden

42.2

Crystal Beach Road

88

Elk
Lake

31

N

0   Kilometers   4

0   Miles   4

MILES AND DIRECTIONS

0.0 Exit the north side of Elk Rapids High School parking lot and turn left onto Third Street. Then make a quick right at the stop sign onto Park Street.

0.3 Stop sign. Turn left onto Buckley Street, and then make a quick right onto Henry Street.

0.4 Stop sign. Turn right onto Ames Street. More traffic, stay in shoulder. Watch edge, which can disappear in sand and gravel.

3.0 Kewadin. Gas station and market.

3.4 Turn left onto Cairn Highway before Milton Township Park and tennis courts.

3.6 Turn right onto Indian Road after Milton Township Fire Department. Use caution on the long downhill in a mile and a half, watching for sand on roads.

5.1 Sharp right.

5.3 Sharp left going downhill. Large quarry/gravel pit on right can be distracting; watch road instead. Lots of sand and gravel on road.

5.8 Turn left on North West Torch Lake Drive.

13.5 Road curves left, away from lake, becoming Barnes Road. Two-tiered hill ahead.

14.5 Stop sign. Turn right on US 31. Stay on shoulder, and watch for heavier, fast traffic on this highway, as well as gravel/sand on road.

17.5 Sonny's Torch Lake Market. Turn right after store on Public Dock Road to go to Torch Lake Township Park. Restrooms.

17.9 Leave park and turn right onto Prospect Street. At yield sign, turn left onto Third Street.

18.0 Stop sign. Turn right onto US 31, again using caution.

20.2 Turn right onto Michigan Highway 88.

20.8 Turn right onto North East Torch Lake Drive, halfway up the hill.

23.8 Torch Tip Ironworks. Combination home/blacksmithy/shop.

23.9 Brownwood Acres. Flea markets on Sundays.

(continued)

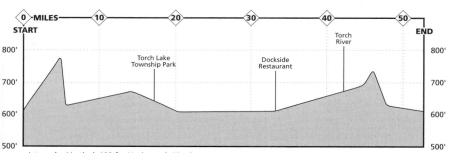

Intervals: Vertical, 100 ft.; Horizontal, 10 mi.

31.1 Stop sign. Turn right on Bellaire Highway (South East Torch Lake Drive), following sign to Alden.

33.4 Turn right to enter Dockside restaurant premises. Leave turning right to continue south on East Torch Lake Drive.

37.1 Stop sign. Turn right onto Alden Highway.

37.9 Enter Alden. S-curve through town. Turn right on East Street for public restrooms. Alden Depot and Museum on your right as you leave town, open Thursday to Sundays, 1:00 to 4:00 P.M.

39.9 Turn right on Crystal Beach Road, at Alden Marine Sports.

42.1 Narrow bridge over Torch River. Ace Hardware, Mobil station.

42.2 Turn right at flashing light onto South West Torch Lake Drive. Shoreline riding.

44.1 Bear left on Hickin Road. Uphill.

44.7 Turn right on Western Road. Patchy, rough pavement ahead.

47.0 Stop sign. Turn left on Bussa Road.

48.0 Stop sign. Turn right onto Cherry Avenue. Elk Lake visible.

49.2 Kewadin. Mobil station, Elk Lake Market.

51.8 Reenter Elk Rapids.

52.3 Turn left on Henry Street just after Pearl's restaurant and curve. Orange sign points to Elk Rapids Schools. Stop sign at Buckley Street, turn left.

52.4 Turn right onto Park Street.

52.7 Turn left onto Third Street to return to Elk Rapids High School parking lot.

around Traverse City's Open Space. Area population usually triples, putting accommodations at a premium. (231) 947–4230.

♦ Music House, 7377 US 31 North, Acme. Restored collection of antique automated instruments and memorabilia. (231) 938–9300.

RESTAURANTS

♦ Pearl's New Orleans Kitchen, 617 Ames Street, Elk Rapids; (231) 264–0530. If you go on a weekend, expect a wait. Creole and Cajun specialties, bayou decor, great atmosphere, and live entertainment some weekends. Outdoor deck.

♦ Dockside, 6340 East Torch Lake Drive; (231) 377–7859. Burgers, sandwiches, salads, wet burritos served on the deck overlooking Torch Lake.

♦ Tapawingo, 9502 Lake Street, Ellsworth; (231) 588–7351. Eclectic, upscale cuisine drawing diners from as far as Detroit and Chicago. Make a reservation and bring your wallet.

ACCOMMODATIONS

Accommodations are a bit scarce in immediate area, but try one of the following:

♦ Cairn House Bed and Breakfast, 8160 Cairn Highway, Elk Rapids; (231) 264–8994; www.cairnhouse.com.

♦ North Wind Resort, 2553 South West Torch Lake Drive, Rapid City; (231) 322–4554.

♦ Stony Waters Inn, 226 North Bridge Street, Bellaire; (231) 533–6131. Cozy motel on Cedar River. Nice lobby fireplace.

♦ Shanty Creek Resort, MI 88, Bellaire; (800) 678–4111. Full-service golf and ski resort.

♦ Grand Traverse Resort, 100 Grand Traverse Village Boulevard, Acme; (800) 236–1577. Full-service golf resort and spa.

Many resorts also offer weekly rentals. See "Local Information" for more information.

RESTROOMS

♦ Mile 3.0: gas station in Kewadin.
♦ Mile 17.6: Torch Lake Township Park.
♦ Mile 33.4: Dockside Restaurant.
♦ Mile 37.9: Alden.
♦ Mile 42.1: various establishments in Torch River.
♦ Mile 49.2: gas station in Kewadin.

Old Mission Peninsula Cruise

The 18-mile-long, 2-mile-wide finger of land that divides Lake Michigan's Grand Traverse Bay is a cyclist's serendipity. Most of the 40-mile route is along flat shoreline, but there are scattered steep hills too, clustered at the tip. Atop them cyclists are rewarded with views of both bays, cherry orchards, and vineyards and then a blow-back-the-helmet descent. Several restaurants offer respite along the route, from a haunted inn to a belly-up-to-the bar pub to an old-time general store serving homemade ice cream. The Old Mission Lighthouse and Park at the tip of the peninsula (also the forty-fifth parallel, halfway between the equator and the North Pole) makes a perfect rest stop.

Traverse City bills itself as the world's cherry capital, and indeed, the region grows more than three-quarters of the world's tart variety, the kind used in pies. You'll see many of these orchards on the Old Mission Peninsula Cruise. It's favored by local cyclists, including members of the aptly named Cherry Capital Cyclists, for its beautiful scenery, good roads, and lack of traffic. This counterclockwise outer loop is the easiest of the many routes around the peninsula.

Pedaling east from the high school, in just a few blocks you'll see the waters of East Grand Traverse Bay (locally known simply as East Bay). Turn left on East Shore Road and enjoy shady, quiet roads through this residential neighborhood. Ignore the many markings on the road, which indicate the routes for various Traverse City running and biking events.

East Shore Road will T into MI 37, also known as Center Road, the peninsula's main drag. Use caution on this, the busiest portion of the ride, especially on summer weekends. At the first opportunity to turn right, do so, onto Bluff Road.

Bluff intersects Smokey Hollow Road, which is the first and worst climb. As you're spinning the pedals, look up to your left. The big house perched on the bluff is Chateau Chantal, one of about a half-dozen wineries growing grapes and producing wine on the peninsula.

A few words about the fruit industry: The microclimate on this spit of land creates ideal conditions for fruit growing. Summer heat and winter cold are moderated by winds and precipitation blowing across the peninsula. Hilly terrain means trees and vines can be planted in tiers, allowing them all maximum exposure to sunlight. Snowfall is also heavier on the peninsula than in Traverse City, which insulates trees and vines in winter.

Such idyllic surroundings are equally attractive to people, however, and several years of hard times for the cherry industry have led to subdivisions standing where orchards once did. But the grape

THE BASICS

Start: Traverse City Central High School.

Length: 39.5-mile loop, with 2-mile optional sidetrip.

Terrain: Mostly flat, with scattered short but steep hills midride, at the tip of the peninsula.

Traffic and hazards: Use caution on Center Road/Michigan Highway 37, a state highway and the peninsula's main drag, especially on the first of three stretches you'll ride on. All stretches offer a wide shoulder, however. The route consists entirely of two-lane roads and is curving and at times hilly, meaning cars can appear suddenly. Special Note: In July and early August, watch for slow-moving trucks carrying tanks of cherries and for slippery patches of spilled cherries, especially on the northern half of the route.

Getting there: In Traverse City, go north onto MI 37 at the intersection of Garfield Road and U.S. Highway 31/MI 37. Turn right at the first light, in about a quarter mile, onto Eastern Avenue. The high school is in the second block on your right.

and wine industry, with its higher profit margins and value-added product, are giving the peninsula's agricultural community new hope for survival. Stop at any of the wineries, perhaps after you've put away the bike. You'll find a complimentary tasting glass and ready conversation.

A great downhill follows the Smokey Hollow climb, and you can coast nearly all the way into the settlement of Old Mission. The general store with the homemade ice cream, plus pickles in barrels, penny candy, beverages, and deli items, is on your right. After you've rested, walk down to the cabin just past the store/post office. It's a replica of the original church built in 1839 by the Rev. Peter Dougherty, who came here to Christianize the Native Americans. Dougherty's other legacy is that of the cherry. He planted the first orchard on Old Mission in 1852.

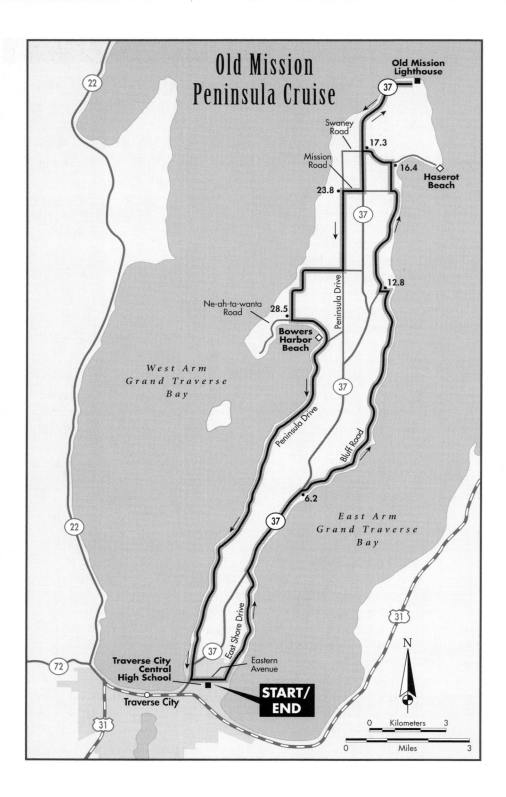

0.0 Turn right out of the Traverse City Central High School parking lot onto Eastern Avenue. You can get on a bike path paralleling Eastern in about 0.2 mile.

0.7 Turn left on East Shore Drive.

3.8 Turn right on Center Road/MI 37. Fast traffic, stay on paved shoulder. Pit toilet on right at East Bay Public Boat Launch.

5.9 Archie Park on left. Pit toilet.

6.2 Turn right onto Bluff Road, just past Gray Road.

11.8 Nice rest stop overlooking East Bay on left, with benches.

12.8 Turn right at stop sign (T intersection). No sign for road you are turning onto, but it is Smokey Hollow Road. Big hill ahead.

14.0 Begin fast descent, which includes a sharp left turn at about mile 14.4.

15.6 Right on Mission Road, after Old Mission sign.

15.9 Old Mission General Store and post office, featuring homemade ice cream, pickles in barrels, penny candy, beverages and deli items.

16.4 Turn left on Swaney Road. (For restroom, turn right on Swaney and go 0.2 mile to Haserot Beach, then retrace route.)

17.3 Right on Center Road/MI 37. Faster traffic, stay on shoulder.

18.1 Enter Lighthouse Park.

19.9 Loop around cul-de-sac and enter lighthouse driveway. Pit toilet, drinking fountain, lighthouse, beach, and park. Leave park the same way you came.

23.4 Turn right on unmarked road, which is Mission Road, opposite direction from sign pointing to Old Mission.

23.8 Turn left on Peninsula Drive.

25.9 Turn right on Kroupa Road. Kroupa Fruit Processing plant on right. Use extreme caution in July and August if spilled cherries are on road.

26.9 Kroupa takes a series of sharp curves, first left, then right, then left, and then goes downhill. Be prepared to stop abruptly at stop sign.

(continued)

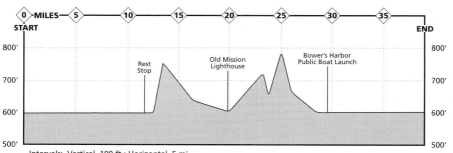

Intervals: Vertical, 100 ft.; Horizontal, 5 mi.

28.5 Turn left at stop sign onto Ne-ah-ta-wanta Road. **Sidetrip:** For an extra 2 miles, turn right and follow Ne-ah-ta-wanta until it dead-ends, then retrace route.

29.6 Bowers Harbor Public Boat Launch. Pit toilet.

29.7 Turn right onto Peninsula Drive.

29.8 Boathouse Restaurant.

30.4 Bowers Harbor Inn and Bowery restaurants.

39.0 Right on Center Road/MI 37 at traffic light. Stay on shoulder.

39.3 Turn left onto Eastern Avenue at traffic light.

39.5 Turn right into high school parking lot to finish ride.

Leave Old Mission by continuing north on Mission Road. For a bathroom break, take the first right and you'll see Haserot Park, which has pit toilets. Otherwise, turn left and ride back up for the second stretch on MI 37/Center Road, much less trafficked up here. It's a flat couple miles to the lighthouse park.

Located on the forty-fifth parallel, halfway between the North Pole and the equator, the Old Mission Lighthouse is a private residence, but you can freely wander the beach and the park. Water levels have always been shallow here, but the extreme drop in Great Lakes water levels over the past few years has created a yawning expanse of exposed lake bottom. Amenities include a pit toilet and drinking fountain.

Leave the lighthouse park as you came. You'll turn right, opposite the Old Mission sign, and start heading down the West Bay side of the peninsula. Power Island, a county park, is visible midbay.

At Ne-ah-ta-wanta Road, turn right to add a couple miles. To stay on the route, turn left. Bowers Harbor Public Boat Launch is on your right in 1 mile, offering pit toilets. For more-civilized facilities plus a bite to eat, stay in the saddle a few minutes longer and turn right onto Peninsula Drive. Three dining options are coming up in the next half mile. Up first is the Boathouse, followed by the purportedly haunted and pricey Bowers Harbor Inn and its unhaunted and easier-on-the-wallet sister, the Bowery.

Peninsula Drive will take you all the way back to town. Turn left at the second light—the only two you'll encounter all ride—and you're back at the high school.

For those still hungry or who prefer to do the wine tasting by car, head back up Center Road. You'll first see Peninsula Cellars, located on the right in an old schoolhouse. It's followed by Chateau Grand Traverse, the region's oldest winery, whose perch on the left provides a view of both bays. Mapleton, the peninsula's center of commerce, is just beyond Chateau Grand Traverse. It contains a

Catholic church, a hardware store, a mom-and-pop grocery that offers deli fare, and the Peninsula Grill restaurant.

Finally, Chateau Chantal, glimpsed from the back on the route, lies about 2 miles past Mapleton on Center Road. Wend your way up that drive, and you'll see why it was saved for the car. Just imagine plowing it in winter.

LOCAL INFORMATION

♦ Traverse City Convention and Visitors Bureau; (800) TRAVERS; www.my traversecity.com.
♦ Old Mission Peninsula Web site, www.oldmission.com.

LOCAL EVENTS/ATTRACTIONS

♦ The National Cherry Festival is held around the first week in July, usually including the Fourth. Music, cherry food, an air show, and fireworks, centered around Traverse City's Open Space. Area population usually triples, putting accommodations at a premium. For information, call festival headquarters at (231) 947–4230.

Orchard equipment awaits the fruit harvest. Courtesy of Michael O. Henderson

- The lighthouse at Old Mission Lighthouse and Park is a private residence, but visitors are welcome to look, take photos, and wander the park and beach; situated at the forty-fifth parallel, halfway between the North Pole and the equator.
- Wineries. Peninsula Cellars, 11480 Center Road; (231) 933–9787. Chateau Grand Traverse, 12239 Center Road; (231) 223–7355. Chateau Chantal, 15900 Rue de Vin (off Center Road); (231) 223–4110. For more information on these and other wineries, visit www.mytraversecity.com/wine.

RESTAURANTS

- Bowers Harbor Inn, 13512 Peninsula Drive, Traverse City; (231) 223–4222. Regional cuisine in a bayfront mansion. Extensive wine list. Pricey.
- The Bowery, 13512 Peninsula Drive, Traverse City; (231) 223–4222. Cheaper sister to Bowers Harbor Inn. Ribs, rotisserie chicken, steaks, perch. Wide beer selection. Low to midrange prices.
- Boathouse Restaurant, 14039 Peninsula Drive, Traverse City; (231) 223–4030. Seafood, steaks, duck, pasta, burgers. Outdoor dining available. Midrange prices.
- Peninsula Grill, 14091 Center Road, Traverse City; (231) 223–7200. Off route. Steaks, prime rib, fish, pasta, salads, and sandwiches. Pizza after 5:00 P.M. Low to midrange prices.
- Old Mission Tavern, 17015 Center Road, Traverse City; (231) 223–7280. Off route. Attached gallery featuring work of local artists. Prime rib, fresh fish, pasta, and ethnic specials. Midrange prices.

ACCOMMODATIONS

- On the peninsula, Bowers Harbor Inn (13512 Peninsula Drive; 231–223–4222) offers rooms. Chateau Chantal (15900 Rue de Vin; 231–223–4110) offers bed-and-breakfast-style accommodations, as does the Ne-ah-ta-wanta Inn (1308 Ne-ah-ta-wanta Road; 800–220–1415).
- Traverse City has a plethora of both chain and locally run hotels; call the Convention and Visitors Bureau for more options.

RESTROOMS

- Mile 3.8: East Bay Public Boat Launch.
- Mile 5.9: Archie Park.
- Mile 16.6: Haserot Park.
- Mile 19.9: Old Mission Lighthouse Park.
- Mile 29.6: Bowers Harbor Public Boat Launch.
- Mile 29.8: Boathouse Restaurant.
- Mile 30.4: Bowery/Bowers Harbor Inn restaurants.

Leland Ramble

This clockwise, flat loop around the north end of Lake Leelanau departs from the fishing and tourist village of Leland. Riders will pass a lakeside park and through the village of Lake Leelanau, situated at the "narrows" of the hourglass-shaped lake. Traffic will be light on the east side of the lake, but will increase on the trip back into Leland, best known for its Fishtown, a 140-year-old cluster of weathered fishing shanties, most now converted to eateries and shops, situated at the mouth of the Leland River connecting Lake Leelanau with Lake Michigan. After the ride, watch a commercial boat return with the day's catch, sample smoked whitefish in the shanties-turned-shops, or take a ferry to one of the Manitou Islands, part of the Sleeping Bear Dunes National Lakeshore.

Among Leelanau County's many quaint hamlets and burgs, the village of Leland has a distinct flavor. That's likely because it's just about the only one that retains indigenous industry—commercial fishing. Certainly, the trappings of a tourist economy exist, too. However, on the historic Fishtown docks, amid the weather-beaten shanties that now house T-shirt shops and trendy art boutiques, you can still watch fishermen clad in rubber overalls wind nets and discuss the latest weather on the big lake. Postride, you can sample what their nets yield (baked whitefish, smoked whitefish, whitefish pâté . . .) on the menus of many local restaurants.

From the harbor parking lot, turn left up River Street to the main intersection in town. Turn left on MI 22, heading out of town. Lake Leelanau will be on your right. Curving around the tip, turn right on County Road 641. East

The weathered shanties of Leland's Fishtown give the community much of its character. Courtesy of Travel Michigan

Leland Family Park comes up on your right in about a half mile. It's a private park paid for by local residents, but you can still glimpse the great view. As you pedal south, keeping the lake on your right, you'll notice a mix of housing—tiny old summer cottages and cabins among giant new homes, some occupied year-round, many still seasonal.

You'll turn away from the lake for a short jog, turn south again, and then turn west on MI 204 to enter the village of Lake Leelanau, situated at the "narrows" of the lake of the same name. If you've worked up an appetite, on your left will be Dick's Pour House, where author Jim Harrison, most widely known for *Legends of the Fall,* used to lift a few before moving out of the area a few years ago. On the right a little further is Kejara's Bridge, a funky deli/coffeehouse specializing in vegetarian and organic fare. Continue on MI 204 to leave Lake Leelanau.

At MI 22, turn left for a 1-mile detour to the Bibbs Manitou Farm Market and Bakery, or turn right to stay on the route. As you approach Leland, stop at Stonehouse Bread for a fresh, crusty loaf to sample with local wine. (To pick your perfect red or white, try the Leland Mercantile or the Leelanau Cellars tasting room, both just up Main Street.) Van's Beach makes a great place for a postride toast, especially at sunset. To find the beach, turn left on the unmarked road (Cedar Street) before Van's Marathon station. In 1 block it dead-ends into a foot trail to the beach. During the height of summer, you can watch the sun set in between North and South Manitou Islands, part of the Sleeping Bear

Dunes National Lakeshore. Today you can take a ferry from Fishtown out to the islands, which are both open for camping. North Manitou is the more primitive of the two.

LOCAL INFORMATION

♦ Leelanau Peninsula Chamber of Commerce; (231) 271–9895; www .leelanauchamber.com.
♦ Traverse City Convention and Visitors Bureau; (800) TRAVERS; www.mytraversecity.com.

LOCAL EVENTS/ATTRACTIONS

♦ The Leland Wine and Food Festival is typically held on a Saturday in early June. Wine, food, and music in Leland Harbor. (231) 271–9895.
♦ The Cedar Polka Festival in nearby Cedar is held around the first week in July, usually including the Fourth. Polka music, dancing, and beer under a big tent, plus a parade and a polka Catholic mass. (231) 228–3378.

♦ The following are among the Leelanau County wineries with tasting rooms: Black Star Farms, Suttons Bay; (231) 271–4970. Boskydel Vineyards, Lake Leelanau; (231) 256–7272. Good Harbor Vineyards, Lake Leelanau; (231) 256–7165. L. Mawby Vineyards, Suttons Bay; (231) 271–3522. Leelanau Wine Cellars, Omena; (231) 386–5201. All are within a half hour's drive of Leland. For more information on these and other wineries, visit www.mytraverse city.com/wine/.

RESTAURANTS

♦ The Cove, 111 River Street, north of Main Street, Leland; (231) 256–9834. Indoor and outdoor deck dining overlooking Leland River and Fishtown. Open seasonally only.
♦ The Bluebird, 102 East River Street, Leland; (231) 256–9081. Local favorite. Fresh whitefish, seafood, steak, pasta.
♦ The Early Bird, 101 South Main Street, Leland; (231) 256–9656. Casual-fare cousin to the Bluebird. Sandwiches, burgers, soups.

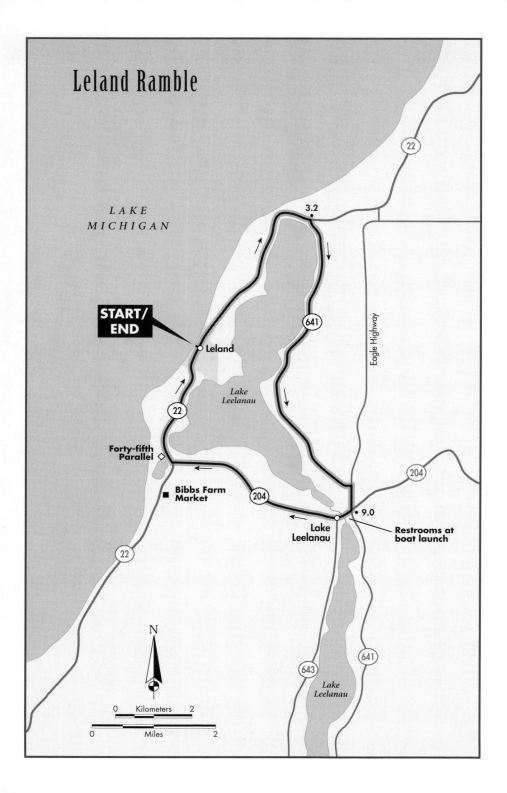

Leland Ramble

LAKE
MICHIGAN

3.2

22

641

Eagle Highway

START/
END

Leland

22

Lake
Leelanau

Forty-fifth
Parallel

204

Bibbs Farm
Market

204

204

9.0

22

Lake
Leelanau

Restrooms at
boat launch

641

N

0   Kilometers   2

0   Miles   2

643

Lake
Leelanau

0.0 Turn left out of Leland Harbor parking lot onto River Street.

0.1 Turn left onto Main Street/MI 22. Ride on shoulder after leaving town.

3.2 Turn right on North Lake Leelanau Drive/County Road 641.

3.9 East Leland Family Park. Private park, but feel free to pull over and admire the view. Road narrows after park.

8.6 Stop sign. Turn right onto Eagle Highway.

9.0 Turn right onto MI 204. To reach restrooms at Lake Leelanau Narrows boat launch, cross MI 204 onto CR 641 and go 0.1 mile. Return to intersection and turn left onto MI 204.

9.4 N.J.'s grocery store on left; Kejara's Bridge on right.

12.3 Turn right on MI 22. **Sidetrip:** To add 2 miles and visit Bibbs Manitou Farm Market, turn left on MI 22 instead, watching for fast-approaching traffic from the south. Shoulder also narrows, curves and pavement is rough in places.

12.7 Forty-fifth parallel sign. You are now halfway between the North Pole and the equator.

14.2 Leland commercial area begins—Stonehouse Bread on right.

14.5 Left on River Street.

14.6 Leland Harbor parking lot on right, Fishtown on left.

♦ Riverside Inn, 302 East River Street, Leland; (231) 256–9971. Menu of eclectic cuisine changes seasonally.

ACCOMMODATIONS

♦ Falling Waters Lodge, P.O. Box 345, Leland 49654; (231) 256–9832. On the Leland River.

♦ Leland Lodge, 565 Pearl Street, Leland; (231) 256–9848. Rooms and cabins. Dining on premises.

♦ Many other bed-and-breakfasts and hotels are available in Leelanau County and nearby Traverse City. Contact the Chamber or Visitors Bureau above.

RESTROOMS

♦ Start/finish: Leland Harbor. There are separate restrooms for the general public and for those who moor boats here. Both are in the brick building in the middle of the parking lot.

♦ Mile 9.1: Lake Leelanau Narrows boat launch on CR 641 (a deviation from route).

♦ Mile 9.4: various restaurants in Lake Leelanau.

Leelanau North Cruise

Native Americans christened the peninsula jutting off the northwest Michigan mainland Leelanau, *which translates variously as "land of delight" or "delight of light." Locals will delight in sharing this definition with you, as well as the fact that they get to live here year-round. With 98 miles of Lake Michigan shoreline, 30 miles of inland lakes and rivers, and a half-dozen hamlets that ooze with history, ethnicity, sophisticated shops, local artwork, and outstanding restaurants, this wedge of hills and valleys does have much to recommend it. You'll hit many of the highlights on the Leelanau North Cruise. Optional spurs will allow you to extend your ride to visit a winery tasting room and a lighthouse.*

The land of delight can be described in three words: water, fruit, and tourism. Like the Old Mission Peninsula to the east, Leelanau's geographic situation creates a unique climate ideal for fruit growing. Historically, that meant cherries, though there's some local dispute surrounding just who was the first to discover that. A monument in Northport credits missionary George Smith with planting the region's first cherry tree in 1849, beating by three years his Old Mission counterpart, the Rev. Peter Daugherty, who is credited with the same achievement on a similar monument just across West Grand Traverse Bay.

The more recent discovery has been wine grapes, and many growers on both peninsulas have grasped grapes as a lifeline for the regional agriculture industry. Wine is also being seen as an enhancement to tourism. Capitalizing on their locations, several wineries offer bed-and-breakfast accommodations.

Combined with the tasting-room rounds that are especially popular during the fall grape harvest, a strain of tourism called "agricultural tourism" has sprung up in north-western Michigan.

As much as they are a way of making a living, the land and the water are a way of life in Leelanau County. There's a strong sense of environmental stewardship here, a desire to protect and preserve the natural heritage. Bikes fit into that mind-set, so you'll find a welcoming attitude here. The Traverse City bicycle club sponsors a fall tour around Leelanau County, so bikes are a familiar sight to many locals.

The land of delight does have one undelightful caveat: the road signs are at times confusing. Most roads have both a name and a number. These roads frequently curve, fork, or come to oddball (three- and five-way) intersections at which point names and numbers change. Once around the curve or through the intersection, however, you may find, the original road name or number reappears. Pay close attention to the mileage and directions for this ride, and you should be fine.

From Lake Leelanau, you'll first ride north and east, including up one big hill, into the heart of Leelanau County's Bohemian region. A historical marker at St. Wenceslas Church, 6.5 miles into the ride, nicely explains the Bohemian connection. Its statement "Bohemia, now a part of Czechoslovakia" is a reminder of how constantly things change.

After the church, you'll continue riding east toward Omena. The first optional spur arrives at just under 11 miles. To stay on the route, you'll turn left at the Overlook Road T intersection. To visit Leelanau Wine Cellars, you'll turn right. Follow the curve to the left onto Tatch Road. The tasting room is on your left in just under a mile. Separate from the tasting room, there's a nice outdoor deck for relaxing. Retrace your route to return to the T intersection and resume the ride, heading north on Overlook Road.

Overlook was well named, with countryside views to the left and bay views to the right. Use caution on the downhill that ends at a stop sign and on the left

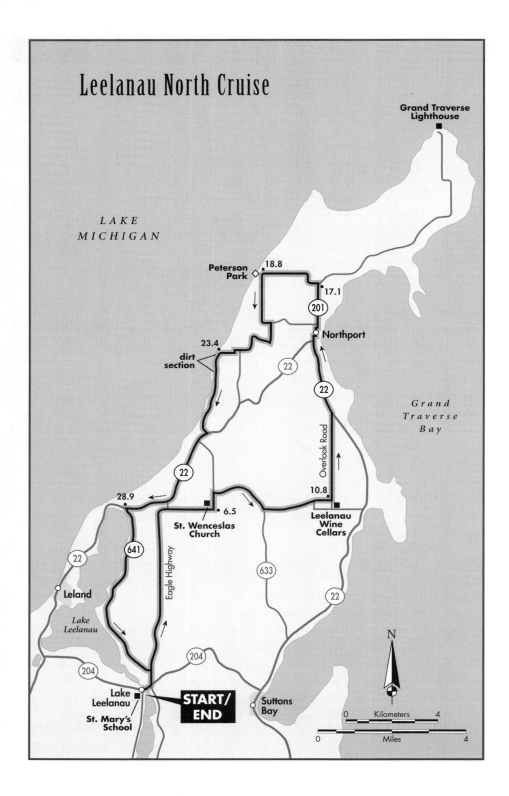

Leelanau North Cruise

Grand Traverse
Lighthouse

*LAKE
MICHIGAN*

Peterson
Park
18.8

17.1
201

Northport

22

23.4

dirt
section

22

*Grand
Traverse
Bay*

Overlook Road

28.9

22

10.8

6.5

St. Wenceslas
Church

Leelanau
Wine
Cellars

641

Eagle Highway

633

22

22

Leland

*Lake
Leelanau*

204

Lake
Leelanau

St. Mary's
School

204

**START/
END**

Suttons
Bay

N

Kilometers
0   4

Miles
0   4

0.0 From the parking lot north of St. Mary's School, turn right onto St. Mary's Street, then right onto MI 204 and cross the bridge over the Lake Leelanau narrows.

0.3 Turn left on CR 641 at Skyler's Resale Furniture.

0.7 Continue straight onto Eagle Highway; CR 641 goes left.

5.5 Big curve right. Stay straight after curve to go onto Kolarik Road; Eagle Highway goes left. Big climb ahead.

6.5 St. Wenceslas Church. Restrooms in community building behind church, which is usually open. Continue on Kolarik past church (turning left if you entered the property) and go straight at the stop sign, using caution and watching for oncoming traffic as you cross the road. Follow the curve to the left to go onto Jelinek Road.

7.2 Turn right on Omena Road after the triple silos.

8.9 Turn left on Omena Road/County Road 626 at white house, following the arrow pointing to Omena.

10.8 Omena Road T's into Overlook Road/CR 626. Turn left to stay on route.
Sidetrip: Turn right for 2-mile detour to Leelanau Wine Cellars. Follow the curve to go onto Tatch Road in 0.2 mile. Winery is 0.9 mile from T intersection on left. Retrace route to T intersection and continue straight.

13.3 Turn left onto MI 22 using caution as you cross against oncoming traffic.

14.7 Northport village limits.

15.4 Flashing light—go straight onto MI 201.

15.7 Flashing light—turn right to stay on MI 201, which then jogs left, becoming Waukazoo Street.

15.9 Turn right onto MI 201/Nagonaba Street. To leave town, follow MI 201's quick jog left. Go straight to visit park, beach, and marina. Turn left at THE DEPOT sign for restrooms on Bay Street. From the water, return to town and turn right on MI 201 to leave town.

(continued)

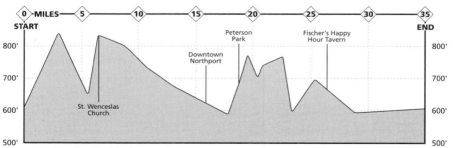

Intervals: Vertical, 100 ft.; Horizontal, 5 mi.

17.1 Y intersection. Go straight or to left of Y and then turn left on Peterson Park Road to stay on 35-mile route. **Sidetrip:** Veer right to right of Y for 14-mile out-and-back spur to lighthouse. Road will have different names in different sections. On your return, keep riding straight until turning right onto Peterson Park Road.

17.4 Road curves right, becomes Kitchen Bay. Road turns left, becomes Peterson Park Road again.

18.8 Peterson Park on right after Foxview Drive. Restrooms, playground, Lake Michigan overlook, and long staircase to rocky beach. Turn right when leaving park.

19.5 Big uphill. Road becomes Foxview Drive.

20.4 Turn right on Clausen. Steep, short uphill.

20.9 Stop sign. Turn right on Johnson Road.

22.2 Turn left at yield sign onto Carlson Road.

22.6 Turn right onto Onomonee Road.

23.4 Turn left onto Gills Pier Road, using caution after the downhill. 1-mile dirt road.

25.4 Turn right on MI 22. Fischer's Happy Hour Tavern at intersection. Restrooms available. Hills are over!

28.9 Turn left on CR 641.

29.6 East Leland Park.

34.3 Turn right on Eagle Highway.

34.7 Turn right on MI 204 to cross narrows.

35.0 Turn left on CR 643 to return to St. Mary's School.

---

turn onto MI 22. You'll be on this busier section of road for about a mile and a half, when it becomes Michigan Highway 201 and enters Northport. MI 201 will jog right, left, and right to take you through the aptly named outpost, the northernmost community in Leelanau County.

Northport has a small cadre of hardy locals, sustained by the school system, grocery store, and single gas station. The population starts to swell on weekends around Memorial Day, becomes a Monday to Friday town from the Fourth of July through Labor Day, returns to weekend activity through the fall color season, and then cocoons itself again for the long winter.

One of the favorite summer establishments is Woody's Settling Inn, on your left after MI 201 takes its second jog. Comedian Tim Allen, a Detroit native, used to settle in here for his up-north weekends. It's got a great shady deck in addition to a fun, friendly indoor bar. Across the street, Stubb's

Sweetwater Grill is another good choice for a bite to eat. If a picnic is more your inclination, continue on MI 201 and follow it right at the gas station. The local branch of Tom's, a Traverse City–based grocery store, is on your right, with a deli, bakery, and everything else you might need for a picnic. Take it down to the park and harbor ahead for a waterside seat. Restrooms are also available.

Leaving Northport on MI 201, you'll come to a Y intersection in just over a mile, and the second optional spur. The 14-mile out-and-back is flat and will take you to the Grand Traverse Lighthouse, a state park facility that also offers camping. They'll usually let bikes in free, but separate admission is required to tour the lighthouse. It's a great detour, but assess your ability and time honestly before setting out. Plan on a minimum of an hour and a half for riding and park wandering. After that you'll have another 25 miles ahead. In those 25 miles there's another great beach and overlook, and several hills. If it is after noon by the time you arrive here, you might be better off saving the lighthouse for a car trip.

To skip the spur, cross MI 201 to go onto the left side of the Y, and then take a left onto Peterson Park Road. After a rolling mile and a half, Peterson Park is on your right, with restrooms, playground equipment, an overlook, and stairs down to the rocky beach, which is a good hunting ground for Michigan's state stone, the petoskey.

The next several miles consist on concentrated hills, both up and down. You'll have the worst behind you when you turn right onto Onomonee Road, which descends down to Lake Michigan. From Onomonee, turn left onto Gills Pier Road, where the road turns to hard-packed dirt for 1 mile.

At the intersection of Gills Pier Road and MI 22 is Fischer's Happy Hour Tavern. It's a good place to celebrate that you've completed two-thirds of the ride and that the hills are behind you. The remaining 10 miles, along MI 22 and then down the eastern shore of Lake Leelanau, are relatively flat.

LOCAL INFORMATION

♦ Leelanau Peninsula Chamber of Commerce; (231) 271–9895; www.leelanau chamber.com.
♦ Traverse City Convention and Visitors Bureau; (800) TRAVERS; www.my traversecity.com.

LOCAL EVENTS/ATTRACTIONS

♦ The Northport Fourth of July is an all-American evening of music and fireworks at the Northport marina on, of course, July 4 at dusk, which can be 10:00 P.M. or later during midsummer up north.
♦ The Leelanau Peninsula Food and Wine Festival is held in early August at Haserot Park. Wine and food alfresco. (231) 271–9895 or (800) 980–9895.

RESTAURANTS

◆ Fischer's Happy Hour Tavern, 7100 West North Manitou Trail, Northport; (231) 386–9923. Favorite with locals. Family-owned and famous for burgers, soups, and fish.

◆ Woody's Settling Inn, 116 Waukazoo Street, Northport; (231) 386–9933. Steaks, seafood, cherry-smoked chicken. Outdoor deck.

◆ Stubb's Sweetwater Grill, 115 Waukazoo Street, Northport; (231) 386–7611. Regional American cuisine. Varied menu.

ACCOMMODATIONS

Most Leelanau County lodging is offered at bed-and-breakfasts. Traditional motels and hotels are available in nearby Traverse City.

◆ Old Mill Pond Inn Bed and Breakfast, 202 West 3rd Street, Northport; (231) 386–7341; www.leelanau.com/lodging/oldmillpond.

◆ Sunrise Landing Motel and Resort, 6530 North West Bay Shore Drive, Northport; (231) 386–5010 or (800) 488–5762 (reservations); www.sunrise landing.com. Motel alongside West Grand Traverse Bay.

◆ Bay Pointe Resort, 6574 North West Bay Shore Drive, Northport; (231) 386–5491 or (800) 700–5491; www.baypointeresort.com. Primarily weeklong rentals of cottages and cabins (they call them condos), but daily or weekend reservations may be available. Condo 5 has the best front deck.

RESTROOMS

◆ Mile 6.5: St. Wenceslas Church (west side of community building behind church).

◆ Mile 16.0: Northport beach/park/marina.

◆ Mile 18.8: Peterson Park.

◆ Mile 25.4: Fischer's Happy Hour Tavern.

Leelanau South Ramble

The rule of thumb is that shoreline riding is flat. Inland, expect to encounter hills. This ramble starts smack in the middle of Leelanau County and heads to its eastern shore. Ergo, this ramble will provide a bit of challenge. The hills come fairly early in the ride and are balanced with downhills, hilltop views of Grand Traverse Bay, a beautiful stretch of flat shoreline, and the village of Suttons Bay, strategically situated to provide the ice-cream cone you'll need to power yourself over the last hill home.

Michiganders often refer to Leelanau County as Michigan's "little finger," continuing the metaphor of the mitten shape that is the Lower Peninsula. Glance at your hand. For this ride you'll depart from somewhere around the knuckle and pedal some of the least-traveled roads in this corner of the "land of delight."

From St. Mary's you'll head briefly north and then east, in order to cross the narrows of Lake Leelanau. The bridge across this hourglass-shaped lake that posed a major barrier to east-west travel dates back to 1864, when a wooden crossing was built. The modern version is a Depression-era works project that was built in 1939 and most recently updated in 2003. It's on the National Register of Historic Places.

Heading south on County Road 641, there's a wide shoulder for the first mile, which then disappears. It will recur off and on, although narrower, until you turn left on Otto Road and begin the first hill. There's an enticing rest point to motivate you: Boskydel Vineyard, one of northern Michigan's vineyards that

Start: St. Mary's School in Lake Leelanau.

Length: 22.2-mile loop.

Terrain: Rolling, a few climbs.

Traffic and hazards: Use greatest caution crossing Michigan Highway 22 and on the short stretch of Michigan Highway 204 returning to Lake Leelanau. As usual up north, traffic is heaviest on weekends.

Getting there: From Traverse City, take MI 22 north to Suttons Bay. Go through downtown and turn left at the flashing light onto MI 204. In Lake Leelanau, cross the "narrows" dividing the lake and turn left at Dick's Pour House onto County Road 643. St. Mary's is on the left. Park in the lot on the north side of the school, on the street, or at the church south of the school.

has remained more local than commercial. I once asked the proprietor to recommend his favorite vintage. "That'd be like asking me to pick my favorite child," he replied.

After the vineyard you'll zigzag south and east for several miles, encountering a few climbs and one beautiful, nearly mile-long downhill to West Grand Traverse Bay. You'll be able to see across the bay to the tip of the Old Mission Peninsula. From the crest you'll understand the sentiment that prompted the state motto: "*Si quaeris peninsulam amoenam, circumspice,*" translated as "If you seek a pleasant peninsula, look about you."

There are the Upper and Lower, of course. Within each of those are sub-peninsulas, like Leelanau and Old Mission in northwestern Michigan. And within those are sub-sub-peninsulas like the one that shapes Suttons Bay. You're about to ride around that.

First there's a half-mile ride up MI 22. Use caution on the left turn onto the highway, which can be very busy in summer. Turn right at the first opportunity, onto Lee Point Road. For the next 8 miles, the route will follow either shorelines or ridge lines as it takes you out to Stoney Point, at the mouth of Suttons Bay. You'll ride along the shoreline to reach the community of the same name.

The largest community in Leelanau County, Suttons Bay is a bona fide year-round town. Certainly, the sidewalks thin in winter, but they don't roll up the way they do in Northport, Leland, and Glen Arbor. In addition to the usual shops and restaurants, there's a movie theater that draws audiences from miles around with its winter "Beyond the Bay" foreign film series, a bank, and two grocery stores. Suttons Bay is also known for the red phone booth on St. Joseph Avenue, the main drag. If you've got people riding at different paces, it's a good place to rendezvous before (depending on your appetite and the time of day) you seek out a cinnamon roll, a slice of pizza, or a full meal. 45th Parallel Café is a place to try for a quick bite. The geographic line bisecting the Northern Hemisphere actually lies offshore, a little north of Stoney Point, but it's still a unique claim to fame.

Grand Traverse Bay, beyond the cherry trees, moderates northwest Michigan's climate for ideal fruit growing conditions. Courtesy of Travel Michigan

Linger in Suttons Bay as long as you like. It's just a flat 4 miles home. Continuing through downtown, you'll turn left at the flashing light onto MI 204. Ride straight west, staying on the wide shoulder. Back in Lake Leelanau you'll cross the narrows again, turn left on CR 643, and return to St. Mary's.

LOCAL INFORMATION

◆ Leelanau Peninsula Chamber of Commerce; (231) 271–9895; www.leelanau chamber.com.

LOCAL EVENTS/ATTRACTIONS

◆ Taste the bounty of Leelanau County farms and orchards at the Suttons Bay Farmers Market held Saturday mornings from Memorial Day through the end of September in the skating park on Broadway Street, at the south end of town.

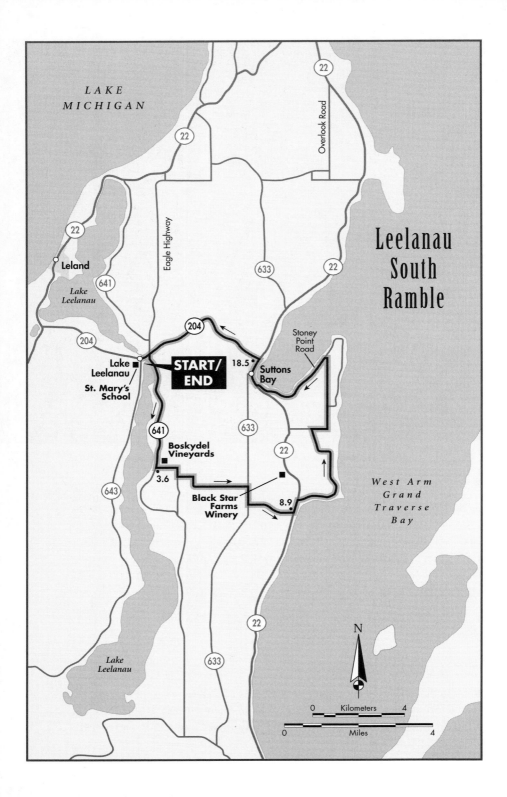

LAKE
MICHIGAN

Leelanau
South
Ramble

Leland

Lake
Leelanau

Eagle Highway

Overlook Road

Stoney
Point
Road

18.5
Suttons
Bay

Lake
Leelanau
St. Mary's
School

START/
END

Boskydel
Vineyards

3.6

Black Star
Farms
Winery

8.9

West Arm
Grand
Traverse
Bay

Lake
Leelanau

N

0   Kilometers   4

0   Miles   4

0.0 From the parking lot on the north side of St. Mary's School, turn right onto St. Mary's Street/(CR 643). Then turn right onto MI 204 to cross bridge.

0.3 Turn right on County Road 641.

0.4 Lake Leelanau Narrows boat launch. Restrooms.

3.6 Turn left on Otto Road. Uphill climb. Entrance to Boskydel Vineyards at top of hill on left.

4.3 Turn right on Maple Valley Road.

4.6 Turn left on Otto Road. Uphill climb.

5.0 Stop sign. Turn right on Otto Road, which will climb, level, then climb again.

6.7 Stop sign. Turn right on Center Road/County Road 633.

7.1 Turn left on Fort Road.

8.1 Long downhill. Be prepared to stop at bottom.

8.9 Stop sign. Turn left on MI 22.

9.3 Turn right onto Lee Point Road.

12.5 Yield sign. Turn right onto McAlister Road.

14.0 Smith Road intersects on the left. Downhill and bay view.

15.1 Stop sign. Turn left on Stoney Point Road.

16.7 Road curves, becomes South Shore Drive.

17.6 Sutton Park. Restrooms.

17.7 Turn right onto MI 22.

17.9 Flashing light. Veer right onto St. Joseph Avenue, the main drag through downtown Suttons Bay.

18.2 Turn right on Adams Street and then right on Front Street to reach public restrooms.

18.5 Turn left on MI 204 at flashing light.

22.2 Turn left on St. Mary's Street/CR 643 after crossing bridge.

♦ Take in a show at Bay Theatre, a family-owned cinema. Annual "Beyond the Bay" foreign film series runs once a month in the fall through the spring and brings films northern Michigan would never see otherwise. On St. Joseph Avenue in downtown Suttons Bay. (231) 271–3841.

♦ At the flower farm on MI 22 between Suttons Bay and Omena, pick your own bouquet from the wide selection of wildflowers. Scissors provided and even take-home water jugs to keep flowers fresh. Most priced at less than $1.00 per stem; you'll get a big bouquet for less than $5.00.

♦ The Cedar Polka Festival in nearby Cedar is held around the first week in July, usually including the Fourth. Polka music, dancing, and beer under a giant tent, plus a parade and a polka Catholic mass. (231) 228–3378.

• The following are among the Leelanau County wineries with tasting rooms: Black Star Farms, Suttons Bay; (231) 271–4970. Boskydel Vineyards, Lake Leelanau; (231) 256–7272. Good Harbor Vineyards, Lake Leelanau; (231) 256–7165. L. Mawby Vineyards, Suttons Bay; (231) 271–3522. Leelanau Wine Cellars, Omena; (231) 386–5201. All are within a half hour's drive of Leland. For more information on these and other wineries, visit www.mytraverse city.com/wine.

RESTAURANTS

• Café Bliss, 420 St. Joseph Avenue, Suttons Bay; (231) 271–5000. Open seasonally. Pricey but worth it. Organic and vegetarian specials. Fabulous desserts. Outdoor dining available.
• Hattie's, 111 St. Joseph Avenue, Suttons Bay; (231) 271–6222. Pricier yet, but outstanding reputation for regional cuisine. Herbs grown in window boxes used in the kitchen. Local art displayed. Try the early-bird special to go a little easier on the wallet.
• For burgers, salads, and sandwiches that go easier on the budget, try Fireside Pub, Boone's Primetime Pub, or Eddie's Village Inn, all on St. Joseph Avenue in downtown Suttons Bay.
• Kejara's Bridge, 202 North Main Street, Lake Leelanau; (231) 256–5397. Funky coffeehouse atmosphere. Breakfast and deli sandwiches. Entertainment Saturdays.

ACCOMMODATIONS

If you're looking for mainstream motels, go back to Traverse City. Bed-and-breakfasts abound in Leelanau County. A few to try:
• Fig Leaf Bed and Breakfast, 112 West Race Street (MI 204 at the corner of MI 22), Suttons Bay; (231) 271–3995. Painted purple, you can't miss it. Proprietress has turned her penchant for color on the place—not for those who prefer white walls.
• Guest House, 504 St. Joseph Avenue, Suttons Bay; (231) 271–3776. Kitchen facilities available. Screened front porch, deck overlooking Grand Traverse Bay.
• Sunset Lodge Bed and Breakfast, 12819 Tatch Road, Omena; (231) 386–9080. Six miles north of Suttons Bay. Rooms with private baths in main house, facilities with kitchen in adjacent cottages. Wraparound porch. Leelanau Wine Cellars tasting room just up the road, Omena beach just down the road.

RESTROOMS

• Mile 0.4: Lake Leelanau Narrows boat launch.
• Mile 17.1: Sutton Park.
• Mile 18.2: Front Street, east of and parallel to St. Joseph Avenue, between Jefferson Avenue and Adams Street. Watch for sign on St. Joseph.

14

Glen Arbor Cruise

R iders who take on this route will come away with a true
sense of place about northwest Michigan: its hilly topography
edged with shoreline, its seemingly contrary environment of sand and
woods, and its maritime history. While the distance is relatively short,
one extremely challenging uphill and the rapid descent that follows
bump this ride up into the cruise category. Numerous points of interest
within the Sleeping Bear Dunes National Lakeshore, from the Maritime
Museum in Glen Haven to the Dune Climb, can easily make this a full
day's ride.

Shipping and lumbering were the industries that built many Lake
Michigan communities, including Glen Haven. It's a sign of the times and the
new economic base that Glen Haven is now a ghost town, while a couple miles
east, the artsy community of Glen Arbor is thriving. This ride starts out going
back in time. Leave Glen Arbor heading west on MI 109. At the T intersection
in about 2 miles, turn right to go to Glen Haven, which is in the process of
being resurrected by the National Park Service as part of the Sleeping Bear
Dunes National Lakeshore.

Once a busy refueling station for steamers traversing the Great Lakes, Glen
Haven was a company town, owned by the Northern Transportation Company.
The number of workers needed and the isolation of the area also required
houses, a school, and a company store. Paid in scrip redeemable only at the
store, workers' wages quickly returned to the company. In 2003 the Glen Haven
General Store opened, a replica of the 1920s-era store with several original
touches, including the steamship ticket booth. It stocks merchandise typical of
the early twentieth century. Today you can pay with cash or credit cards. But

Big Glen Lake is renowned for its beautiful, turquoise-blue waters. Courtesy of Travel Michigan

kids can get an idea of the concept by doing small jobs around the park like picking up litter. They report it to park staff and receive a scrip coupon redeemable for a piece of candy at the store.

A half mile beyond the store is the Maritime Museum, located at the former Coast Guard Lifesaving Station. Originally built south of Glen Haven, the lifesaving station was necessary due to the dangerous waters of the Manitou Passage. The shortcut between the mainland and the islands allowed ships to stay close to shoreline communities and supplies. However, it also presented ships with the risk of either running aground in shallower waters rife with shoals or sinking in storms. The museum is well done and well worth at least a half hour's detour.

Leave the lighthouse the way you came, continuing south on MI 109. Coming up on your right is the Dune Climb, one of the most popular attractions within the national lakeshore, home of the largest freshwater dunes in the world. A Chippewa Indian legend is the source of the unusual name. In the tale, a mother bear and her two cubs swim across Lake Michigan to escape a great forest fire in Wisconsin. The mother bear arrives on the Michigan shore first and climbs to the highest hill to watch for her cubs. The swim proved to be too much for the cubs, however. Taking pity on the grieving mother bear, the Great

Spirit turns her into the mainland part of the park, which to the Indians appeared to be shaped like a sleeping bear. The cubs are raised up into the offshore Manitou Islands, forever under her eye.

In order to preserve the fragile dune environment, hiking is confined to certain areas of the park. The Dune Climb is one of them. It's exactly what it sounds like, a huge sand dune 130 feet high. You can climb to your heart's content. Be advised that hiking on sand is far more strenuous than on hard-packed ground, however. Park admission is required to enter the Dune Climb. A bike pass costs $5.00. Restrooms are available at the foot of the Climb.

From the Dune Climb, continue south on MI 109. A few more miles brings you to Welch Road. Turn left. Or, to visit Pierce Stocking Scenic Drive, another highlight of the park (see ride 15), which will add 7 tough miles to your ride, continue straight less than a tenth of a mile and turn right to enter the Scenic Drive.

As you ride down Welch, you'll see Glen Lake off in the distance and get a good look at Alligator Hill ahead and to your left. It's an odd name to find this far north, but from a distance you can really see how the bumpy hill nosing into the narrows earned its name.

The Little Bear Deli at the narrows between the Glen Lakes offers you a chance to grab a bite to fuel you up for the climb of just over a mile up MacFarlane Road/County Road 616 that awaits. At the crest, turn into the Inspiration Point overlook to take in a well-earned view. A breakneck descent follows. Speeds can easily exceed 40 miles per hour, so use extreme caution.

THE BASICS

Start: Glen Arbor Township Park.

Length: 19.6-mile loop.

Terrain: Rolling to hilly.

Traffic and hazards: Watch for heavier traffic on Michigan Highway 109, especially turning into the Dune Climb and Pierce Stocking Drive. Watch for sand on the roads, and use caution on the long, winding, fast descent after Inspiration Point.

Getting there: From Traverse City, take Michigan Highway 72 west. After 13 miles the highway takes a sharp jog to the right, or north, then turns left (west) again at the flashing light. At 20 miles, turn right onto County Road 677, after the Sleepy Bear Campground. The sign says TO GLEN ARBOR. In about 2.5 miles, CR 677 intersects Michigan Highway 22 at the three-way intersection just south of the "narrows" between Big Glen and Little Glen Lakes. Turn right and then veer left to cross the bridge over the narrows. Follow MI 22 another 2.5 miles into the village of Glen Arbor. Turn right on State Street, after the sign for Glen Arbor Township Park and the tennis courts. Park in the lot at the corner of State and Lake Streets.

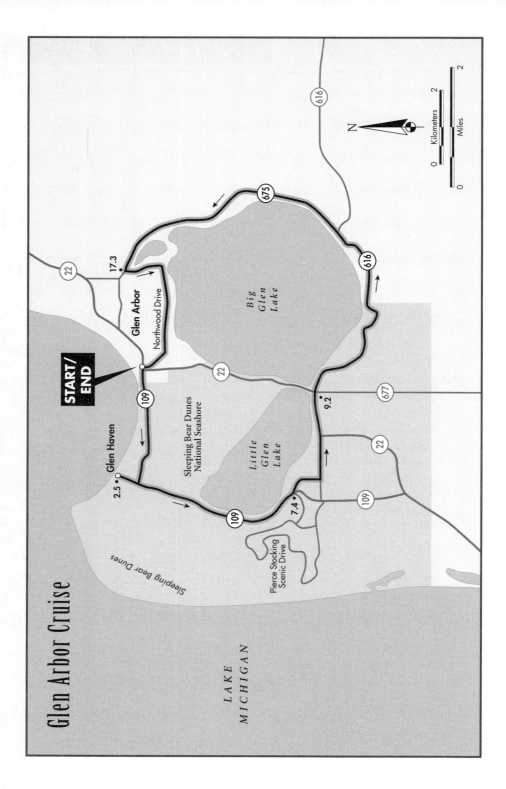

Glen Arbor Cruise

0.0 From parking lot at Glen Arbor Township Park, turn left on Lake Street.

0.1 Turn left at stop sign onto Western Avenue/MI 22.

2.1 T intersection. Turn right onto MI 109 to go to Glen Haven, period store, and Maritime Museum.

2.5 Glen Haven. Restrooms. Glen Haven General Store. Follow road to left to visit Maritime Museum.

2.9 Museum entrance/cul-de-sac. Turn around to go back.

3.5 Stop sign. Turn right to pass general store and restrooms again.

4.0 Stop sign. Continue straight on MI 109. Hill ahead.

5.0 Glen Lake Picnic Area on left. Restrooms.

5.3 Dune Climb on right. Restrooms.

7.4 Turn left on Welch Road. Fast downhill. Continue straight on Welch at yield sign at bottom of hill.

8.4 Stop sign. Turn left onto Glenmere/MI 22, toward Glen Arbor.

9.2 Irregular intersection. Little Bear Deli and Catering on your right. Restrooms inside. Pass it, continuing straight on McFarlane Road/CR 616. MI 22 veers off left. Biggest climb and descent of ride ahead.

10.8 Turnoff for Inspiration Point on left. Watch traffic coming around curve. Safer to use second entrance. Turn left to leave, and use caution on winding downhill.

12.8 Veer right onto Dunns Farm Road/CR 675.

13.2 Old Settlers Park on left. Restrooms.

15.2 Foothills Motel and Foothills Cafe. Breakfast and lunch till 3:00 P.M. Cheap and hearty fare.

17.3 Make a sharp left turn onto Fisher Road. Electrical substation on right.

17.8 Turn right on Northwood Drive at T intersection.

19.3 Stop sign. Turn right on Lake Street.

19.6 Turn left on State Street to return to park parking lot.

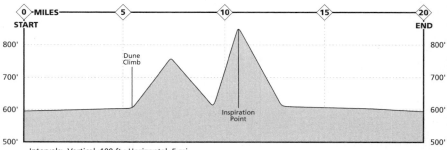

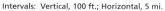

Intervals: Vertical, 100 ft.; Horizontal, 5 mi.

Rounding the southern end of Glen Lake, you'll veer right onto Dunns Farm Road/County Road 675. Old Settlers Park is on the left, with restrooms and a drinking fountain. CR 675 hugs the shoreline of Big Glen, until a sharp left onto Fisher Road takes you back into town.

Glen Arbor is full of restaurants, whether your hankering is for a burger and a beer or prime rib and a good red. Shopping runs the gamut from sophisticated art galleries in media that you can put on your walls or wear (jewelry, fiber, and fabric shops are particularly good) to T-shirt shops and Wildflowers, a wonderful garden store.

LOCAL INFORMATION

♦ Sleeping Bear Area Chamber of Commerce, Glen Arbor; (231) 334–3238; www.sleepingbeararea.com.

LOCAL EVENTS/ATTRACTIONS

♦ Sleeping Bear Dunes National Lakeshore is one of four national parks in Michigan, with beaches, hiking, and camping. Its headquarters are at 9922 Front Street, Empire; (231) 326–5134; www.nps.gov/slbe.
♦ The Dunegrass and Blues Festival held in August in nearby Empire, headquarters of the Sleeping Bear Dunes National Lakeshore.

RESTAURANTS

♦ Art's Tavern, 6847 Western Avenue, Glen Arbor; (231) 334–3754. Local favorite. Burgers, whitefish, steaks, pizza.
♦ Boone Docks, 5858 Manitou Boulevard, Glen Arbor; (231) 334–6444. Huge deck with outdoor bar in summer. Large menu includes sandwiches and salads and full dinners.
♦ Funistrada, 4566 MacFarlane Road, Maple City; (231) 334–3900. Italian food in casual setting. Reservations suggested.
♦ While menus are limited, the Leelanau Coffee Roasting Company (6443 Western Avenue, Glen Arbor; 800–424–JAVA) and Cherry Republic (6026 South Lake Street, Glen Arbor; 800–206–6949) are two local purveyors of foodstuffs not to be missed. Take home some local flavors.

ACCOMMODATIONS

You won't find any chain hotels or motels in Glen Arbor or most of Leelanau County. Traverse City, forty minutes away, has this style of accommodations in abundance—visit www.mytraversecity.com for more information.

- Glen Arbor Bed & Breakfast and Cottages, 6458 Western Avenue, Glen Arbor; (231) 334–6789 or (877) 253–4200.
- North Oak Bed & Breakfast, 5760 North Oak Street, Glen Arbor; (231) 334–6445.
- Foothills Motel and Restaurant, 7097 South Dunns Farm Road, Maple City; (231) 334–3495.

RESTROOMS

- Start/finish: Glen Arbor Township Park (portable toilet).
- Mile 2.5: Glen Haven.
- Mile 5.3: Dune Climb.
- Mile 9.2: inside Little Bear Deli and Catering.
- Mile 13.2: Old Settlers Park (pit toilet).

Pierce Stocking Cruise

Don't be misled by the low mileage—you'll want to dedicate at least an afternoon to Pierce Stocking Scenic Drive's 6.9 miles. Located within the Sleeping Bear Dunes National Lakeshore, it is recommended by the National Park Service for "expert" cyclists only, due to the steep terrain, sharp curves, and traffic. Combined with the Glen Arbor Cruise, it can easily fill a day. Pierce Stocking is a microcosm of the entire park, which stretches for 35 miles along Michigan's west "coast." The winding, hilly, one-way road with a dedicated bike lane is designed with twelve stopping points where the highlights and contrasting environments within the park are explained. While picnic areas are provided, there are no restaurants or vending machines on Pierce Stocking Drive, so stash snacks in the bike bag before setting off.

The drive is named for its creator, lumberman Pierce Stocking, a self-taught student of nature and lover of northern Michigan's woods, water, and dunes. It's to the public's benefit that he lived when he did. Today the attitude of many who might discover such beauty would be to keep others away, particularly those who arrive in motorized transportation.

But Stocking wanted to share the beauty with others, so he decided to build a road through the area in southwest Leelanau County. In 1967, seven years after planning for the road began, it opened to the public. Known at the time as Sleeping Bear Dunes Park, the road was operated by Stocking until his death in 1976. It was named in his honor several years later.

Pierce Stocking Drive is a one-way, seasonal road. Admission to the park is $5.00 per cyclist. The pass is valid for seven days. The National Park Service recommends that those considering bicycling the route drive it first to be sure that their abilities are up to it. I don't consider that necessary, but don't overestimate your abilities based on the low mileage. If you can handle a 50-mile flat ride or a 30-mile ride with moderate hills, you can probably handle this route.

Be sure to pick up an interpretive guide as you enter the drive, which will explain each of the dozen stopping points along the drive. My favorites are 2, 4, 9, 10, and 11.

From the drive entrance you'll first ride through a shady, deciduous forest area. Stop 1 is a covered bridge, included in the drive simply as a picturesque detail. Stop 2 overlooks the two Glen Lakes, which only appear to be separate where they are bridged at the "narrows." Connected to Lake Michigan millennia ago, Glen Lake was separated from it when a sandbar developed in the post-glacial era. Alligator Hill, nosing into the narrows from the north, is also visible.

Between stops 2 and 3, the environment starts to evolve from dense forest to open dune. Trees turn to dunegrass and scrub brush. At stop 3 a viewing platform allows you an overall view of the dunes from atop one of the highest, some 200 feet.

At stop 4 you can take an up-close look on the Cottonwood Trail, a mile-and-a-half trail looping through the constantly changing dunes. At the whim of the wind, some dunes advance up to a meter a year. In other places, plants stabilize them. Bowls are blown out, then filled in. Trees are buried and then revealed. Wildflowers bloom, seemingly impossibly, out of the sand.

At stop 5, you'll learn about dune ecology and the conditions plants must adapt to in order to survive in what appears to be a desert. You'll turn back east for stops 6 and 7, leaving the dunes and entering a beech and maple forest. The ride will turn blissfully shady and cool.

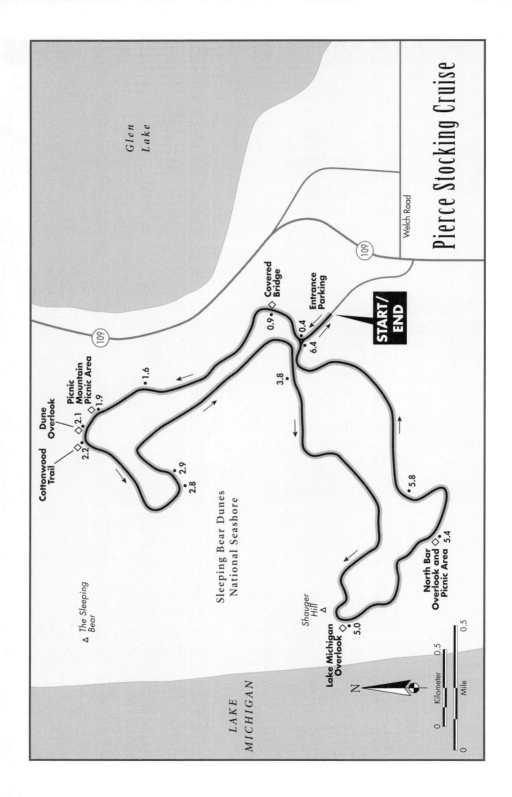

Pierce Stocking Cruise

Glen Lake

Welch Road

109

Covered Bridge

Entrance Parking

START/ END

0.9
0.4
6.4
3.8
1.6
1.9
2.1
2.2
2.8
2.9
5.8
5.4
5.0

Dune Overlook

Picnic Mountain Picnic Area

Cottonwood Trail

△ The Sleeping Bear

Sleeping Bear Dunes National Seashore

Shauger Hill △

North Bar Overlook and Picnic Area

Lake Michigan Overlook

LAKE MICHIGAN

N

0   Kilometer   0.5

0   Mile   0.5

0.0 Turn right out of parking lot toward payment booth.

0.4 Take first right at fork onto one-way part of drive.

0.9 Stop 1. Covered bridge, followed by hill.

1.6 Stop 2. Little Glen Lake in foreground.

1.9 Picnic Mountain. Restrooms.

2.1 Stop 3. Dune Overlook.

2.2 Stop 4. Cottonwood Trail. Optional hike. Go around cul-de-sac and turn right back onto scenic drive.

2.3 Stop 5. Downhill follows.

2.8 Stop 6.

2.9 Stop 7.

3.8 Stop 8.

5.0 Stops 9 and 10. Lake Michigan Overlook. Restrooms.

5.4 Stop 11. North Bar Overlook. Restrooms.

5.8 Stop 12, followed by downhill.

6.4 Turn right onto two-way part of road.

6.9 Parking lot on left.

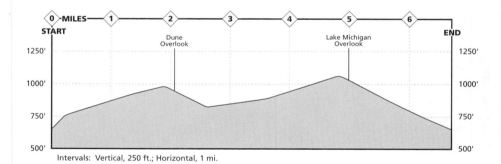

Intervals: Vertical, 250 ft.; Horizontal, 1 mi.

Stop 8 invites you to imagine 11,800 years ago, when the glaciers retreated.

Stops 9 and 10 are where you'll find the biggest crowds on the Scenic Drive. On a clear day you can see Point Betsie, 15 miles to the south, and the Manitou Islands to the northwest from stop 9, the Lake Michigan Overlook. An Indian word meaning "great water" or "big water," Lake Michigan, the largest lake entirely within the United States and the fourth-largest freshwater lake in the world, was named appropriately. The overlook is not perched atop a dune, however, but on a glacial hill. While you will likely see people descending it, the Park Service strongly discourages it. Climbers exacerbate the erosion from the lake, not to mention that the climb is extremely strenuous. As the signs note, the only way to stage a rescue off the bluff slope is by helicopter, which can be expensive! Stick to the Cottonwood Trail for a better, safer look at actual dunes.

Stop 10 is the viewing point for the Sleeping Bear Dune, for which the park is named. Trying to find it now is a little like trying to see the shapes of star constellations. Due to the wind and weather, it's changed significantly since the Chippewa Indians noted it as a landmark and created what is now called the Legend of Sleeping Bear. Now half the height it once stood, it is only a matter of time until the sleeping bear disappears, leaving only her legend.

Two more stops complete the Scenic Drive. Stop 11, North Bar Lake, takes its name from its formation. A former bay on Lake Michigan, it was transformed into a lake when a sand bar gradually built up as the shoreline straightened over time. The deeper parts of the bay remain ponded behind the sandbar. This process also formed Glen Lake and Torch Lake.

Last stop is the pine plantation. These trees are intruders in the Sleeping Bear Dunes, planted after loggers depleted the area's natural hardwoods. Since the park's purpose is to preserve the natural environment, some of the pine plantation stands have been cut to encourage regrowth of the native trees.

This covered bridge on Pierce Stocking Drive serves as a kind of gateway to the dunes.
Courtesy of National Park Service

LOCAL INFORMATION

◆ Sleeping Bear Area Chamber of Commerce, P.O. Box 217, Glen Arbor 49636; (231) 334–3238; www.sleepingbeararea.com, click on Empire.

LOCAL EVENTS/ATTRACTIONS

◆ The Sleeping Bear Dunegrass and Blues Festival is an outdoor music fest featuring bluegrass and rock music, arts and crafts, food booths, and shuttle rides to the beach. Held in early August. (231) 326–5249.

◆ The Empire Anchor Days Weekend in July features a parade, games, arts and crafts, pancake breakfast, chicken barbeque, farmers' market, and beach dance. (231) 326–5249.

◆ Sleeping Bear Dunes National Lakeshore, Park Headquarters, 9922 Front Street, Empire; (231) 326–5134; www.nps.gov/slbe/pssd.htm.

RESTAURANTS

◆ Empire Village Inn, MI 22, Empire; (231) 326–5101. Sandwiches, pizza, soups, chili, and full dinners.

◆ Joe's Friendly Tavern, Front Street, Empire; (231) 326–5506. Whitefish, burgers, sandwiches, chili, soup.

ACCOMMODATIONS

You won't find any chain hotels or motels in Empire or most of Leelanau County. Traverse City, forty minutes away, has this style of accommodations in abundance—visit www.mytraversecity.com or call (800) TRAVERS for more information.

◆ Empire House Bed and Breakfast, 11015 South LaCore Road, Empire; (231) 326–5524.

◆ Lakeshore Inn of Empire, MI 22 and Front Street, Empire; (231) 326–5145.

◆ Sleeping Bear Bed & Breakfast, 11977 Gilbert Road, Empire; (231) 326–5375.

RESTROOMS

◆ Start/finish of the Scenic Drive (pit toilet).
◆ Picnic Mountain Area between stops 2 and 3.
◆ Stops 9 and 10 (seasonal portable toilets).
◆ Stop 11 (seasonal portable toilet).

Crystal Lake Ramble

This ride is a microcosm of everything that northern Michigan has to offer. In the 26 miles you'll see beautiful lakeshore, two Lake Michigan lighthouses, and a garden center that is a riot of color. You'll pass through a sleepy village perfectly positioned for lunch and a swim. All this on roads that are fairly level and relatively lightly traveled. There's only one traffic light in all of Benzie County, and it's not on this ride. If you're looking for a great family ride, one within almost everyone's ability level, yet with enough highlights and scenery to satisfy more experienced riders, this is it.

Compared to Leelanau County, its neighbor to the north, Benzie County remains relatively rural. Vacation homes do abound, and there are plenty of golf courses and a ski resort. But somehow all that remains more hidden, and Benzie retains more of the original up-north flavor that's harder and harder to find.

It's a wonder, because everything that draws tourists to northern Michigan can be found on this ride: quiet back roads, quaint villages, sandy beaches, two lighthouses, and miles of blue shoreline. Start in Frankfort. Sunsets are an event here at the harbor, where the lighthouse beckons at the end of a long breakwall, but save that for after the ride.

Leaving the parking lot, you'll soon be on MI 22. The road undulates as it heads north, and you'll have the closest thing to a climb just after you leave the town. Crystal Gardens is less than 2 miles outside town. Flower fanatics could spend hours here.

Point Betsie Lighthouse, about 3 miles outside of Frankfort, is the next highlight. Gear down before you turn left on Point Betsie Road in order to make it up the short but steep hill over the dune. Built in 1858 and still used and occupied, Point Betsie is one of the most photographed lighthouses on the lake. The surf is often loud and rough here, giving you a good idea why Lake Michigan is a Great Lake. On your way out, remember that you'll have to stop abruptly at the bottom of that steep hill before turning left onto MI 22.

Curving around the northwest corner of the lake, you'll have the lake on your right and steep bluffs on your left. Turn right onto County Road 704/Crystal Drive after MI 22 curves away from the lake. Crystal Lake used to be higher, until back in 1873 an attempt was made to create a channel from the lake out to Lake Michigan. The project failed and lowered the level of the lake dramatically. It did expose beach around much of the lake, allowing for the later development of the bordering roads and, in 1880, the village of Beulah. A sign at the intersection of CR 704 and Warren Road is set at the original water level. There's another one in Beulah, at the park next to the public beach.

Crystal Drive leads you to Beulah, where you might enjoy a slice of cherry pie at the Cherry Hut, a sandwich at L'Chayim deli, or a swim at the public beach, where restrooms and picnic tables are also available.

Leaving Beulah, you'll have a 9-mile bike path to take you back to Frankfort. This leg of the trip used to involve the biggest hills and heaviest traffic of the ride. But the Betsie Valley Trail has spared you that. While two-thirds of it is paved, the first third is not. You can ride on a parallel side street for the first mile, but you will have to get your wheels dusty for 2 more, watching for soft spots. In Frankfort, browse at The Bookstore, grab lunch at the Coho Cafe, or head down to the beach.

THE BASICS

Start: Frankfort.

Length: 26.4-mile loop.

Terrain: A few rollers in the first couple miles, then flat. Ends on a 9-mile stretch of bike path, 2 miles of which are gravel.

Traffic and hazards: The route follows lightly traveled roads. Watch for sand on the road, especially on the early stretch along Michigan Highway 22 and the access road to Point Betsie Lighthouse.

Getting there: From Traverse City, take U.S. Highway 31/Michigan Highway 37 south. At Chums Corners, MI 37 continues south while US 31 turns west toward Interlochen. Turn right, following US 31 some 25 miles to Benzonia. At the traffic light (the only one in the county), turn right onto Michigan Highway 115. In Frankfort turn left on 10th Street and then right on Main Street. At 5th Street, turn left to park in the municipal lot along the channel leading to Lake Michigan. Do not park in numbered spaces, which are assigned.

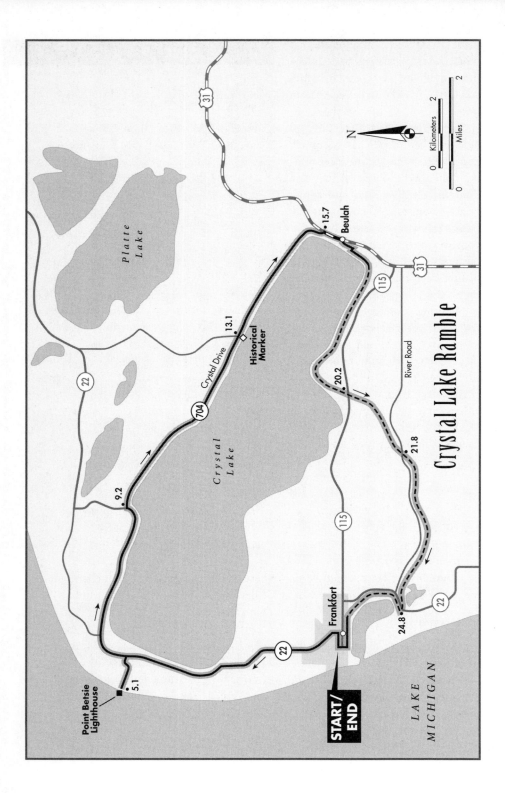

Crystal Lake Ramble

Point Betsie Lighthouse
5.1

22

704 Crystal Drive

Crystal Lake

Platte Lake

9.2

13.1

◇ Historical Marker

15.7
● Beulah

31

115

20.2

River Road

21.8

115

Frankfort

22

24.8

22

START / END

LAKE MICHIGAN

N

31

0 Kilometers 2
0 Miles 2

0.0 From municipal lot, ride up 5th Street. Stop sign at Main Street. Cross Main.

0.1 Stop sign at Forest Avenue. Continue straight. Turn right at stop sign on next block onto Leelanau Avenue.

0.3 Stop sign. Turn left onto 7th Street. Follow out of town. It becomes Crystal Avenue and then MI 22.

1.7 Crystal Gardens. Wonderful flowers and nursery.

4.5 Turn left on Point Betsie Road to visit Point Betsie Lighthouse. Gear down before turn in order to make it up short but steep hill.

5.1 Lighthouse and beach.

5.9 Stop sign. Use caution as you will be coming downhill. Turn left onto MI 22.

9.2 Turn right onto CR 704/Crystal Drive.

12.5 Public lake access.

13.1 Intersection of CR 704 and Warren Road—historical marker about Crystal Lake.

15.7 Turn right at stop sign onto US 31. Stay on shoulder.

16.1 Turn right on North Benzie Boulevard, after sign to downtown business district.

16.7 Turn right on Crystal Avenue, paralleling Betsie River Trail.

17.8 Pavement ends. Cross over to Betsie Valley Trail, for 2 miles of crushed limestone. Path can be soft in spots.

18.1 Turn right at the fork in the path so that you are still riding alongside Crystal Lake, though farther away than before.

19.9 Stop sign. Cross Mollineaux Road and continue on now-paved path.

25.7 Stop sign at East Shore Marina. Continue straight.

26.0 Turn right from path as it emerges between Frankfort Cold Storage and D & R Automotive toward Main Street. Turn left on Main Street.

26.4 Turn left on 5th Street to return to parking lot.

LOCAL INFORMATION

♦ Benzie Area Visitors Bureau; (800) 882–5801; www.visitbenzie.com, www.benzie.org.

LOCAL EVENTS/ATTRACTIONS

♦ The Annual Beulah Art Fair, a juried art show in Beulah Park on Crystal Lake, is held in mid-July and features eighty-five artists and crafters, food, and music. (231) 325–6642.

♦ The Cherry Bowl Drive-In is one of the few remaining drive-ins in Michigan. Open first weekend in May through September. No movies rated

above PG-13. 9812 Honor Highway, Honor; (231) 325–3413; www.cherry
bowldrivein.com.

♦ Gwen Frostic Prints/Presscraft Papers is highly recommended. The late
artist used the natural environment as her inspiration, and the studio itself
blends in with its surroundings. On River Road between Frankfort and
Benzonia. Open 9:00 A.M. to 5:30 P.M. seven days a week May to November;
9:00 A.M. to 4:30 P.M. Monday through Saturday November to April. (231)
882–5505.

♦ The Michigan Legacy Art Park at Crystal Mountain Resort features twenty
works by Michigan artists along wooded trails. Summer concerts. 12500
Crystal Mountain Drive, Thompsonville; (800) 968–7686, ext. 7101;
www.michiganlegacyartpark.org.

RESTAURANTS

♦ The Roadhouse, 1058 US 31, Benzonia; (231) 882–9631. At the top of the
hill in Benzonia, a reference point everyone around here uses. Tex-Mex bar and
grill.

♦ The Cherry Hut, US 31, Beulah; (231) 882–4431. An institution since 1922.
Cherry pie, cherry sundaes, cherry jelly, etc. Also lunch and dinner. Open
Memorial Day to mid-October.

♦ L'Chayim, 274 South Benzie Boulevard, Beulah; (231) 882–5221. From the
Golan Heights to Golda Meir, this deli has a sandwich for you. Also soups,
bagels, cheese.

♦ Cabbage Shed Waterfront Pub, 198 Frankfort Avenue, Elberta; (231)
352–9391. On Betsie Bay. Steaks, seafood, bar, outdoor dining, and entertainment.

ACCOMMODATIONS

♦ Chimney Corners Resort, 1602 Crystal Drive, Frankfort; (231) 352–7522.
Sentimental bias admitted—I had my wedding reception here. Family-owned.
Weekly cabin rentals and nightly stays in the rustic lodge atop the bluff.

♦ Brookside Inn, US 31, Beulah; (231) 882–9688. Lodging and dining, including outdoor dining.

♦ R & R Motel, 541 Lake Street, Frankfort; (231) 352–9238.

♦ Crystal Mountain Resort, MI 115, Thompsonville; (800) 968–7686. Full-
service golf, ski, and conference resort.

RESTROOMS

♦ Mile 15.0: Beulah Beach, next to park and Betsie Valley Trailhead.

♦ In Frankfort at the beach 5 blocks from the start/finish (seasonal pit toilets).

Sunrise Side Cruise

Michigan's Lake Huron shore is also called the state's "Sunrise Side," a label that you'll see everywhere here, including the name of this ride. Its alliterative ring suggests the presence of a marketing-savvy tourism industry, yet the Sunrise Side doesn't feel nearly as touristy as Michigan's more popular and well-known northwest side. This side feels more homespun than upscale. You're more likely to find camping instead of condos. You'll see fewer PRIVATE signs along beaches. Best of all for bicyclists, you'll see fewer cars on the Sunrise Side. Locals cherish the slower pace over here, so take your time to enjoy the Sunrise Side Cruise.

The ride starts in Harrisville State Park, one of the oldest state parks in the state, which stretches for nearly a mile along Lake Huron. Park at the beach/picnic area, return to the main entrance, and head north on US 23. The major highway was recently resurfaced and is in wonderful condition, including a wide shoulder. You'll skirt downtown Harrisville as you cross MI 72 at the traffic light. The town offers a Saturday farmers' market, weekly evening concerts at the harbor pavilion, and other community events and festivals throughout the summer.

After Harrisville, the ride's first attraction is the Sturgeon Point Lighthouse, about 5 miles outside of town. The light still functions more than 130 years after it became operational in 1870, warning vessels of the reef that extends a mile and a half into Lake Huron at Sturgeon Point. It was automated in 1939 and last occupied in 1941. After the lighthouse fell victim to vandals, the Alcona Historical Society took it under its wing and restored it in the mid-1980s.

The lighthouse is now a maritime museum, open daily from Memorial Day through mid-September. The lighthouse tower is off-limits to the public, but still take the time to peek inside the museum. Nautical artifacts including an anchor, windlass, and ice crusher also dot the grounds.

The most recent addition to the lighthouse property is the old Bailey School, a one-room schoolhouse built in 1907 in Mikado Township, southwest of the present location. It closed in 1941 (a year when it had thirteen students and the teacher earned $125 per month) and was moved to Sturgeon Point in 1998. Furnished as it would have been during the early twentieth century, the school and the lighthouse make an interesting historical complex. Restrooms are also available

After the lighthouse, continue north on Lakeshore Drive. You'll get glimpses of Lake Huron along this residential stretch until Alcona Township Huron Park at mile 14, when you'll get a wide view. There are restrooms, a playground, and picnic tables.

After the park the ride turns away from Lake Huron. Inland you'll encounter some hills, but they are rolling—no climbs of any significance. The scenery also turns rural as you enter farmland. Livestock, particularly dairy cattle, are a large sector of local agriculture, and you might see a herd grazing or a field dotted with just-baled hay. Roads remain lightly traveled.

The village of Lincoln is a good break point, especially if you haven't packed picnic supplies and already eaten en route. The Alcona Historical Society has been busy here, too, where Lincoln Depot and Museum, a tribute to rail transportation, is currently under restoration. Though it's difficult to imagine now, Lincoln was a bustling commercial hub in the late nineteenth and early twentieth century. The Depot recalls that era.

For a little sustenance, try the Iron Skillet or Durfee's Restaurant or pick up picnic supplies at Gloria's, a deli/grocery store on Second Street. There are picnic tables three doors down, next door to the Ice Cream Junction. After Lincoln, it's an easy 8 miles back to Harrisville and the sunset of the Sunrise Side Cruise.

This one-room schoolhouse is part of the historical complex at Sturgeon Point. Courtesy of Michael O. Henderson

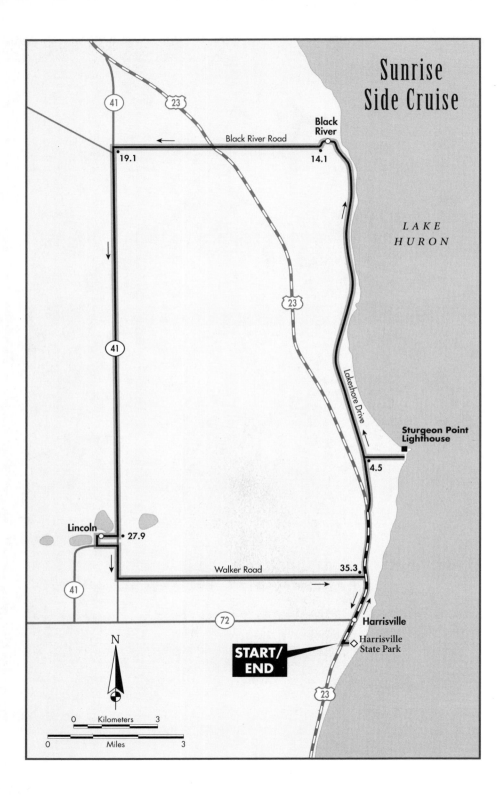

Sunrise Side Cruise

Black River

Black River Road

19.1

14.1

LAKE HURON

Lakeshore Drive

Sturgeon Point Lighthouse

4.5

Lincoln

27.9

Walker Road

35.3

Harrisville

Harrisville State Park

START/ END

N

Kilometers   3

Miles   3

0.0 From the main entrance to Harrisville State Park, turn right onto US 23.

3.3 Turn right on Lakeshore Drive.

3.8 Cedarbrook Trout Farm—public fishing.

4.5 Turn right on Point Road to visit Sturgeon Point Lighthouse. Restrooms.

5.4 Turn left into parking area just before road dead-ends. After visiting lighthouse, retrace route on Point Road and turn right back onto Lakeshore Drive.

9.3 Turn right on Alcona, which then becomes Lakeshore Drive.

13.8 Turn right on Ridge Road/Huron Park into Alcona Township Huron Park. Restrooms. Retrace route into park and turn right at stop sign.

14.1 Turn right on Black River Road at St. Gabriel's Catholic Church.

14.2 Yield sign—rough railroad tracks.

14.5 Follow curve to the right. Watch for traffic merging from left.

19.1 Stop sign. Turn left on County Road F-41 toward Lincoln.

27.9 Turn right, staying on CR F-41, toward Lincoln business district. Becomes Main Street.

28.3 Continue straight on Main Street/CR F-41 curves left and becomes Second Street.

28.4 Stop sign. Turn left on Lake.

28.5 Depot at corner of Lake and Fiske. Turn left on Fiske, then turn right at stop sign onto Second Street/CR F-41.

28.7 Stop sign/flashing red light. Turn left, heading out of Lincoln on Traverse Bay Street Road.

29.1 Stop sign. Turn right on Barlow Road.

29.9 Turn left on Walker Road.

35.3 Stop sign. Turn right on US 23.

37.0 Turn left into Harrisville State Park and return to parking lot.

LOCAL INFORMATION

♦ Huron Shores Chamber of Commerce, P.O. Box 581, Harrisville 48740; (800) 432–2823; www.huronshoreschamber.com.

♦ Michigan's Sunrise Side Travel Association; www.misunriseside.com.

LOCAL EVENTS/ATTRACTIONS

♦ The Sunrise Side Wine and Food Festival at Harrisville Harbor is held in July. Food, live music, and art. (800) 432–2823.

◆ Harrisville Harbor Nights is a weekly concert series at Harrisville Harbor Pavilion. Big band one week, country the next, acoustic folk the next. Thursday nights in July and August. Free.

◆ The Alcona County Fair has everything you'd expect at a fair: livestock competitions, carnival rides, a rodeo, and musical entertainment. First week of August. (989) 736–9550.

RESTAURANTS

◆ The Old Place Inn, 309 East Main Street, Harrisville; (989) 724–6700. Dating back to 1870, the Old Place Inn has served as a home to a sheriff and a hotel to patrons including gangster John Dillinger. Now it's a great place for a quick lunch or a full dinner. Porch dining available.

◆ Harbortown Pizza, corner of MI 72 and US 23; (989) 724–5000. Pizza, subs, salads. Carry-out only. Take one down to the concert at the harbor.

◆ Coffee Talk Cafe, 417 Main Street, Harrisville; (989) 724–6236. Breakfast and lunch. Specializes in Greek salads and hummus. Sidewalk tables available.

◆ For diner/cafe-style establishments with standard menu fare, stop at Backwoods Bistro, the Iron Skillet, or Durfee's, all on the route in Lincoln.

ACCOMMODATIONS

◆ Seaver Country House, 311 McLean Road, Harrisville; (989) 724–6939.

◆ Four Seasons Motel, 797 South US 23, Harrisville; (989) 724–6220.

◆ Copper Inn, 913 South Huron Road/US 23, Harrisville; (989) 724–7338.

RESTROOMS

◆ Start/finish: Harrisville State Park.

◆ Mile 4.5: Sturgeon Point Lighthouse.

◆ Mile 13.8: Alcona Township Huron Park.

◆ Mile 28.5: various establishments in Lincoln.

Au Sable Cruise

*H*istorically, the Au Sable River has served as a commercial waterway, first for Native Americans, then for fur traders, and then for the lumber industry, as white pine logs from inland forests floated down to Lake Huron sawmill towns. Today the "river of sand" is still a workhorse, providing power from six hydroelectric dams. But these days the Au Sable is also a major source of recreation, hosting an annual marathon canoe race, legions of fishermen and boaters, and, of course, bicyclists. River Road, a National Forest Scenic Byway that runs along the Au Sable, is the heart of this ride. Highlights include a monument to the lumbering industry and a picturesque natural spring that feeds the Au Sable, which in turn feeds Lake Huron. You'll probably want to feed yourself before setting off or else stock up your bike bag, as food options are somewhat limited on the route.

Rivers have entirely different personalities than lakes, and a ride along the Au Sable feels very different than the many shoreline rides in this book. Perhaps it's the sense of adventure spiced with mystery that a river stirs within. Though it is often obscured from road view by trees, or from convenient access by high banks, you still know it's there, and you know it's going someplace. There's a purpose to its flow, other than to lap pleasantly at a beach.

This sense of purpose is reinforced on the Au Sable by the very well-done Lumberman's Monument, a rare tribute to the logging industry. You'll reach it after a relatively flat 15 miles on River Road. You'll have had two opportunities already to view the river from overlooks and one chance to pick up picnic

Start: Eastgate Welcome Center to Huron Manistee National Forest.

Length: 41.6-mile lariat.

Terrain: Flat to rolling. Second half of ride, on north side of Au Sable, has more hills.

Traffic and hazards: The road will be busy for the first 4 miles, but traffic thins after Foote Site Village. There's a shoulder through most of the ride, but it has intermittent gaps and widens and narrows.

Getting there: From the U.S. Highway 23 intersection in downtown Oscoda, take River Road west 2.0 miles and park at the Eastgate Welcome Center, located on the right.

supplies, at the Dam Store at mile 4.0. The Lumberman's Monument is a good spot to picnic, again overlooking the river, chewing over what you'll learn there as much as your sandwich.

In hindsight, Michigan's lumbering era is often seen an environmental disaster, responsible for rampant deforestation in much of the state. The Lumberman's Monument offers another point of view. According to the inscription on the 14-foot bronze statue, it was erected in 1931 "to perpetuate the memory of the pioneer lumbermen of Michigan, through whose labors was made possible the development of the prairie states."

The statue depicts a timber cruiser with a compass, a sawyer holding an ax and crosscut saw, and a "river rat" with a peavey, a combination hook-and-prod tool that the logger used to manipulate the floating logs while balancing on them. Besides the statue, there's an educational display area where you can try your hand at wielding a peavey, look at a logjam, and learn about branding logs. If you go down the 200 stairs to the river, you can see a wanigan, a shelter used in lumbering camps.

Two miles after the Lumberman's Monument is the Canoer's Memorial Scenic Overlook. You'll see canoes on the Au Sable every day of the week nearly three seasons of the year, but they culminate in late July, when paddlers run the entire 120-mile length of the Au Sable in an exhausting, overnight canoe marathon.

The Grayling-to-Oscoda canoe marathon has been running since 1947. In the late 1990s, someone came up with the idea of a bicycle chase race, and the Black Bear Bicycle Tour was born. If you're up for a 100-mile ride (or shorter loops), come back the last weekend in July. Otherwise, after you've had your fill of the Canoer's Memorial, head back out to River Road.

In about another mile is the Au Sable's third highlight: Iargo Springs. I counted 289 steps down the bank to the springs; one tourist publication lists 294, and the U.S. Forest Service says it's a 300-step descent. Keep your own count if you like; just remember you'll have to climb back up. A trail was first constructed by the Civilian Conservation Corps in 1934, and it's been periodically upgraded to the current wooden staircase and boardwalks through the springs to the river. After 18 miles of cycling, much of it on open, sunny road,

The Lumberman's Monument, on scenic River Road, commemorates Michigan's lumbering era.
Courtesy of Michael O. Henderson

you'll find it pleasantly cool down at the springs, which have been used as a drinking-water source since presettlement times.

Shortly after Iargo Springs you'll turn north to cross the Au Sable and then begin riding back east along the northern bank. You'll encounter more hills, including one immediately after the river crossing. The Au Sable Hookup at the bottom of that hill is the second opportunity for a snack. On the first section of Bissonette Road, a marshy area separates the river from the road. Eventually you'll again be riding within view of the river, and the road will flatten out. You'll cross back over the Au Sable at Rea Road, again passing the Dam Store, and return to the Eastgate parking area in 4 miles.

This ride is highly recommended in the fall, when the color along the river is breathtaking.

LOCAL INFORMATION

♦ Michigan's Sunrise Side Travel Association; www.misunriseside.com.
♦ Oscoda Area Visitors Center and Chamber; (800) 235–4625; www.oscoda .com.

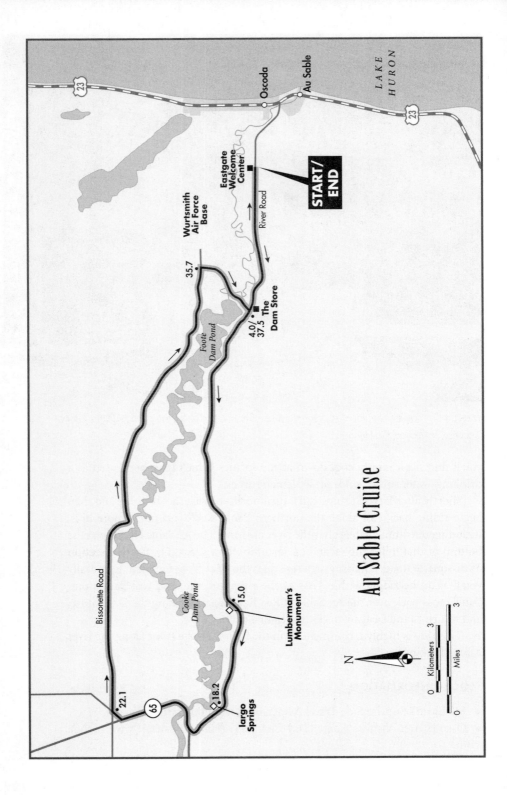

Au Sable Cruise

LAKE HURON

23

Oscoda

Au Sable

23

Eastgate
Welcome
Center

START/
END

River Road

Wurtsmith
Air Force
Base

35.7

Foote
Dam Pond

4.0/
37.5 • The
Dam Store

Bissonette Road

Cooke
Dam Pond

15.0
◇
Lumberman's
Monument

22.1 •

65

18.2
◇
Iargo
Springs

N

0   Kilometers   3

0   Miles   3

0.0 Eastgate Welcome Center. Turn right from parking lot onto River Road.

3.2 Au Sable Overlook. Stairs to river.

4.0 The Dam Store. Food and drinks.

7.6 Foote Pond Scenic Overlook. Turn right to visit, then turn around in cul-de-sac.

9.0 Turn right at stop sign back onto River Road.

15.0 Turn right on Monument Road to visit Lumberman's Monument. Restrooms. Retrace your route to return to River Road and turn right.

17.0 Canoer's Memorial Scenic Overlook.

18.2 Iargo Springs. Three-hundred-step staircase to visit natural springs feeding Au Sable. Restrooms.

19.3 Stop sign. Turn right onto Michigan Highway 65 north. Watch rumble strip on shoulder.

20.0 Road narrows at bridge over Au Sable.

20.3 Au Sable Hookup. Party store and hot dog stand on left. Use caution crossing road, as oncoming traffic is coming downhill.

22.1 Turn right on Bissonette Road. Marked ahead of intersection, not at intersection.

35.7 Turn right on Rea Road.

36.7 River access. Pit toilets.

37.5 Stop sign. Turn left on River Road. The Dam Store on left.

41.6 Turn left into Eastgate Welcome Center parking lot.

♦ River Road Scenic Byway information: Tune radio to 1610 AM.

♦ Lumberman's Monument office; (989) 362–8961.

LOCAL EVENTS/ATTRACTIONS

♦ The Au Sable River Canoe Marathon is a 120-mile overnight canoe race from Grayling to Oscoda. Besides being exhausting for competitors, it's also called the toughest spectator race in the world. Last weekend of July; www.au sablecanoemarathon.org.

♦ The Gagaguwon Pow Wow features costumed traditional dancing and drumming and Native American arts and crafts. Last weekend of July. See the Oscoda Area Visitors Center and Chamber for more information.

♦ At Art on the Beach, 200 artists exhibit their work on the beach in Oscoda. Last weekend in June. See the Oscoda Area Visitors Center and Chamber for more information.

♦ The Sunrise Concert Series includes some free and some ticketed performances at Oscoda Beach Park Band Shell and Oscoda High School. See the Oscoda Area Visitors Center and Chamber for more information.

♦ The Au Sable Inn Finish Line and Sports Bar, 100 South State Street, Oscoda; (989) 747–0350. On the river, at the end of the famous canoe race.
♦ Wiltse's Brew Pub and Family Restaurant, 5606 CR F-41, Oscoda; (989) 739–2231. Microbrewery serving seafood, sandwiches.
♦ The Bavarian Bakery and Restaurant, 5222 North US 23, Oscoda; (989) 739–8077. Salads, sandwiches, specials, breads and pastries.

ACCOMMODATIONS

♦ AmericInn Lodge and Suites, 720 East Harbor Street, Oscoda; (989) 739–1986 or (800) 634–3444.
♦ Super 8, 4270 North US 23, Oscoda; (989) 739–8822. On the beach with an indoor pool.
♦ Huron House Bed and Breakfast, 3124 North US 23, Oscoda; (989) 739–9255; www.huronhouse.com. Calls itself a "couple's retreat on Lake Huron."

RESTROOMS

♦ Start/finish: Eastgate Welcome Center.
♦ Mile 15.0: Lumberman's Monument.
♦ Mile 18.2: Iargo Springs.
♦ Mile 36.7: river access.

White Lake Challenge

Riders will sample Michigan's best on the White Lake Challenge, as the route meanders through orchards, woodlands, and small towns and along Lake Michigan shoreline. Starting in the quaint town of Whitehall the route heads north, weaving through several miles of the Hart-Montague Rail Trail. On the way to Shelby, a long climb will offer panoramic views of unhurried Oceana County, one of the top fruit-growing counties in Michigan, before a winding descent into town. Those who prefer to avoid the climb may choose to ride the paved rail-trail for the first portion of the route. Upon leaving Shelby the route will travel southwest toward the sandy shores of Lake Michigan.

The twin cities of Whitehall and Montague, on opposite sides of White Lake, are the departure point for the White Lake Challenge. The communities played an important role during the Michigan lumber era of the late nineteenth century, as logs floated down the White River to sawmills in the twin cities. Stately Victorian homes in both towns offer a reminder of the prosperous lumbering days. Today the area features excellent outdoor activities, quaint galleries, and antiques shops, without the tourist trappings of fudge and trinket stores typically found further north.

For cyclists in the group who prefer a more leisurely ride before meeting up with their gung-ho riding companions, the paved Hart-Montague Rail Trail travels from Whitehall to Shelby. This will cut off about 5 miles of the 20 to Shelby and eliminate the worst hills.

From Whitehall the route heads north, crossing the border from Muskegon County to Oceana County, home to some 700 farms producing tart and sweet

It's worth the miles to get to this view. Courtesy of Nancy Hulka

cherries, apples, dairy products, beef, and Christmas trees, but especially known for asparagus. Known as the Asparagus Capital of the nation, Oceana County harvests more than four million pounds of the vegetable annually. Women vie for the title of "Mrs. Asparagus" during the National Asparagus Festival in June, which alternates between the Oceana County villages of Shelby and Hart.

Asparagus doesn't provide much in the way of roadside scenery, but the cherry and apple orchards do. In May these fruit trees offer riders the spectacle of beautiful blooms. Michigan's native flora, including white trillium, yellow marsh marigold, and white mayapples, can be glimpsed in woodlots lining the road.

For those taking the road ride, the towns of Rothbury, New Era, and Shelby all offer food and rest stops. The Jubilee Ice Cream Parlor is a popular old-fashioned shop in New Era at mile 14.9. At mile 20 in the village of Shelby, those who took the trail option will rejoin the regular route. Restaurant options include several pizza shops, the Wooden Nickel Restaurant, and Brown Bear Food and Spirits. All the towns offer convenience stores and markets where you can pick up supplies for a picnic lunch. Roadside fruit and vegetable stands are common in the summer and fall and offer fresh-picked produce. From Shelby you'll backtrack south a bit on the rail trail before heading west to Lake Michigan.

Majestic views of Lake Michigan await at mile 37.3 at the Claybanks Park and Campground. A mile down the road, stop at Claybanks Pottery, sitting quietly in the woods off the road.

After passing more orchards the route travels through flat, open cornfields along Chase Road before heading back to the wooded shores of Lake Michigan. At mile 50 be sure to turn right on Ferry Street, next to the Old Channel Inn Restaurant, which will dead-end at Lake Michigan. Walk the beach or take a swim in the cooling waters of the big lake. This is an easy stop to miss, as Ferry Street is at the bottom of a short, fast, winding downhill run.

After leaving Lake Michigan the route will skirt White Lake and pass lovely homes as it heads through the town of Montague and back to Goodrich Park in Whitehall.

LOCAL INFORMATION

♦ White Lake Area Chamber of Commerce and Welcome Center, 124 Hanson Street, Whitehall; (800) 879–9702; www.whitelake.org.
♦ Muskegon County Convention & Visitors Bureau, 610 West Western Avenue, Muskegon; (800) 250–WAVE.
♦ Shelby Area Chamber of Commerce, P.O. Box 193, Shelby, 49455; (231) 861–4050; www.oceanacounty.net.

LOCAL EVENTS/ATTRACTIONS

♦ The National Asparagus Festival in Oceana County celebrates the asparagus harvest. Parade, arts-and-crafts fair, asparagus smorgasbord. Second weekend in June, with villages of Hart and Shelby alternating as host.

THE BASICS

Start: Goodrich Park in Whitehall.

Length: 56.1-mile loop with an optional 5-mile shortcut.

Terrain: Mostly flat to gently rolling, with some steep climbs and fast downhill runs.

Traffic and hazards: Traffic is light on most roads. Due to the popularity of the Hart-Montague Rail Trail, motorists are accustomed to bicyclists in the area. Use caution while crossing busy Oceana Drive and while riding a 1-block section of Oceana Drive. You will encounter more traffic on Stony Lake Road, and the shoulder is sand. There is also more traffic in and around Montague and Whitehall.

Getting there: From Grand Rapids, take Interstate 96 west to Muskegon and then U.S. Highway 31 north. Exit at the Whitehall/Montague/Colby Street exit. Downtown Whitehall is approximately 2 miles from the exit. After passing through downtown, Colby Street will take a sharp right turn. Lake Street is on the left. Turn left on Lake Street (prior to crossing the White River bridge) and park in the lot at Goodrich Park.

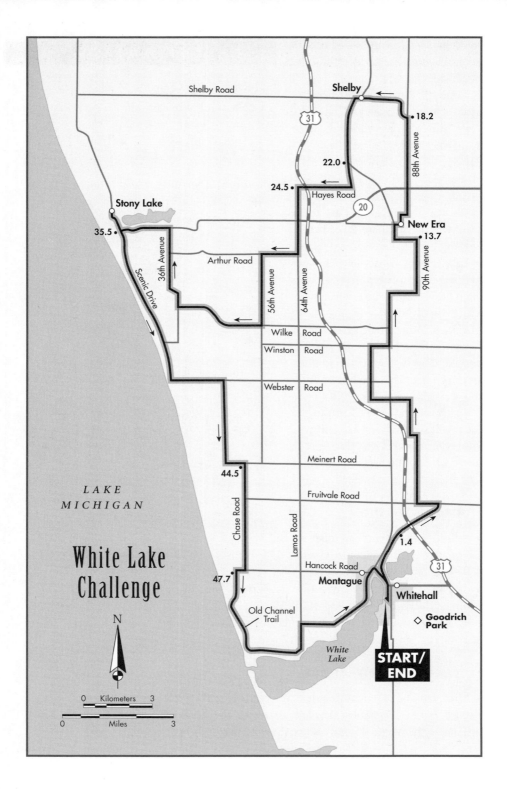

White Lake Challenge

LAKE
MICHIGAN

Shelby Road

Shelby

31

18.2

22.0

24.5

Hayes Road

20

Stony Lake

35.5

New Era

13.7

36th Avenue

Scenic Drive

Arthur Road

56th Avenue

64th Avenue

90th Avenue

Wilke   Road

Winston   Road

Webster   Road

Meinert Road

44.5

Fruitvale Road

Chase Road

Lamos Road

1.4

Hancock Road

47.7

Montague

31

Whitehall

Goodrich
Park

Old Channel
Trail

White
Lake

START/
END

N

0   Kilometers   3

0   Miles   3

0.0 From the parking lot turn right onto Lake Street and then left onto the Hart-Montague Rail Trail located behind Pinheads restaurant.

1.4 Turn right on Walsh Road. **Option:** Stay on the trail until mile 19.8 in Shelby, cutting about 5 miles off the trip.

3.3 Turn left on Fruitvale Road. (There may not be a street sign.)

3.8 Turn right on Henderson Road.

5.7 Turn left on Skeels Road.

6.0 Turn right on Henderson Road.

7.0 Turn left on unmarked road (Roosevelt Road).

7.5 Continue straight on Roosevelt. Use caution crossing Oceana Drive.

7.6 Jog right (road will turn into 80th Avenue).

9.5 Turn right on Winston Road.

10.0 Stop sign. Continue straight. Town of Rothbury (Wesco gas station has food, snacks, and restrooms).

10.5 Turn left on 88th Avenue.

11.0 Stop at T intersection. Turn right on unmarked road.

12.2 Turn left on 90th Avenue.

13.7 Bear left on Yale Road.

14.3 Turn right on Hart-Montague Trail.

14.9 Turn right on Ray Street in New Era. (Turn left to visit New Era. Ice cream available at the Jubilee in the red building. Portable toilet behind the picnic shelter located next to the rail trail.)

15.1 Turn left on James Street.

15.2 Turn right on Oak Street.

15.3 Bear left on Redwood. You will be on 88th Avenue once out of town.

16.2 Stop sign. Continue straight, using caution while crossing Michigan Highway 20. Pause at the hilltop to enjoy the orchard views.

18.2 Stop sign. Turn left on Shelby Road. Cruise into the town of Shelby on a fast, winding downhill.

19.8 Stop in Shelby. Turn right on State Street, then left on Second Street. (If you're coming off the trail, take a right on Second.)

19.9 Turn right on Michigan Street, Shelby's main drag (Brown Bear and Wooden Nickel restaurants). If you're coming off the trail take a left on Michigan.

20.1 Turn left on Fourth Street.

20.1 Turn left on rail trail. Picnic tables and outhouses available.

22.0 Turn right on Grant Road and then left on Oceana Drive using caution, more traffic. Oceana Drive will curve to the left. Stay straight, going onto Water Road.

(continued)

23.1 Turn right on Hayes Road.

24.5 Stop at T intersection. Turn left on 64th Avenue.

26.4 Bear right onto Arthur Road.

27.3 Bear left on 56th Avenue.

29.3 Turn right on Wilke Road.

30.4 Stop at T intersection. Turn right on Wilke.

32.5 Bear right on 36th Avenue. Claybanks Township Hall on corner.

34.1 Turn left on Stony Lake Road. Caution, more traffic.

35.5 Turn left on Scenic Drive. (Turn right for a quarter-mile ride to Stony Lake and a convenience store and a restroom at the park across the street, then backtrack.) Scenic Drive will become Webster Road.

37.3 Claybanks Park. Well water, pit toilets, beautiful view of Lake Michigan.

38.2 Claybanks Pottery. An interesting shop.

41.6 Turn right on 48th Avenue.

44.0 Turn left on Meinert Road.

44.5 Turn right on Chase Road.

47.4 Stop at T intersection. Turn right on Hancock Road.

47.7 Turn left on Old Channel Trail.

50.0 Old Channel Trail Restaurant and Ferry Street. For Lake Michigan beach access, turn right on Ferry Street. Watch carefully. Located at the bottom of a curving downhill, this turn is easy to miss.

52.4 Turn right on Wilkes Road.

55.5 At T intersection turn right on Dowling Street, which will bridge over White Lake.

55.6 Continue straight at the stoplight, riding on the sidewalk/bike trail.

56.1 Turn right on Lake Street and return to parking lot.

♦ At Pumpkinfest in Montague, roll pumpkins down the Dowling Street Hill or enter a pumpkin-carving, pie-eating, or seed-spitting contest. Second Saturday in October.

♦ The White River Light Station, built in 1875 is said to be haunted and was featured in a Discovery Channel program about haunted lighthouses. Museum displays of the area's lighthouses and shipping, fishing, and logging industries. 6199 Murray Road, Whitehall; (231) 894–8265; www.whiteriver lightstation.org.

RESTAURANTS

♦ Riverview Cafe & Bakery, 115 North Mears Avenue, Whitehall; (231) 893–5163. Gourmet sandwiches, pastries and bread, French dinners. Gourmet chocolate. Overlooking the White River.
♦ Pinheads Gutters and Grub, 115 South Lake Street, Whitehall; (231) 894–4103. Wood-fired pizza, pasta, sandwiches, fish, and steak. Deck overlooking White Lake.
♦ Trailside Restaurant, 4723 First Street, New Era; (231) 861–6446. Mom-and-pop place serving American food. Good homemade desserts.
♦ Brown Bear Food and Spirits, 142 Michigan Street, Shelby; (231) 861–5014. A local favorite. Burgers, sandwiches, soup.

ACCOMMODATIONS

♦ Cocoa Cottage Bed & Breakfast, 223 South Mears Avenue, Whitehall; (231) 893–0674 or (800) 204–7596. Chocolate reception, chocolate at breakfast, and chocolate-themed rooms with private baths. Covered, locked bike storage.
♦ Super 8 Motel, 3080 Colby, Whitehall; (231) 894–4848 or (800) 800–8000. Moderate rates at this well-known chain.
♦ Lakeside Inn, 5700 Scenic Drive, Whitehall; (888) 442–3304. Resort on White Lake. Heated pool. Hotel rooms and housekeeping unit. Restaurant on site. Covered, locked bicycle storage.

RESTROOMS

♦ Start/finish: Goodrich Park.
♦ Mile 10.0: Wesco gas station and convenience store.
♦ Mile 14.9: New Era White Pine Picnic Shelter.
♦ Mile 20.2: Shelby White Pine Picnic Area.
♦ Mile 37.3: Claybanks Park.

Big Rapids Cruise

*L*ocal bicyclists love the rolling hills, steep climbs, and twisting roads of Mecosta County, territory often overlooked and unknown by others. Only an hour's drive from Grand Rapids, Michigan's second-largest city, the Big Rapids Cruise offers quiet roads, interesting stops, and a taste of Amish farm country. Starting in the college town of Big Rapids, the route heads north to the village of Paris—complete with a replica of the Eiffel Tower, scaled down of course—before looping south to the village of Stanwood. There you might pass an Amish carriage bound for supplies at the local feed store or market."

Up North without the drive" is Mecosta County's slogan, and it lives up to it on the Big Rapids Cruise. The ride's hub takes its name from the "big" rapids of the Muskegon River, where the town's first sawmill was built in the 1850s. Today it is better known as the home of Ferris State University, one of Michigan's public four-year universities. Riders can thank the long and mighty Muskegon, one of the major tributaries to Lake Michigan, for the geography of the area, featuring rolling grades, steep hills, and more than one hundred lakes. Wildflowers line the route in spring and summer, and brightly colored leaves in autumn.

The route starts at the Old Train Depot in Big Rapids and heads north to the village of Paris. Cyclists who want to eliminate some hills, although not distance, can instead take the White Pine Rail Trail to Paris. While the entire trail is not paved, the sections used for this ride are.

Unlike the French capital, you won't find fashion runways, art museums, or sidewalk cafes in the small village of Paris, established in 1867 by John Parish. His name was mistaken for "Paris," and it's stuck ever since. Michigan's Paris does offer the Market/Hardware store, where locals drop by for a soda pop or plumbing supplies. And it has its own replica of the ultimate French icon, in the back section of Hatchery Park. High school students welded the 20-foot-high steel Eiffel Tower and placed it in the park in 1980.

After viewing the tower you'll be brought back to the United States by the 8-foot-tall concrete Indian standing in full headdress. This vintage 1938 statue is an example of the Depression-era Work Projects Administration.

Just north of Paris is the Paris Fish Hatchery, an enjoyable side trip. Dating back to 1881, it holds the title as the largest and oldest operating hatchery in the state of Michigan. Today, the hatchery is operated by the Mecosta County Park Service. Using the pole and bait provided, you can fish here without a license.

One final Paris-area attraction is the cross-cultural elm tree adjacent to the hatchery building. Planted in 1910, this unique tree is an American elm on the bottom with a Japanese elm grafted on top. It looks like one tree stuck on top of another. The bark is especially distinctive, with long vertical lines on the bottom and an elephant-skin pattern on top.

After saying "*au revoir*" to Paris, head east on Hoover Road to ascend and descend some rather large hills. Enjoy streams, ponds, forested vistas, and scenic farms.

At mileage point 16.5, nearing Big Rapids again, you'll turn off 165th Avenue onto Sixteen Mile Road. Use extreme caution on the half-mile stretch of Sixteen Mile Road, as traffic is heavy and fast.

THE BASICS

Start: White Pine Rail Trail staging area.

Length: 40.3-mile loop.

Terrain: Rolling hills, steep climbs, some fast descents and several flat sections.

Traffic and hazards: Traffic is usually very light throughout the entire route, with a few exceptions. A half-mile section of Sixteen Mile Road must be cycled with caution, as traffic is fast and heavy and the shoulder is not paved. Heavier traffic may also be found on the 2-mile stretch of Pierce Road. Caution is also warranted on a 1.5-mile section of McKinley Road, as traffic will be heavier and the shoulder is gravel.

Getting there: From Grand Rapids, take U.S. Highway 131 north to the Big Rapids exit (# 139, Business Route 131/Michigan Highway 20. After exiting, turn right onto Perry Street (MI 20). At the corner of Perry and State Street, turn left onto State Street/MI 20. Then continue on MI 20 by turning right onto Maple Street/MI 20. Continue straight at the traffic light where Maple intersects Third Street. The White Pine Rail Trail staging area at the Old Train Depot is 1 block farther on the right. Parking is free.

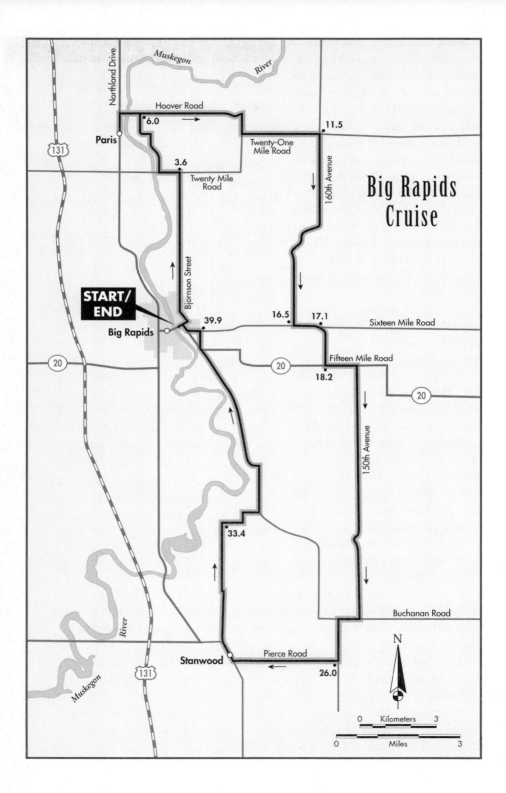

Big Rapids Cruise

0.0 From the White Pine Rail Trail staging area, turn right on Maple Street and then make a quick left on Bjornson Street. **Option:** To eliminate some hills, enter the trail (next direction at mile 5.8).

0.6 Stop sign. Continue straight on what is now called 195th Avenue.

3.6 Stop sign. Left on Twenty Mile Road.

4.3 Jog right on Ash Road.

5.3 Jog left on Twenty-one Mile Road.

5.6 Jog right on 205th Avenue.

5.8 If you took the trail, turn left on unmarked road (Hoover Road).

6.0 Hoover Road. Turn left to visit the village of Paris and the Paris Fish Hatchery. Hoover Road ends at a T intersection with Northland Drive. Caution: More traffic. Turn left and in a half mile enter Paris. Turn right on bike path where it intersects Hoover Road for a quarter-mile trip to the Paris Fish Hatchery. Retrace your route and head east on Hoover.

8.9 Veer right on 180th Avenue.

9.4 Veer left on Twenty-one Mile Road.

11.5 Four-way stop. Turn right on 160th Avenue.

13.8 Pond. Veer right.

16.5 Turn left on Sixteen Mile Road. Caution: Heavier traffic, gravel shoulder.

17.1 Turn right on 157th Avenue.

18.2 Four-way stop. Turn left on Fifteen Mile Road.

18.9 Bear right on 150th Avenue.

25.5 Stop at T intersection. Turn right on Buchanan Road.

26.0 Bear left on 155th Avenue.

27.0 Turn right on Pierce Road. Heavier traffic.

29.8 Turn right on Stanwood Road. Village of Stanwood. Convenience store, Corner Cafe. Turn left on Jefferson Street for Stanwood Pizza and Ice Cream. Upon leaving Stanwood, continue straight (north) on Stanwood Road.

30.4 Four-way stop. Continue straight.

33.4 Stop at T intersection. Bear right on Eleven Mile Road.

33.9 Yield sign. Turn left on 180th Avenue.

35.8 Bear left on 175th Avenue. Road will make several twists.

37.9 Two-way stop. Turn left on McKinley Road. Caution: Heavier traffic, gravel shoulder.

39.3 Stop sign. Turn right on Taft, then make a quick left on 190th Avenue. Use caution at intersections.

39.9 Stop sign. Turn left on Colburn Street.

40.1 Turn right on White Pine Rail Trail.

40.3 Parking lot.

Heading into the village of Stanwood, on the southernmost part of the ride, you'll see Amish farms along Pierce Road. Amish horse-and-buggies are common in the village itself. Take a break from the bike and peruse Stanwood's several antiques shops. If you've worked up an appetite, try the Corner Cafe for burgers, sandwiches, and fish. Stanwood Ice Cream and Pizza serves up, naturally, ice cream and pizza.

From Stanwood, 10 miles of twisting roads take the route back to Big Rapids. Use caution on McKinley Road. A small section of the paved White Pine Rail Trail deposits you back at the parking lot.

After visiting Paris and climbing the hills of Mecosta County, riders may have visions of having finished the Tour de France.

LOCAL INFORMATION

♦ Big Rapids Convention and Visitors Bureau, 246 North State Street, Big Rapids; (888) 229–4FUN; www.bigrapids.org.

LOCAL EVENTS/ATTRACTIONS

♦ Sawmill Tube and Canoe runs canoeing and tubing trips on the Muskegon River. 230 Baldwin Street, Big Rapids; (231) 796–6408.

The Muskegon River flows out to Lake Michigan. Courtesy of Nancy Hulka

- The Wheatland Music Festival offers a weekend of camping and bluegrass. It marked its 30th anniversary in 2002. Held in Remus, in southeastern Mecosta County. www.wheatlandmusic.org.

RESTAURANTS

- Shuberg's Bar, 109 North Main Street, Big Rapids; (231) 796–5333. A local favorite. Burgers, soup, dinners.
- Bennigan's Grill and Tavern in the Holiday Inn, 1005 Perry, Big Rapids; (231) 796–4400.
- The Sawmill Saloon, 1003 Maple Street, Big Rapids; (231) 796–9812; www.sawmillsaloon.com. Off the rail trail. Patio cookouts and live music.

ACCOMMODATIONS

- Best Western of Big Rapids, 1705 State Street, Big Rapids; (231) 592–5150. Moderate prices, continental breakfast.
- Outback Lodge Bed & Breakfast, 12600 Buchanan Road, Stanwood; (231) 972–7255. Located on a horse ranch. Handcrafted Amish furniture and crafts.

RESTROOMS

- Start/finish: White Pine Rail Trail staging area (portable toilet).
- Mile 5.8: Paris County Park.
- Mile 29.8: Stanwood village. Ask to use restrooms at local establishments.

Kent County Ramble

E scape the urban bustle of Michigan's second-largest city, Grand Rapids, on this relaxing rural ride in northeast Kent County. The gently rolling route departs from the large and scenic Warren Townsend Park and wanders north past wooded lots, scenic farmland, and five lakes. An artesian spring, a historic church, and five cemeteries are some of the highlights. On Wednesdays you can also watch—or participate in—road bike races at Grattan Raceway.

The ramble starts with a delightful departure point. Bear Creek meanders through the heavily wooded Warren Townsend Park, which also offers picnic facilities, walking trails, and a beautiful stone pavilion built in 1926. If you're visiting on the weekend, it's likely you can enjoy a wedding, as nuptials frequently are celebrated on the park's footbridges.

Leave the park heading east on Six Mile Road, which runs through the park. Three miles of country roads will take you to a busy crossing at Ramsdell Drive and Belding Road. Be sure to use extreme caution at this crossing. A few more miles and suburban surroundings will give way to farmland filled with crops and horses. You'll enjoy a couple of nice downhills before arriving at Wabasis Park at mile 10.8. Take some time to explore the park. Fill your water bottle at the artesian spring, or cool off at the swimming beach on a hot day. The park also offers snacks and restrooms.

After Wabasis Park, 5 more miles brings you to Grattan Raceway. The raceway normally hosts car and motorcycle races, but on Wednesday nights it is transformed into a bicycle racing track. From May to September at 6:45 P.M., spectators can enjoy fast-paced, wheel-to-wheel road bicycle racing excitement as pros and amateurs race the 2-mile course. Anybody is welcome to race, but keep in mind that the Grattan track is fast and accidents do happen. Admission is free and visitors are encouraged to bring cookies, cake, and pies to reward the racers.

If you don't get a piece of cake or pie at the raceway, there's food to be had at the Grattan General Store or the Grattan Bar and Restaurant a mile from the speedway. After leaving the village of Grattan, a mile of riding on Belding Road takes you to Gavin Lake Avenue. Belding Road is extremely busy, but there is a very wide shoulder.

Parnell Grocery at the 20-mile mark offers ice cream and snacks. Enjoy your cone in the shade of beautiful, towering St. Patrick's Catholic Church or explore the church's cemetery. The parish, founded in 1844, erected the present sanctuary in 1877.

Continue south on Parnell Avenue for a 6-mile loop through wooded countryside before emerging on Five Mile Road, where you'll encounter more traffic. (For a 23.2-mile option, continue straight on Five Mile Road instead of turning left on Parnell.)

At mile 28 Five Mile Road will turn to the right and become Cannonsburg Road. In another mile, Ramsdall will take you back to the Townsend Park, where you can dangle your cycling feet in Bear Creek.

LOCAL INFORMATION

♦ Grand Rapids/Kent County Convention and Visitors Bureau; (800) 678–9859; www.visitgrandrapids.org.

LOCAL EVENTS/ATTRACTIONS

♦ The Festival of the Arts celebrates music, art, and food. Live entertainment. Free admission. Held in downtown Grand Rapids on the first weekend in June.
♦ Picnic Pops: Outdoor concerts by the Grand Rapids Symphony, held at the Cannonsburg Ski Area near Warren Townsend Park in July and August. For information about dates and tickets, contact the Grand Rapids Symphony at (616) 454–9451.
♦ The Gerald R. Ford Museum, a monument to the only Michigander to

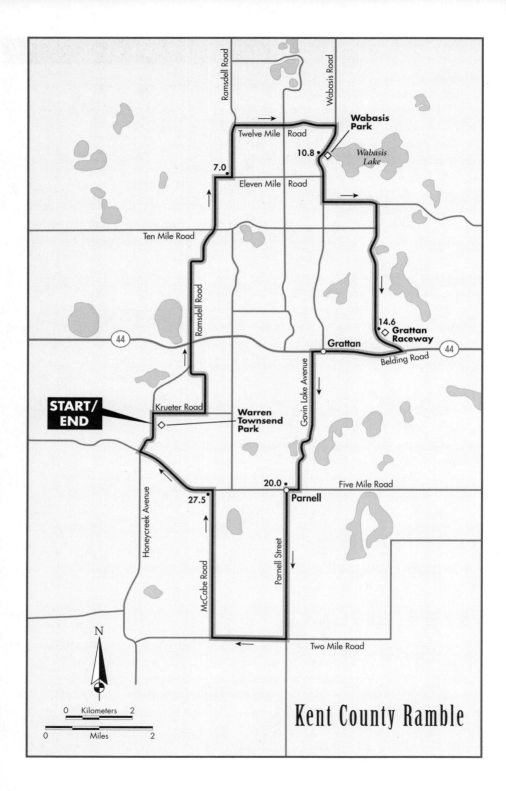

Ramsdell Road

Wabasis Road

Twelve Mile Road

Wabasis Park

10.8 •

Wabasis Lake

7.0 •

Eleven Mile Road

Ten Mile Road

Ramsdell Road

44

14.6 •
◇ **Grattan Raceway**

Grattan •

44

Belding Road

Gavin Lake Avenue

START/ END

Krueter Road

◇ **Warren Townsend Park**

20.0 •

Five Mile Road

Parnell •

Honeycreek Avenue

27.5 •

McCabe Road

Parnell Street

Two Mile Road

N

0 Kilometers 2

0 Miles 2

Kent County Ramble

0.0 From Warren Townsend Park turn right (east) out of the parking lot onto Six Mile Road.

0.7 Turn left on Giles Avenue.

1.2 Turn right on Kreuter Road.

1.5 Turn left on Greeley Road.

2.6 Turn right on Ramsdell Drive. Watch for more traffic.

3.1 At the stop sign Ramsdell intersects with busy Michigan Highway 44/Belding Road. Continue straight on Ramsdell Road while using extreme caution when crossing.

6.6 At the T intersection turn right on Eleven Mile Road/Ramsdell Drive. Ramsdell will split off from Eleven Mile Road in less than half a mile.

7.0 Turn left on the Ramsdell Drive split-off.

8.0 Turn right on Twelve Mile Road.

10.0 Turn right on Wabasis Avenue, watching for more traffic and enjoying the downhill run.

10.5 Wabasis Park Overlook and Picnic Area. A nice high bluff looks out over of Wabasis Lake.

10.8 Wabasis Park. Upon entering the park turn left to visit the artesian spring. Continuing straight on the main park road leads to the swimming beach. Flush toilets, drinking water, and snacks available at the beach. When leaving the park turn left to continue heading south on Wabasis Road.

11.7 Turn left on Hart Street.

12.7 Right on Lessiter Avenue.

14.6 Grattan Raceway. Wednesday night fast-action road bike track racing.

15.5 Turn right on Belding Road to enter the village of Grattan. Snacks at the general store. Meals available at the Grattan Bar and Restaurant.

15.9 Turn left on Belding Road, riding on the wide, paved shoulder.

16.9 Turn left on Gavin Lake Avenue.

19.6 Turn right on Five Mile Road.

20.0 Turn left on Parnell Avenue. Parnell Grocery on the corner offers snacks and ice cream. Restrooms inside the store. On the corner of Parnell is St. Patrick's Catholic Church and cemetery. **Option:** For a 23.2-mile ride, continue straight on Five Mile Road and rejoin route at mile 27.5 below.

23.0 Turn right on Two Mile Road.

24.5 Turn right on McCabe Avenue.

27.5 Turn left on Five Mile Road, riding on the paved shoulder. Watch for more traffic.

(continued)

St. Patrick's Catholic Church in Parnell. Courtesy of Nancy Hulka

28.0 Five Mile Road will turn to the right and become Cannonsburg Road. Veer right onto Cannonsburg. Five Mile Road continues straight.
29.0 Turn right on Ramsdell Drive.
29.2 Warren Townsend Park.

occupy the Oval Office, also the only occupant not elected to the office; 303 Pearl Street Northwest, Grand Rapids; (616) 254–0400.

RESTAURANTS

♦ Honey Creek Inn, 8000 Cannonsburg Road, Cannon Township; (616) 874–7849. Excellent hamburgers, sandwiches, fish, and soup.
♦ Grattan Bar and Restaurant, 11817 Old Belding Road, Grattan Township; (616) 691–8221. Old-fashioned country hospitality and down-home cooking.
♦ The Cottage Bar, 18 LaGrave Avenue Southeast, Grand Rapids; (616) 454–9088. Burgers and great cheese fries in the oldest operating bar and restaurant downtown.

ACCOMMODATIONS

♦ Amway Grand Plaza, 187 Monroe Avenue Northwest, Grand Rapids; (616) 776–6425. Restored historic hotel in downtown Grand Rapids. Fine shops, restaurant, pool, exercise room.
♦ Fountain Hill Bed and Breakfast, 222 Fountain Street Northeast, Grand Rapids; (616) 458–6621. Beautiful 1874 Italianate home located in the historic Heritage Hill district overlooking downtown Grand Rapids. Private baths, Jacuzzi rooms available.
♦ Days Inn Downtown, 310 Pearl Street, Grand Rapids; (616) 235–7611. Reasonable rates, indoor pool, free parking.

RESTROOMS

♦ Start/finish: Warren Townsend Park.
♦ Mile 10.8: Wabasis Park (pit toilets at the picnic area, flush toilets at the swimming beach).
♦ Mile 20.0: inside Parnell Grocery.

22

Tawas Ramble

The cove carved into Lake Huron, the sister cities along its shore, the point where protected bay meets open water, and the light-house that sits on it all take their name from a former Indian chief, O-ta-was. Today, from a bike seat, you can still appreciate some of the things that must have given O-ta-was great pride: clear water, sandy beaches, cool woods, and fertile fields inland. The ride starts at Tawas Point State Park, a particularly popular spot in the spring, when bird-watchers converge on what's considered a "migration trap." From there the 26 miles takes you along shoreline, through neighborhoods and farm country, and to downtown East Tawas.

The Tawas Ramble follows a sort of distorted figure-eight path, consisting of two loops that pass through East Tawas and Tawas City twice. The east loop takes you through a pleasant shady stretch of riding along Tawas Bay and then through a residential area along Lake Huron north of Tawas Point. The west loop takes you first through farmland and then back along the bay. But I think one of the nicest things about this ride is the portion where the loops connect, in the neighborhoods in between. Shoreline, lighthouses, and dramatic views tend to exist away from ordinary neighborhoods. But the Tawas Ramble takes you through some of the older neighborhoods of East Tawas. The charm of their architecture, their flower gardens, and their porches might make you envy the residents, who enjoy it all and still live within walking distance of the lake-front and its attractions. Outside the city limits, on MI 55, you'll notice a road sign alerting traffic to Amish buggies in the area. This is definitely farm country, and you might also meet a tractor on the road.

On the second pass through town, stop and stroll the streets of East Tawas, the more resortlike of the two communities. A must-do stop is at Marion's Dairy Bar, across the street from the East Tawas Harbor. The line for their waffle cones might be out the door, but they'll move you through lickety-split. Read the wish list compiled by employees taped to the tip jar to pass the time.

At the end of the ride, Tawas Point State Park has wonderful facilities for both day visitors and campers, including a lighthouse, nature trails, playground areas, and beaches on both the bay and the open lake. Its situation on the peninsula that forms Tawas Bay also gives visitors the unique opportunity to see both sunrises and sunsets over water. As you'll no doubt have noticed by this point, the northeast side of Michigan calls itself the Sunrise Side, and daybreak over Lake Huron is indeed a spectacular sight. But if you're not up quite that early, come back to the state park at sunset and look out over Tawas Bay. Voila! A sunset on the Sunrise Side.

THE BASICS

Start: Tawas Point State Park.

Length: 26-mile double loop.

Terrain: Relatively flat.

Traffic and hazards: Traffic can be heavy on a 4-mile stretch of U.S. Highway 23 and a 4-mile stretch of Michigan Highway 55, but both have good shoulders. Also, note that while most of the Tawas-area tourist publications mention a bike path along Tawas Bay, it actually varies from a dedicated bike path to a bike lane to a road shoulder to even a sidewalk. It is used for this ride, but be aware that it is not entirely a dedicated path, isolated from vehicular traffic, as you might be led to believe.

Getting there: From northbound US 23 just north of East Tawas, turn right onto Tawas Beach Road. Stay to the right at the Y intersection in 1.7 miles. The state park is another mile ahead. Pay the $6.00 day-pass fee and follow the signs straight back to the lighthouse/beach/picnic area.

LOCAL INFORMATION

◆ Tawas Bay Tourist and Convention Bureau; (877) TO–TAWAS; www.tawas bay.com.

LOCAL EVENTS/ATTRACTIONS

◆ A farm market is held on Saturdays from 8:00 A.M. to 1:00 P.M. on East Bay Street in East Tawas, in front of Marion's Dairy Bar.
◆ Summerfest includes kids' events, a car show and cruise, and a fly-in. Held in mid-July. (877) TO–TAWAS.

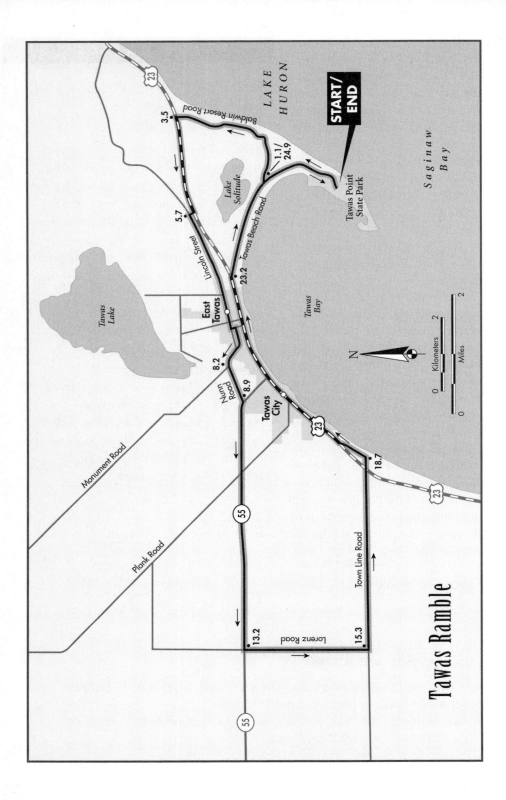

Tawas Ramble

0.0 Go straight out of Tawas Point State Park entrance onto Tawas Bay Road, riding on shoulder.

0.4 Cross over road to ride on two-way bike path alongside road.

1.1 Leave bike path to turn right on Baldwin Resort Road. You will need to cross two lanes of traffic to make this turn.

3.5 Stop sign. Turn left on US 23, staying on wide shoulder.

5.6 Turn right on Cemetery Road. Immediate railroad track crossing.

5.7 Turn left onto unmarked road (Lincoln Street) where it T's at cemetery.

7.3 Flashing light four-way stop. Continue straight.

7.4 Turn left on Sawyer.

7.5 Turn right onto West State Street.

7.8 After Huron, follow curve to right. Becomes Bridge Street.

8.2 Intersection with Monument. Continue straight. Road becomes Nunn.

8.9 Stop sign. Turn right onto MI 55.

13.2 Turn left on Lorenz Road.

15.3 Stop sign. Left on Town Line Road.

18.0 Rough railroad crossing. Recommend stopping and walking bike.

18.7 Stop sign. Turn left on Bay Street.

19.1 Stop sign. Turn right on Lake Street/US 23. For the next 4 miles, you may choose to ride on the shoulder/bike path or on the sidewalk, depending on traffic and preference.

19.5 Tawas River.

20.3 Tawas City Park. Playground, concession stand, restrooms, beach.

21.3 Enter East Tawas. Park and picnic area.

21.7 Iosco County Historical Museum.

22.0 East Tawas State Harbor. Turn right for restrooms, harbor, docks, beach. Turn left onto Newman Street to visit downtown East Tawas. Return to this intersection and continue north along US 23.

23.2 Turn right onto Tawas Beach Road.

24.9 At Y, veer to the right, staying on bike path along Tawas Beach Road.

26.0 Tawas Point State Park. Follow signs straight to beach/picnic/lighthouse to return to day parking area.

♦ The Tawas Bay Waterfront Fine Art Festival and Wine Tasting Social takes place in early August.

♦ Blues by the Bay is a weekend of blues in downtown East Tawas. Late August. (877) 362–3636; www.bluesbythebaytawas.com.

East Tawas Harbor. Courtesy of Michael O. Henderson

RESTAURANTS

◆ Marion's Dairy Bar, 111 East Bay Street/US 23, East Tawas; (989) 362–2991. Homemade waffle cones, baked fresh daily. Look for the man licking a cone on the roof.

◆ Chum's, 105 West Westover Street, East Tawas; (989) 362–3681. Sandwiches, salads, burgers. Outdoor patio dining in downtown East Tawas.

◆ Falco Rosso Restaurant, 350 West Davison Road, East Tawas; (989) 362–1061. Italian specialties, fish, seafood, ribs, steak. Located at the Red Hawk Golf Club.

◆ Mitch's Pizzeria, 703 Lake Street/US 23, Tawas City; (989) 362–8012.

ACCOMMODATIONS

◆ Tawas Bay Holiday Inn, 300 North US 23, East Tawas; (800) 336–8601. On Tawas Bay.

◆ Days Inn of Tawas City, Lake Street, Tawas City; (989) 362–0088.

◆ Martin's Motel, 708 East Bay Street/US 23, East Tawas; (989) 362–2061.

RESTROOMS

◆ Start/finish: Tawas Point State Park.

◆ Mile 20.3: Tawas City Park.

◆ Mile 22.0: East Tawas State Harbor.

Frankenmuth Ramble

Frankenmuth is Michigan's "Little Bavaria," the home of the world's largest Christmas store and all-you-can-eat chicken dinners and the most popular tourist destination in the state. It might be the last place you'd think of for a relaxing bike ride. But the Frankenmuth Ramble circles the strip where the tourist trappings are concentrated, avoiding the crowds. You'll follow a most pleasant, quiet route through Saginaw County farmland. The ride is mostly flat, with a few pulls and glides—nothing big enough to be called a climb or descent. Still, postride, you'll be able to justify second helpings at Zehnder's or the Bavarian Inn.

This route is a modified version of the Frankenmuth Fahrrad, a fundraising ride held by the city's Optimist Club. But *fahrrad*, German for "cycling," isn't what most people associate with Michigan's "Little Bavaria," as the community bills itself. The town is renowned for three things: its German heritage, displayed in everything from architecture to food; Bronner's Christmas Wonderland, which crams Christmas items into a building on the outskirts of town bigger than five football fields; and all-you-can-eat chicken dinners at the twin giant restaurants owned by members of the same family.

After riding the Frankenmuth Ramble, however, riders will be able to add *fahrrad* to the list. With some of the historical monuments it passes, the ramble allows you to appreciate not only Frankenmuth's German heritage but its Native American roots. You'll enjoy quiet country roads and return to Frankenmuth having earned one of the two million chicken dinners Zehnder's and the Bavarian Inn will serve this year.

Start: Frankenmuth Memorial Park and Palmer Schau Platz band shell.

Length: 21.9-mile loop.

Terrain: Mostly flat.

Traffic and hazards: The ride bypasses most of the tourist traffic. Use greatest caution when crossing Main Street in downtown, on the covered bridge, and going through the parking lot after it.

Getting there: From Interstate 75, take exit 136 for the Birch Run Outlet Mall/ Frankenmuth and go east on Michigan Highway 54/83. Turn left at the traffic light in 2 miles, continuing north on MI 83. After 4 more miles, follow the road to the left, following the TOURIST DISTRICTS and DOWNTOWN signs. Go through downtown and turn right at the light on Genesee Street after 2 more miles. Go past the high school and turn right on Park Street. Park next to the restrooms by the Palmer Schau Platz band shell.

The ride starts at the parking area for Frankenmuth Memorial Park and the Palmer Schau Platz band shell, located behind Frankenmuth High School on the north side of town. The first highlight, at mile 1.8, is the magnificent St. Lorenz Evangelical Lutheran Church. The current church was dedicated in 1880 and displays the original stained glass. The congregation, however, dates back another thirty-five years, when a Lutheran missionary colony was established to bring the gospel to Saginaw Valley Chippewa Indians. The settlers named their community by combining the name of their home region, Franconia, and the German word *mut* for "courage."

After passing St. Lorenz you'll ride into the southern end of Frankenmuth's Main Street strip, where most of the three million annual visitors spend their time. Ride across the covered bridge, through the Bavarian Inn Lodge parking lot, and out into the farmland east of Frankenmuth. Saginaw is one of Michigan's most farming-intensive counties, with more than 180,000 acres of corn, soybeans, and sugar beets, the broad-leafed, low-growing crop you'll no doubt notice from the bike seat.

One of the prettiest parts of the ride comes at mile 12.0, when you'll turn onto Loren Road, which parallels a local creek. The trees drooping over it make you feel almost cozy as you ride under the canopy.

Turning off Loren, you'll enter the community of Tuscola. C & K Corner Store is the only place for a snack on the ride. Drinks, ice cream, pizza, and convenience store items are available here.

Leaving Tuscola, you'll ride a 4-mile square around more fields and then head back west into Frankenmuth. Just outside town—you'll see the band shell across the way—is the Chippewa Indian Memorial. Frankenmuth may trumpet its German heritage on Main Street, but here it pays respectful tribute to the

You'll ride over the covered bridge as you leave the Frankenmuth city limits.

Chippewa Indians, who inhabited the Saginaw Valley for 4,750 years before the Germans arrived. From the design of the memorial to its geographic orientation and the choice of plants, trees, and inanimate objects, the memorial acknowledges and offers respect to Chippewa culture.

Near the Indian Memorial is an equatorial sundial and a rose garden dedicated to Frankenmuth's sister city, Gunzenhauzen, in Bavaria, Germany. Plan to spend at least a half hour off the bike, wandering around the grounds.

Back in Frankenmuth you can partake of the famous chicken dinners, watch the glockenspiel toll the hour, and watch a laser light show at River Place. Even if you've come to Frankenmuth for the Fahrrad, you can't help but be a tourist, too.

LOCAL INFORMATION

♦ Frankenmuth Chamber of Commerce and Convention and Visitors Bureau, 635 South Main Street; (800) FUN–TOWN; www.frankenmuth.org. Good maps available at office.

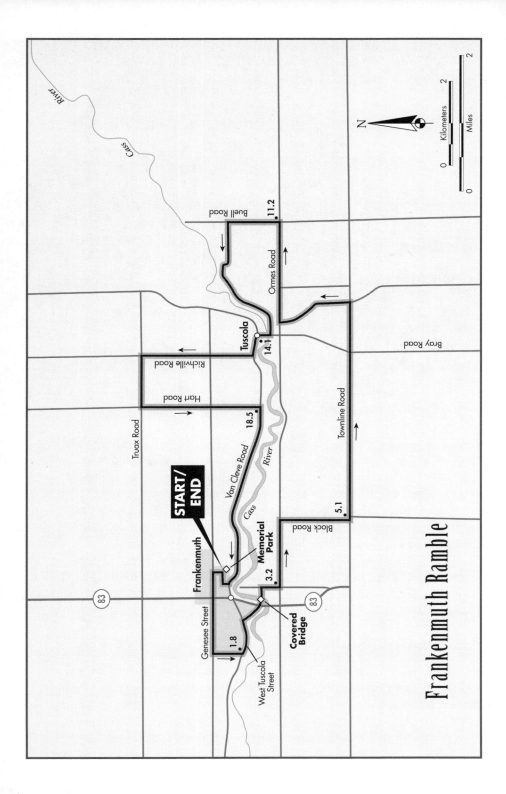

Frankenmuth Ramble

0.0 From the parking lot next to the restrooms, turn right on Park Street.

0.1 Stop sign. Turn left on Genesee Street.

1.3 Turn left on Mayer Road at the Frankenmuth Travel Agency.

1.8 Turn left at stop sign onto West Tuscola Street. St. Lorenz Evangelical Lutheran Church on your right.

2.2 Right on Gunzenhauzen Street at cemetery.

2.6 Road becomes Mill Street. Turn right at stop sign onto Covered Bridge Lane. Cross through light and cross bridge, entering Bavarian Inn parking lot.

2.9 Turn right at the exit sign in the parking lot, down the last parking row, away from Bavarian Inn, and exit parking lot.

3.1 Stop sign. Turn right on Weiss Street.

3.2 Stop sign. Turn left on Jefferson Street.

4.2 Turn right on Block Road.

5.1 Turn left on Townline Road. Some rougher pavement.

8.5 Turn left on Barkley.

9.7 Stop sign. Turn right on Ormes Road.

11.2 Turn left on Buell.

11.9 Turn left on Loren Road.

13.7 Stop for one-lane bridge.

13.9 Stop sign. T intersection. Turn right on Bray.

14.1 Stop sign. C & K Corner Store. Turn left on Van Cleve.

14.4 Turn right on Richville Road.

16.0 Turn left on Truax Road.

16.6 Stop sign. Turn left on Hart Road.

18.5 Stop sign. T intersection. Turn right on Van Cleve.

21.1 Chippewa Indian Memorial Park.

21.4 Turn right on South Hass Street.

21.5 Stop sign. Turn right on East School Street.

21.7 Enter Frankenmuth Memorial Park.

21.9 Parking lot on right.

LOCAL EVENTS/ATTRACTIONS

♦ Michigan's "Little Bavaria," the No. 1 destination in Michigan, attains that status with a number of different annual festivals. Check out www.franken muthfestivals.com for a current list or call (989) 652–FEST. There is the World Expo of Beer in May, Summer Music Fest in August, and Oktoberfest in September. The Bavarian Festival is in June; www.bavarianfestival.com or (989) 652–8155.

♦ A laser light show is held nightly April to December at Frankenmuth River Place, an Alpine-styled (of course) collection of shops at 925 South Main Street. Held on Friday and Saturday only from January to May. Free.

RESTAURANTS

♦ Zehnder's, 730 South Main Street, Frankenmuth; (800) 863–7999; www .zehnders.com. A little more formal-feeling than the Bavarian Inn across the street.

♦ The Bavarian Inn, 713 South Main Street, Frankenmuth; (800) 228–2742; www.bavarianinn.com. Across the street from Zehnder's, owned by another branch of the Zehnder family. A bit more kitsch, including nutcracker sentinels and a 50-foot glockenspiel, but the same all-you-can-eat chicken dinners.

♦ Frankenmuth Brewery, 425 South Main Street, Frankenmuth; (989) 652–6183. If all-you-can-eat chicken dinners aren't what you had in mind, try this brewpub and restaurant. Brewery tours, too; the $4.00 ticket includes two sample brews.

ACCOMMODATIONS

♦ Zehnder's Bavarian Haus (1365 South Main Street) and Bavarian Inn Lodge (One Covered Bridge Lane). Frankenmuth's not quite a company town, but the Zehnder influence is everywhere. See phone numbers and Web sites above. Bavarian Inn Lodge does have a different phone number than the restaurant: (888) 775–6343.

♦ Fairfield Inn, 430 South Main Street, Frankenmuth; (989) 652–5000. Heart of downtown.

♦ Tuscola Street Bed and Breakfast, 210 West Tuscola Street, Frankenmuth; (989) 652–6424. Prairie-style home with a great front porch. Half a block from downtown.

RESTROOMS

♦ Start/finish: Frankenmuth Memorial Park and band shell.

24

Thumb Ramble

Port Austin, the departure point for this ride, is at the very tip of Michigan's "Thumb," a wide peninsula covered with farm fields that pokes into Lake Huron. While it's the Thumb that gives Michigan its distinctive mitten shape, many Michiganders write off this defining region as rural, flat, and uninteresting, not worth going out of your way (as you must) to get there. As a resident of the real "Up north," I was one of them. But the bicycling was a pleasant surprise. First, it wasn't completely flat. Second, the roads were lightly traveled. Third, the shoreline still contains undeveloped stretches, with great open lake views. And finally, I love to feel like I've made a discovery. The Thumb Ramble is just that.

"Where the countryside meets the lakeshore." "Less than a tank of gas away!" (from population centers like Detroit and Flint) "The closer 'Up North.'" Marketing testimonials to the virtues of the Thumb abound. And there's truth in all of them. You'll see both farms (the Thumb is particularly renowned for growing sugar beets) and Lake Huron shore on the Thumb Ramble. If you're coming from southeastern Michigan, it won't take you more than a tank of gas. And in places it does feel like farther up north.

My first surprise: The Thumb isn't completely flat. In fact, there's a very subtle uphill grade for the first 4 miles of the ride, the inland stretch along Grindstone Road. Whether uphill or downhill, most of the grades around here are subtle. You won't find thigh-screaming climbs or lift-the-helmet descents. But it's not a pancake, either.

Start: Port Austin city parking lot, 1 block west of Lake Street, the main drag in Port Austin, and 1 block south of Michigan Highway 25 as it parallels Lake Huron through town.

Length: 25.8-mile double loop.

Terrain: Relatively flat, but some gradual uphill and downhill grades. Wind coming off Lake Huron can be strong.

Traffic and hazards: There are practically none. Only two traffic lights are on the entire route. For the first 9 miles on Grindstone Road, cracks at regular intervals in the concrete shoulder can make for a bumpy ride. But the road is so lightly traveled you can ride on it, keeping an eye on your rearview mirror and moving onto the shoulder when cars appear.

Getting there: From Bad Axe, go north on Michigan Highway 53 to Port Austin. In Port Austin, turn left on State Street (1 block before the harbor and 0.3 mile after Grindstone Road), then right on Line Street to enter the parking lot.

Grindstone has a nice wide shoulder, almost wide enough for two to ride abreast. Unfortunately, there are regularly spaced bumps due to cracks in the concrete. Since the road is so lightly traveled, however, it's possible to ride in the road, as long as you check your rearview mirror frequently, moving onto the shoulder when a car approaches.

After about 9 miles, you'll come to Huron City, a bona fide ghost town. In 1871 and 1881 forest fires destroyed Huron City. Then, as the era of lumbering and the railroad ended, it just kind of faded away. The ten buildings now open to the public, including a church, general store, log cabin, and lifesaving station, are collectively a museum, and the whole town is on the National Register of Historic Places. You can wander the grounds for free, but tours inside are $6.00 to $10.00 for adults.

After Huron City, the road becomes asphalt and you'll have a smooth ride around the Thumb's northeast corner, with a rare open lake view, unmarred by development. (A FOR SALE sign was up, however.) As you begin to ride back west, you'll come to the Pointe Aux Barques Lighthouse Park and Museum. The ominous translation—point of ships or boats—tells the story of Pointe Aux Barques Lighthouse. More than one-hundred ships have sunk off this point. These and other historical facts are explained inside the museum. There's also a playground and campground. If you need to make a pit stop, turn right down the dirt road toward the campground. The cinder-block building there has flush toilets and running water, much nicer than the outhouse facilities by the lighthouse and playground.

Leaving the lighthouse, you'll pass through Huron City again. If you didn't stop before, you'll have a better chance to look at the historic buildings, as most of them face Pioneer Drive. As you turn away from the water, you'll also get more of that woodsy, shady, up-north feeling. You'll also head up, literally, with a short climb to the turn on Lakeshore/Grindstone Road.

The Thumb Ramble departs Port Austin whenever you're ready.

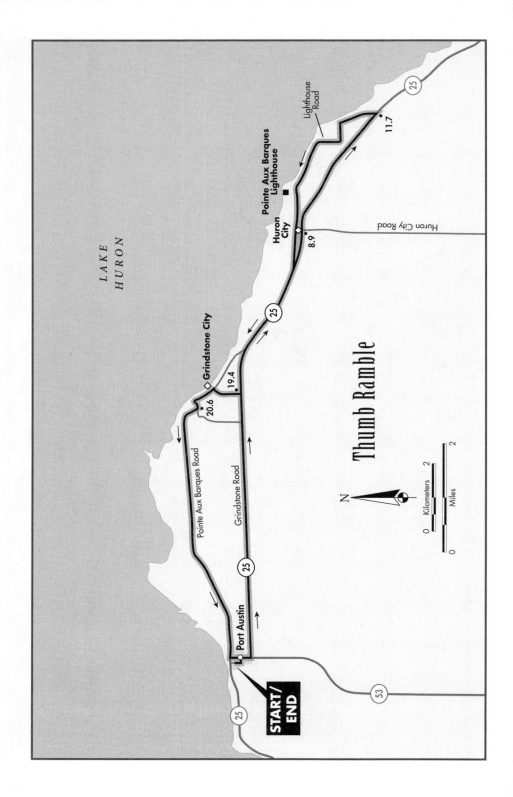

LAKE
HURON

25

Lighthouse
Road

11.7

Pointe Aux Barques
Lighthouse

Huron
City

8.9

Huron City Road

Grindstone City

19.4

20.6

Pointe Aux Barques Road

Grindstone Road

25

25

Thumb Ramble

N

0   Kilometers   2

0   Miles   2

Port Austin

25

START/
END

25

53

MILES AND DIRECTIONS

0.0 From the parking lot, turn right on Line Street. Make a quick left at the stop sign onto State Street, then a quick right at the next stop sign onto Lake Street, heading south out of town.

0.3 Turn left on Grindstone Road/MI 25 south.

6.4 Grindstone Road becomes Lakeshore.

8.9 Huron City historic district, open July 1 to Labor Day.

11.7 Turn left on Lighthouse Road.

12.5 Turn right into Lighthouse Park. At entrance drive's T, turn right down dirt road toward campground to go to modern restrooms with running water.

13.6 Stop sign. Turn right back onto Lighthouse Road.

15.9 Stop sign. Turn right on Pioneer Drive.

16.1 Huron City. Historical buildings.

16.8 Stop sign. Turn right on Lakeshore/MI 25 north.

19.4 Turn right on Pearson Road, toward Grindstone City.

20.2 Harbor marina and DNR boat launch. Pit toilet.

20.4 Captain Morgan's.

20.6 Bear right onto Pointe Aux Barques Road.

25.7 Traffic light. Turn left on Lake Street.

25.8 Turn right on unmarked road (State Street), and then right on Line Street to return to parking lot.

You'll repeat a mile along Lakeshore/Grindstone before turning back toward the lake toward Grindstone City, home of Captain Morgan's, the only restaurant along the route. If you've timed it right, you can watch the charter fishing boats bring in the day's catch at noon, 1:00, and 8:00 P.M. Take Pointe Aux Barques road out of Grindstone City all the way back to Port Austin. It's such a nice ride that if you have time, you might want to ride it again.

LOCAL INFORMATION

♦ Port Austin Chamber of Commerce; (989) 738–7600; www.portaustinarea .com.

♦ Thumb Promotions; www.thumbtravels.com.

LOCAL EVENTS/ATTRACTIONS

♦ Huron City Museums: Wander around the grounds of these ten buildings dating to the late nineteenth century, or take a paid tour. Adult tickets $6.00. 7995 Pioneer Drive, Huron City; (989) 428–4123.

♦ Take a half-day or all-day charter fishing cruise on Lake Huron. www.thumb areacharterboats.com, click on "Port Austin" or "Grindstone City" for the closest boats.

♦ Sunset cruises: Looking across Saginaw Bay, you can see sunsets on Michigan's Sunrise Side. Friday and Saturday nights aboard the *Miss Port Austin*, departing from Port Austin State Dock. (989) 738–5271.

RESTAURANTS

♦ Captain Morgan's, 3337 Pointe Aux Barques Road, Grindstone City; (989) 738–7665. On the route. Bar and grill on the water. Watch the charter boats show off their catch at noon, 1:00 and 8:00 P.M.

♦ Joe's Pizzeria and Restaurant, 8725 Lake Street, Port Austin; (989) 738–8711.

♦ The Bank, 8646 Lake Street, Port Austin; (989) 738–5353; www.thebank 1884.com. A bank from 1884 to 1957, you'll have to pony up a pretty penny (relatively speaking) for dinner here. Seasonal.

♦ Chuck and Jane's Restaurant, 8714 Lake Street, Port Austin; (989) 738–7111. A little bit of everything—salads, Mexican, fish, sandwiches.

♦ Finan's Old Fashioned Soda Fountain, 8687 Lake Street, Port Austin; (989) 738–8412. Lunch counter and ice cream. Check out the menus from when store opened in 1949, when pancakes were 30 cents.

ACCOMMODATIONS

♦ The Captain's Inn, 8586 Lake Street, Port Austin; (989) 738–8321. Restored and updated B&B.

♦ Garfield Inn, 8544 Lake Street, Port Austin; (989) 738–5254. President James Garfield reportedly had an affair with the mistress of the house, where he was taken after the assassination attempt that ended his life.

♦ Lake Vista Resort, 168 West Spring Street, Port Austin; (989) 738–8612. Motel and cottages. View of Lake Huron across street.

RESTROOMS

♦ Mile 12.5: Lighthouse Park (turn right at dirt road toward campground to use restrooms with flush toilets and running water; lighthouse and playground have outhouse facilities).

♦ Mile 20.2: DNR boat launch.

Saugatuck Ramble

Saugatuck bills itself as Michigan's "art coast" and lives up to the slogan, with more than two dozen galleries featuring art in every medium. Some are also working studios. The artistic sensibilities of many residents lend a funky, energetic vibe to the community, which is also known for being gay-friendly. From Saugatuck you'll ride north to Holland, with a stop at a state park featuring dramatic dunes and Lake Michigan views. In Holland you can explore another bustling downtown—except on Sundays. A community with strong religious roots, Holland reserves Sundays for church and family. The ride back to Saugatuck is more direct—with a long stretch on the aptly named Beeline—but with the same lightly traveled roads.

Like so many other Lake Michigan communities, Saugatuck began its life in the mid-1800s as a lumber and sawmill town. As the trees disappeared around the beginning of the twentieth century, it evolved into a summer resort community. Its reputation as a haven for artists began in 1910, when a group of Chicago artists established the Summer School of Painting on Ox-Bow Lagoon in Saugatuck. Now offering studies in media ranging from metalsmithing to printmaking to ceramics to performance art, this prestigious school continues today, affiliated with the Art Institute of Chicago.

This history makes Saugatuck a haven for artists year-round. The abundance of creativity concentrated in a small town has a critical-mass effect on the community. Even those who haven't cultivated an appreciation for art can't help but notice the public restrooms painted with a visage of Georges Seurat's work, or the outdoor sculptures displayed outside galleries.

You'll start the ride on the north end of Saugatuck. Parking is always at a premium in this town. If you can't find a space in the lot north of the tennis courts (park facing the courts, not the hardware store) or on a nearby street, try at the south end of town.

From the tennis courts you'll ride north out of town, crossing Blue Star Highway twice before settling into a wonderful 8-mile section that zigs and zags its way north to Holland parallel to Lake Michigan. Midway through this section you'll come to Saugatuck Dunes State Park, which isn't marked at the intersection where you'll turn. The lack of signage is an indication of how little-used the park is; perhaps beachgoers are deterred by the 140-step staircase they must climb and then descend to get over the dune to Lake Michigan. The view at the top is definitely worth the small hill on the road in, the only one on the ride, as well as the climb. There's also a portable toilet at the cul-de-sac. Unfortunately, it is seldom serviced.

After the state park you'll ride another 4 miles into Holland. You'll ride past beautiful homes along Lake Macatawa as you head inland to the city renowned

Saugatuck features block after block of shops and galleries. Courtesy of Charles Cook

for its Dutch heritage. Holland celebrates it every May with the Tulip Time Festival, when the city's millions of tulips bloom. It also has a wooden-shoe factory and a working windmill. Founded by Dutch who came to America seeking religious freedom, devout Reformed Christianity remains a key part of life today. Consequently, most of Holland's business establishments are closed on Sunday. If you choose to ride then, it's wise to pack snacks in your bike bag.

Downtown Holland is pedestrian-friendly, and it's easiest to lock your bikes up somewhere along 9th Street and explore downtown on foot. Watch for the public statues, especially the one of Ben Franklin reading the Declaration of Independence.

From downtown you'll ride through some of Holland's historic district before turning south on Graafschap Road. New subdivisions are cropping up here, spreading into what was rural territory, but the two-lane roads are still pleasant and lightly traveled. The route back to Saugatuck is more direct than the ride out. From the Burger King on Blue Star Highway, you'll retrace your route back into Saugatuck. From there you can go on to South Haven, the Southwest Shore Cruise, to make it an 80-mile day.

THE BASICS

Start: City park in Saugatuck, on Butler Street between Wilkins Hardware and the tennis courts. Spaces facing tennis courts are public spots. There are only a handful, though, and since parking is always at a premium in Saugatuck, you may need to hunt for a space. Return to this intersection to begin following directions.

Length: 29.8-mile lariat.

Terrain: Flat to rolling.

Traffic and hazards: Use greatest caution crossing Blue Star Highway to leave and enter Saugatuck, as well as on the one-way streets in downtown Holland.

Getting there: Saugatuck is located west of Interstate 196/U.S. Highway 31 between exits 36 and 41. From exit 36, south of Saugatuck, take Blue Star Highway (A2) through Douglas. Turn left on Lake Street after crossing the bridge over the Kalamazoo River, then right on Butler Street in downtown Saugatuck. The parking lot is located in the middle of the fourth block on the right, in between the tennis courts and Wilkins Hardware. From exit 41 take Blue Star Highway south and turn right on Washington Street. Follow this to downtown and turn left on Butler. The parking lot will be in the middle of the fourth block on your left.

LOCAL INFORMATION

♦ Saugatuck/Douglas Convention and Visitors Bureau and Chamber of Commerce; (269) 857–1701; www.saugatuck.com.
♦ Holland Convention and Visitors Bureau; (800) 506–1299; www.holland.org.

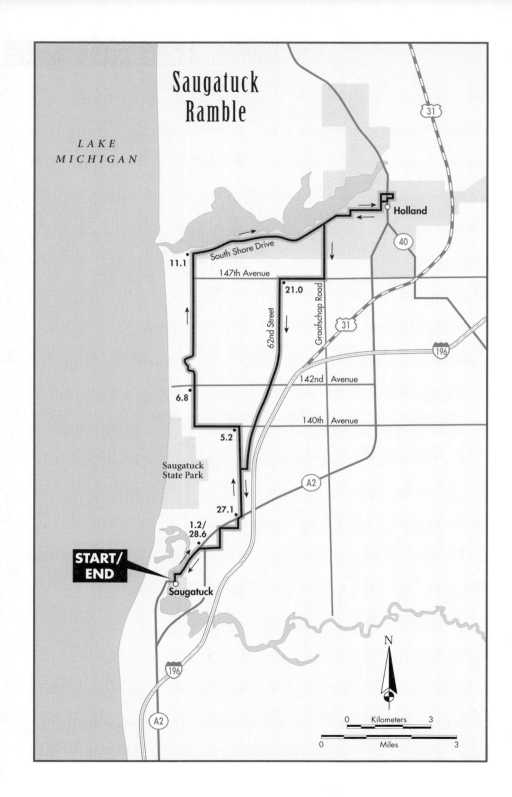

Saugatuck Ramble

LAKE MICHIGAN

Holland

South Shore Drive

11.1

147th Avenue

21.0

62nd Street

Graafschap Road

6.8

142nd Avenue

140th Avenue

5.2

Saugatuck State Park

27.1

1.2/ 28.6

START/ END

Saugatuck

N

0 Kilometers 3

0 Miles 3

0.0 From the parking lot on Butler Street between the tennis courts and Wilkins Hardware (between Main and Mary Streets), turn right on Butler.

0.2 Stop sign at Lucy. Turn right.

0.3 Stop sign at Holland. Turn left.

0.7 Holland becomes Washington Avenue. Continue straight.

1.0 Turn right onto Clearbrook.

1.6 Turn left on 65th Street at the Clearbrook Golf Club clubhouse.

2.0 Turn right on 135th Avenue before intersecting Blue Star Highway again.

2.3 Turn left onto 64th Street.

2.6 Stop sign for Blue Star Highway. Turn right and then take an immediate left after the Burger King onto 64th Street.

2.9 Turn left on Island Lake Road.

5.2 Stop sign. Turn left on 140th Avenue.

5.8 Road curves right, becomes 66th Street.

6.8 Turn left on 142nd Avenue to visit Saugatuck Dunes State Park. No sign at intersection.

7.2 Cul-de-sac/portable toilet/staircase up and down dune to beach. Retrace route to stop sign.

7.8 Stop sign. Turn left on 66th Street, continuing north.

10.5 Bike path begins paralleling southbound 66th Street at 147th Avenue.

11.0 Stop sign at Ottagan. Turn left, going around shipyard. **Option:** Ride the bike path that parallels the street.

11.1 Turn right on South Shore Drive.

13.1 Bike path ends at Holland city limits. South Shore becomes 17th Street.

15.5 Turn left on Harrison Street at Macatawa Dairy Dock. Stop sign at 16th Street in less than 0.1 mile, continue straight.

15.6 Turn right on 15th Street.

16.2 Turn left on Pine Street.

16.4 Turn right on 10th Street, before Pine becomes one-way.

16.5 Turn left on River Avenue (one-way street) using caution. Turn right onto 9th Street in 1 block (one-way street), and left onto Central Avenue in another block. Public restrooms located on Central between 8th and 9th. Lock bikes near here and explore downtown, concentrated on 8th and 9th between River and College Avenues. Holland Museum at River and 10th.

16.6 From the public restrooms on Central, ride north to 8th Street and turn left.

16.8 Stop sign. Turn left on Pine Street (one-way here), staying in right lane. At next traffic light, go straight through 9th Street, after which Pine becomes two-way.

(continued)

17.2 Turn right on 15th Street.

17.8 Turn left on Harrison Avenue. Continue straight through stop sign for 16th Street in less than 0.1 mile.

17.9 Stop sign. Turn right on 17th Street. Macatawa Dairy Dock on corner.

18.7 Turn left on Graafschap Road.

20.0 Turn right on 147th Avenue. Bike path parallels road.

21.0 Turn left on 62nd Street.

21.6 Stop sign at 146th Street. Continue straight through this and the next three stop signs at 145th, 144th (62nd becomes Beeline Road here), and 140th Avenue.

26.0 Stop sign. Turn left on 64th Street.

27.1 Turn right into Burger King parking lot. Go around restaurant, past drive-thru pick up window to exit on Blue Star Highway. Cross Blue Star onto 64th Street. Lighthouse Realty house on corner.

27.5 T intersection. Turn right on 135th Avenue.

27.8 Turn left on 65th Street, following signs for Clearbrook Golf Club/Grill Room. Do not cross Blue Star again.

28.2 Stop sign at golf clubhouse (T intersection.) Turn right onto Clearbrook.

28.6 Stop sign. Cross Blue Star Highway.

28.8 Stop sign. Turn left on Washington Avenue.

29.6 Turn left on Butler Street.

29.8 Parking lot on left before tennis courts.

LOCAL EVENTS/ATTRACTIONS

♦ At the Ox-Bow Friday Night Open House, students at the prestigious summer art program affiliated with the Art Institute of Chicago mount a show Friday evenings from late June to August. Includes artistic demonstrations and performances. 7:30 to 10:00 P.M. Friday at the Ox-Bow School of Art, on Park Street on the west side of Kalamazoo Harbor. (269) 857–5811.

♦ Tulip Time Festival is one of Michigan's biggest festivals, with entertainment, parades, and millions of tulips celebrating Holland's Dutch heritage. (800) 822–2770; www.tuliptime.org.

RESTAURANTS

♦ Eighth Street Grille, 20 West 8th Street, Holland; (616) 392–5888. Pub fare in a historic building dating to 1898.

♦ Butch's Dry Dock, 44 East 8th Street, Holland; (616) 396–8227; www.butchs.net. New York–style deli menu, offering a half-dozen different Reubens alone.

♦ Windmill Restaurant, 28 West 8th Street, Holland; (616) 392–2726. Family restaurant. Wooden shoes in the window, windmill on the sign, but open Sundays.

♦ New Holland Brewing Company, 66 East 8th Street, Holland; (616) 355–NHBC; www.newhollandbrew.com. Makers of "art in fermented form." Typical brewpub menu: sandwiches, salads, pizzas.

ACCOMMODATIONS

♦ The Park House, 888 Holland Street, Saugatuck; (800) 321–4535; www.parkhouseinn.com. Saugatuck's oldest residence, dating to 1857.

♦ Ivy Inn, 421 Water Street, Saugatuck; (269) 857–4643; www.ivy_inn.com.

♦ Holiday Inn Express, 3457 Blue Star Highway, Saugatuck; (269) 857–7178. On the route, and knocks a couple miles off.

RESTROOMS

♦ Start/finish: south of tennis courts in Saugatuck.

♦ Mile 7.2: Saugatuck Dunes State Park (portable toilet).

♦ Mile 16.5: downtown Holland, on Central Avenue between 8th and 9th Streets.

Southwest Shore Cruise

T his ride connects South Haven and Saugatuck, two of south-west Michigan's most popular destinations. Featuring rolling, rural terrain and Lake Michigan breezes, the area is wonderful for bicy-cling. It is also a fruit belt, and a vineyard and tasting room is a first-half highlight of the ride. Blueberry farms and orchards with apples and peaches are also along the route, and you'll probably be able to sample whatever produce is in season from a roadside farm stand. You'll encounter more rolling hills on the first half of the route, heading north to Saugatuck, where a short ferry crossing is an option during summer months. Flatter terrain closer to Lake Michigan will take you back to South Haven.

On any summer weekend, South Haven will undoubtedly be smothered with boaters, beachgoers, and shoppers. You'll quickly leave the tourist traffic behind, riding out of town across a drawbridge over the Black River and then alongside Lake Michigan before turning inland as you leave the city limits. Use caution riding on Blue Star Highway, which you'll be on for a 3-mile northward leg before heading east and inland. The hilliest section is a 4-mile leg on 66th Street, again heading north, followed by 2 miles east on 122nd Avenue. The sec-tion is rolling, however, meaning no cold-start climbs. You'll be able to get at least partway up each hill from your speed down the previous one. A conven-ience store at mile 16.3, in the middle of that 6 miles, is an opportunity to refuel or pick up picnic supplies for later.

Two miles after the convenience store you'll come to Fenn Valley Vineyard. It was established in 1973, and more than a dozen varieties of grapes are grown here today. Try a few varieties in the tasting room, or peek at next year's vintage out in the vineyards.

After Fenn Valley, the scenery remains similarly rural but the terrain flattens a bit as you ride into the communities of Douglas and Saugatuck. They are artists' colonies in the truest sense of the phrase, and you'll find more than two dozen galleries in the two communities that straddle the Kalamazoo River. Some are also working studios. Douglas, which you'll enter first, is by far the smaller and calmer (and thus, in my opinion, more enjoyable) of the two. While the route turns right at Main Street in Douglas, you may want to go another 2 blocks to explore the rest of the town.

Cross the Kalamazoo River on Blue Star Highway and turn into Saugatuck. You'll ride through the heart of downtown along Water Street to the Saugatuck Chain Ferry.

Dating to the nineteenth century, the hand-cranked ferry plies its back-and-forth path along a chain that runs below the water's surface. From Memorial Day to Labor Day, you can ride across with your bike for $1.00 and continue the route on the other side. For spring and fall, the directions below include an all-land option.

If you choose the land option, you'll ride a block east on Mary Street to Butler Street. This is the starting point for the Saugatuck Ramble, which goes farther north to Holland and would add 30 miles to your trip. Combined, the Southwest Shore Cruise and the Saugatuck Ramble constitute a classic ride.

If you stick with a cruise, turn right on Butler through downtown Saugatuck's other main drag. You'll ride across the Kalamazoo River and through Douglas again in order to bypass intersections with merging interstate highway traffic. After a few more miles south, you'll turn west and cross over I–196, using caution as there are exit and on-ramps at this intersection. The road will dead-end and you'll ride south along a 5-mile stretch of Lake Michigan shore. There are homes between you and the water, but you will have glimpses of blue, especially at West Side County Park a little more than a mile after the turn.

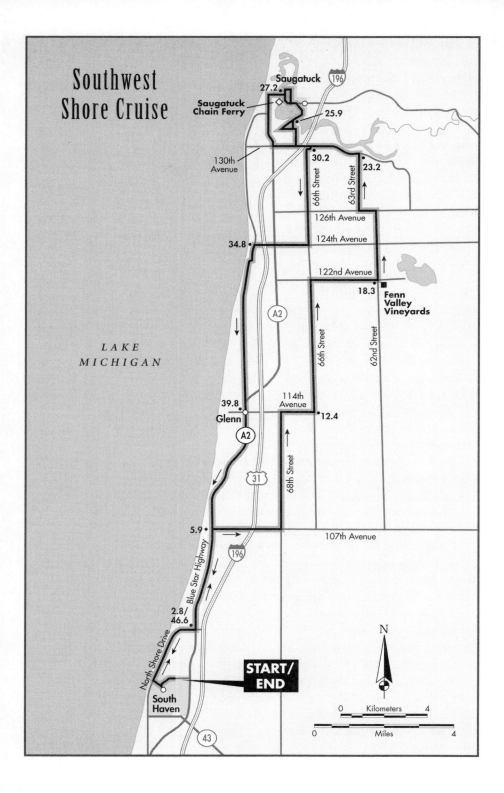

Southwest
Shore Cruise

Saugatuck

27.2

Saugatuck
Chain Ferry

25.9

130th
Avenue

30.2

23.2

66th Street

63rd Street

126th Avenue

124th Avenue

34.8

122nd Avenue

18.3

Fenn
Valley
Vineyards

A2

66th Street

62nd Street

LAKE
MICHIGAN

114th
Avenue

39.8

Glenn

12.4

A2

68th Street

31

5.9

107th Avenue

196

Blue Star Highway

2.8/
46.6

North Shore Drive

START/
END

South
Haven

43

N

0   Kilometers   4

0   Miles   4

0.0 From the Kal-Haven Trail parking lot, turn left onto Bailey Avenue.

0.1 Stop sign. Turn right onto Wells Street.

0.5 Stop sign. Turn left on Black River Street.

0.6 Stop sign. Turn right onto Dyckman Avenue and cross drawbridge.

0.9 Stop sign. Turn right onto North Shore Drive.

1.1 Park on left; restrooms.

2.8 Stop for flashing red light. Use caution turning left onto Blue Star Highway, a divided highway at this point.

5.9 Turn right onto 107th Avenue.

8.0 Turn left onto 68th Street.

11.4 Stop sign. Turn right on 114th Avenue.

12.4 Stop sign. Turn left on 66th Street.

16.3 Stop sign. Turn right on 122nd Avenue. The Little Store on corner.

18.3 Intersection with 62nd Street. Continue straight for 0.3 mile to Fenn Valley Vineyard on the right. Turn left from vineyard back to intersection and turn right onto 62nd Street at mile 19.0.

21.1 Turn left on 126th Avenue.

21.6 Stop sign. Turn right on 63rd Street.

23.2 Stop sign. Turn left on Riverside.

24.1 Riverside becomes 130th Avenue, then Wiley Road.

25.0 Turn right on Water.

25.0 Water becomes Center Street in downtown Douglas.

25.7 Stop sign. Turn right on Main Street.

25.9 Stop sign. Turn right on Blue Star Highway, going over Kalamazoo Lake.

26.2 Turn left on Lake Street after crossing bridge to enter Saugatuck.

26.8 Stop sign for Griffith Street. Continue straight through traffic light at Butler Street in less than 0.1 mile, following the curve to the right. Road becomes Water Street.

27.2 Saugatuck Chain Ferry. Restrooms. It costs $1.00 to cross, from Memorial Day to Labor Day. If crossing, follow Option A directions. If not, follow Option B directions. The two options rejoin south of Douglas.

Option A: After crossing on chain ferry, turn left onto Park Street.

27.8 Park Street becomes Ferry Street.

28.7 Stop sign. Turn right on Blue Star Highway, and make an immediate left at the flashing light onto Wiley Road.

29.7 I–196/US 31 overpass. Rejoin Option B below. Your mileage from this point will reflect 0.4 mile less than Option B.

(continued)

Option B: From the chain ferry dock on Water Street in Saugatuck, turn right on Mary Street.

27.3 Turn right onto Butler Street. Restrooms ahead on left, after tennis courts.

27.5 Traffic light. Turn left onto Culver.

27.6 Stop sign for Griffith Street. Continue straight.

28.1 Stop sign. Turn right on Blue Star Highway, riding on path/sidewalk.

28.9 Traffic light. Turn left on Center Street into Douglas.

29.2 Stop sign at Main Street. Continue straight. Center Street becomes Water and curves to the right.

29.9 Turn left on Wiley Road at T intersection.

30.1 I-196/US 31 overpass. Rejoin Option A below.

Rejoined Route

30.2 Turn right on Mountain Ash/66th Street, immediately after highway overpass.

33.2 Stop sign. Turn right on Michigan Highway 89.

34.4 I-196/US 31 overpass. Use caution passing exit and on-ramps.

34.8 Stop sign. Turn left on Lakeshore Road.

35.3 Stop sign at T intersection. Turn right.

36.2 West Side County Park. Restrooms.

39.6 Stop sign. Continue straight, merging with Blue Star Highway, which comes in from the left.

39.8 Flashing light. Glenn. Glenn Restaurant, open till 2:00 P.M., and convenience store.

46.6 Right on North Shore Drive.

48.5 Stop sign. Turn left on Dyckman Avenue.

48.8 Light for drawbridge. Turn left immediately after crossing drawbridge onto Dunkley Avenue.

48.9 Turn right onto Wells Street.

49.3 Turn left onto Bailey Avenue. Parking lot on right.

Lakeshore Road will hit Blue Star Highway, which you'll take for 7 miles back into South Haven. At the parking lot, the Kal-Haven Trail awaits if your legs have more miles in them.

At 33.5 miles one-way, the crushed limestone Kal-Haven Trail is one of the longest trails in Michigan and runs between a west trailhead in South Haven (used as the departure point for the Southwest Shore Cruise) and an east trailhead just outside Kalamazoo. Six miles is the longest stretch you'll have

From Memorial Day to Labor Day, you can ride Saugatuck's hand-cranked ferry as part of the route. Courtesy of David F. Wisse

between water and restroom stops. Food is available in Grand Junction, 10 miles east of South Haven; in Bloomingdale, 16 miles east; and in Gobles, 20.5 miles east.

Wildflowers and several railroad trestle bridges, including one covered bridge and one camelback bridge, are some of the highlights of the Kal-Haven Trail.

LOCAL INFORMATION

- ◆ South Haven Visitors Bureau; (800) SO–HAVEN; www.southhaven.org.
- ◆ Saugatuck/Douglas Convention and Visitors Bureau and Chamber of Commerce; (269) 857–1701; www.saugatuck.com.

LOCAL EVENTS/ATTRACTIONS

- ◆ South Haven hosts the Fine Arts Fair on the Fourth of July weekend, the Blueberry Festival on the second weekend of August, and the All Crafts Fair on Labor Day weekend. (800) SO–HAVEN.
- ◆ Taste of Saugatuck, sample foods and stroll the streets of Saugatuck on Labor Day weekend. (269) 857–1701.

♦ Lake Michigan's moderating effect on the climate and the rolling terrain make southwest Michigan ideal for fruit production. Several wineries, including Fenn Valley, have united to form the Southwest Michigan Wine Trail. Visit www.miwinetrail.com for a list of winery locations.

RESTAURANTS

♦ Pumpernickel's Eatery, Butler Street at Main Street, Saugatuck; (269) 857–1196. Great sandwiches with everything laid on thick.

♦ Mermaid Bar and Grill, Boardwalk Market Place, on Water Street between Main and Mary Streets, Saugatuck; (269) 857–8208. Outdoor dining along Kalamazoo River channel. Menu has standard bar-and-grill fare and a few surprises.

♦ North Side Memories Deli, 112 Dyckman Avenue, South Haven; (269) 637–8319. Boxed lunches for your day on the . . . boat? So they say, but I'm sure they'll provide for bikes, too.

ACCOMMODATIONS

♦ Holiday Inn Express, 1741 Phoenix Road, South Haven; (269) 637–8810. One mile to trailhead.

♦ North Beach Inn, 51 North Shore Drive, South Haven; (269) 637–6738. On Lake Michigan in South Haven. Pigozzi's Italian restaurant with outdoor dining on premises.

♦ Martha's Vineyard Bed and Breakfast, 473 Blue Star Highway, South Haven; (269) 637–9373; www.marthasvy.com. Just outside town. A good way to cut a couple miles off the route.

RESTROOMS

♦ Start/finish: Kal-Haven Trail trailhead.
♦ Mile 1.1: lakeside park.
♦ Mile 18.6: Fenn Valley Winery.
♦ Mile 27.2: Saugatuck Chain Ferry.
♦ Mile 27.3: next to tennis courts on Butler Street in Saugatuck.
♦ Mile 36.2: West Side County Park.

Kalamazoo County Ramble

*L*ocated almost smack dab between Kalamazoo and Battle Creek is a rural area that combines the character of the hillier fruit-producing regions farther west and the flatter field crop terrain found to the north and east. Here in southeast Kalamazoo County, the land still has some roll to it, but it's gentler than in the Lake Michigan border counties. Roads are laid out on an orderly grid of numerical and alphabetical names, so it's easy to find your way around. An ice cream shop serving 1950s-era nostalgia with its sundaes and shakes and a small winery tasting room are highlights of this relaxing route.

Every few years a supposed sighting of Elvis occurs in Kalamazoo, where he supposedly visited a Burger King after his death. So if you spot the King on this ride, be sure to let the publisher know, so it can be included in future editions. But chances are slim that you'll find Elvis tooling around in the countryside in between Kalamazoo and Battle Creek. In fact, you won't find many people at all on this 22-mile ride through rural southeast Kalamazoo County.

The area straddles the Lake Michigan fruit belt to the west and the grain production found to the east. You'll coast up and down some undulations in the landscape, especially after you leave Coldbrook County Park and head south on 42nd Street, but nothing as dramatic as the rolling orchards and vine-yards to the west.

While the roads are laid out in an orderly grid, with east-west roads named alphabetically starting north and working south, and north-south roads named numerically starting west and working east, they can all blur together as you bike on by. Remember that you're bound by MN Avenue on the north, R

Start: Coldbrook County Park.

Length: 22.3-mile lariat.

Terrain: Flat to rolling.

Traffic and hazards: The ride follows two-lane roads, mostly without shoulders but highly rural. Use caution crossing rough railroad tracks.

Getting there: From Interstate 94, take exit 92 to Mercury. Follow Mercury to MN Avenue and turn right. Coldbrook County Park will be on your right in a couple miles. There is a $5.00 entry fee. From the park entrance, go straight past the payment booth to the parking area.

Avenue on the south, 29th Street on the west, and 42nd Street on the east, and you can't get lost.

After 7 miles you'll come to the town of Scotts, four corners with a name. One of the corners has a convenience store and another has Scooter's Malt Shoppe, a restaurant in the tradition of the old soda fountains, serving foot-long hot dogs and banana splits. Here you will find Elvis—on the menu and on the jukebox. Leave with a "taste of '50s nostalgia," and probably a full stomach.

Leaving Scotts, you'll ride a bit farther south and then head west. A 2-mile stretch on 29th Street has a nice shoulder. Signs begin announcing the Peterson and Sons Winery at mile 13.4, and the winery itself is at mile 15.4. If you've visited any of the wineries on other rides in this book, this "world's smallest winery" with its basement tasting room will be quite a contrast. First of all, you won't see a vineyard outside. Though they don't grow their own, Peterson wines do use Michigan fruit, and they don't confine themselves to grapes. Apricot, cranberry, rhubarb, and wild elderberry are some of the more unusual fruit wines produced at Peterson and Sons, who are happy to tell you about their wines, especially their practice of not adding sulfites.

Use caution crossing 34th Street, the busiest in the area, after the winery. You'll have one small hill on OP Avenue as you cross the Portage River, and then a pleasant 6-mile meander back to Coldbrook County Park.

LOCAL INFORMATION

♦ Kalamazoo County Convention and Visitors Bureau; (800) 530–9192; www.discoverkalamazoo.com.

♦ Greater Battle Creek/Calhoun County Visitor and Convention Bureau; (800) 397–2240; www.battlecreekvisitors.org.

LOCAL EVENTS/ATTRACTIONS

♦ The Kalamazoo Air Zoo has more than seventy vintage aircraft on display and an F-16 fighter simulator. 3101 East Milham Road, Kalamazoo; (269) 382–6555; www.airzoo.com.

♦ The Island Festival features Caribbean and reggae music, entertainment,

Farm stands dot Michigan's roadsides during summer and fall. Here's a fresh-picked bargain: $1.50 for a dozen ears. Courtesy of Michael O. Henderson

and food. Mid-June in downtown Kalamazoo. (800) 530–9192.

♦ Taste of Kalamazoo is held in downtown Kalamazoo in late July. (800) 530–9192.

♦ The World's Longest Breakfast Table: As the home of Kellogg, Battle Creek calls itself Cereal City USA. Every June the whole town gathers for breakfast on Jackson Street in downtown Battle Creek. (800) 397–2240.

♦ Kellogg's Cereal City USA offers fun facts, history, and samples of cereal. 171 West Michigan Avenue, Battle Creek; (800) 970–7020; www.kelloggscerealcity .com.

RESTAURANTS

♦ Scooter's Malt Shoppe, 8399 South 36th Street; (269) 626–8860. 1950s nostalgia reflected in decor and menu items. Open late April to Labor Day and weekends through September.

♦ Olde Peninsula Brewpub and Restaurant, 200 East Michigan Avenue, Kalamazoo; (269) 343–2739. High marks for the brewpub dip.

♦ Kalamazoo Brewing Co./Bell's Brewery, 315 East Kalamazoo Avenue, Kalamazoo; (269) 382–2338. Bell's is a favorite microbrew statewide. English-style pub.

♦ District 211, 211 East Water Street, Kalamazoo; (269) 226–9000; www .district211.com. Casual fine dining in a historic building downtown. Fish, pasta, chicken, lamb.

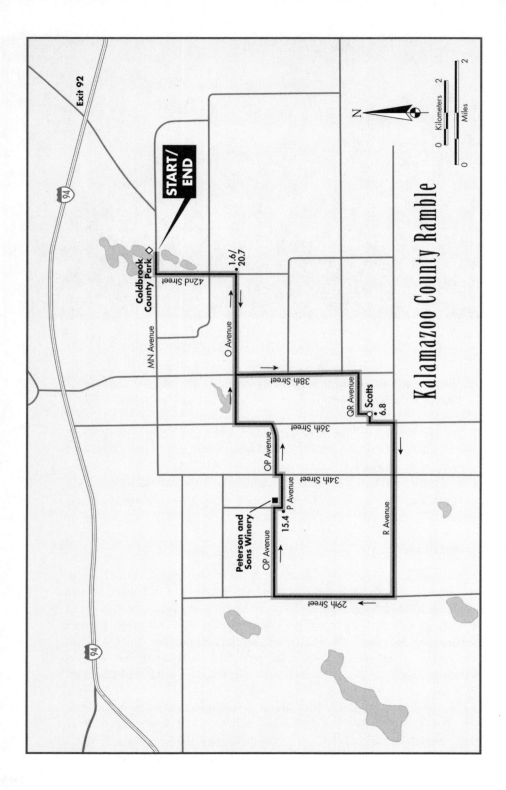

Kalamazoo County Ramble

MILES AND DIRECTIONS

0.0 From the entrance to Coldbrook County Park, turn right at the stop sign onto MN Avenue.

0.1 Turn left on 42nd Street.

1.6 Turn right on O Avenue.

3.6 Stop sign. Turn left on 38th Street.

5.1 Rough railroad tracks just after PQ Avenue.

6.0 Turn right on QR Avenue.

6.8 QR becomes Woodin as you enter Scotts. Turn right on Norscot.

7.0 Stop sign at 36th Street. Main intersection. Scooter's Malt Shoppe on corner. To leave town, turn left on 36th Street.

7.6 Turn right on R Avenue.

8.7 Stop sign. Turn right on 34th Street/R Avenue jog. Cross railroad tracks and make an immediate left on R Avenue again.

11.2 Stop sign. T intersection. Turn right on 29th Street.

13.4 Turn right on OP Avenue. Sign for winery.

15.1 Stop sign. Turn right on 32nd Street, following sign for winery.

15.2 Curve to the left. Road becomes P Avenue.

15.4 Peterson and Sons Winery. Upon leaving, turn left from winery, continuing east on P Avenue.

16.0 Stop sign. Turn left on 34th Street. Make an immediate right onto OP Avenue in less than 0.1 mile.

17.1 Stop sign. Turn left on 36th Street.

17.8 Turn right on O Avenue.

20.7 Stop sign. T intersection. Turn left on 42nd Street.

22.3 Stop sign. Turn right on MN Avenue and then left into Coldbrook County Park.

♦ Coney Island, 266 East Michigan Avenue, Kalamazoo; (269) 382–0377. Serving since 1915, so it's got to be good.

ACCOMMODATIONS

♦ Fairfield Inn East, 3800 East Cork Street, Kalamazoo; (269) 344–8300.
♦ Red Roof Inn East, 3701 East Cork Street, Kalamazoo; (269) 382–6350.

RESTROOMS

♦ Start/finish: Coldbrook County Park.
♦ Mile 7.0: Scooter's Malt Shoppe.

Three Oaks Challenge

*O*ne of the best parts of this ride occurs even before you start—visiting the Bicycle Museum operated by the Three Oaks Spokes bicycle club. Within the small brick building is the history of two-wheeled, human-powered transportation, from the "boneshaker" velocipede of the 1860s to one of the bikes Greg LeMond rode to his Tour de France victory in 1989. In addition to the museum, the Three Oaks Spokes has developed a dozen different routes departing from it. This ride is an adapted combination of two of those routes. A winery, Warren Dunes State Park on Lake Michigan, and acres of rolling farmland are the highlights.

Thanks to the Three Oaks Spokes, Three Oaks is probably the closest thing to a bicycling mecca in Michigan. In addition to the Bicycle Museum, it sponsors the largest one-day ride in Michigan, the Apple Cider Century. Held on the last Sunday in September, it attracts 6,000 cyclists from Michigan, Indiana, and Chicago.

For a little more solitude, avoid that weekend and start your day in the Bicycle Museum, where about two dozen bikes trace the history of two-wheeled transportation. There's the velocipede, the granddaddy of two-wheelers, which dates to the 1860s and is otherwise known as the "boneshaker," for reasons obvious when you look at the metal strip wrapped around the wooden wheel. Also on display from the late nineteenth century are a unique side-by-side "companion" tandem and one of only three Tally-Ho tandems, in which the courteous gent rode on an elevated seat behind the lady. There's the banana-seat Schwinn Sting Ray, circa the 1960s, and a Bottecchia ridden by American

Greg LeMond in 1989, when he won his second Tour de France. All in all it taps into nostalgia and history.

Outside the museum there are Backroads Bikeway signs directing you to the north and south routes designed by the Three Oaks Spokes. You'll follow the signs for the north routes. These signs are posted at most of the turns. However, they do not identify the particular route you're riding by name. Some intersections may also feature two signs, where a shorter route turns off and a longer one continues on. As mentioned, this ride combines two Backroads Bikeway routes: the Grand Mere Trail north of the museum and the Lake Michigan Trail from south of Warren Dunes State Park. This route covers the Lake Michigan Trail in reverse. Therefore, while they can reassure you that you are on designated bikeways familiar to drivers, don't depend on the Backroads Bikeway signs to ride this route.

From the Bicycle Museum you'll ride through rural country past corn, hay, and soybean fields and farmhouses. There are no shoulders, but traffic is light. You'll also ride past vineyards and orchards, made possible by the area's proximity to Lake Michigan's moderating effect on climate. You'll have a couple opportunities to stroll a vineyard and taste local wines at Tabor Hill Winery at the 15-mile mark. Besides tasting, you can have lunch at their restaurant, where the menu changes daily.

After Tabor Hill the hills get a little bigger en route to the next hamlet, Baroda, big enough for a restaurant and gas station, if you need a restroom or a bite to eat. It's another 4 miles into Stevensville, the northernmost point on the route. While you'll pass places to pick up a snack, the Stevensville Station is your best opportunity for a meal until New Buffalo in another 25 miles. From Stevensville you'll be sticking close to the Lake Michigan shore, and the terrain will flatten.

It's another 10 miles through countryside roads to Warren Dunes State Park. There's a beautiful swimming beach about a mile into the park and great sand dunes to climb.

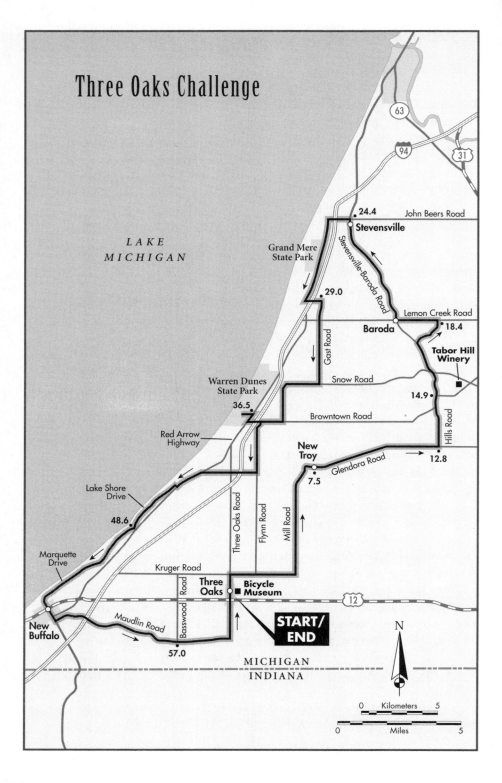

Three Oaks Challenge

LAKE
MICHIGAN

Stevensville 24.4 • John Beers Road

Grand Mere
State Park

29.0 •

Stevensville-Baroda Road

Lemon Creek Road

Baroda • 18.4

**Tabor Hill
Winery**

Gast Road

Snow Road

14.9 •

Warren Dunes
State Park

36.5 •

Browntown Road

Hills Road

Red Arrow
Highway

**New
Troy**

• 12.8

Glendora Road

7.5 •

Lake Shore
Drive

48.6 •

Three Oaks Road

Flynn Road

Mill Road

Marquette
Drive

Kruger Road

Basswood Road

**Three
Oaks**

**Bicycle
Museum**

12

**New
Buffalo**

Maudlin Road

**START/
END**

57.0

MICHIGAN
INDIANA

N

0 Kilometers 5

0 Miles 5

0.0 From the Bicycle Museum, turn right out of the parking lot, riding west on Southcentral Street. Follow the signs for the Backroads Bikeway north routes.

0.1 Stop sign. Turn right on Elm Street. Immediately cross railroad tracks.

1.0 Turn right on Kruger Road.

3.4 Turn left on Mill Road.

7.5 New Troy. On the other side of "town," Mill Road becomes Glendora Road.

12.8 Turn left on Hills Road. Bouncy pavement.

14.9 Turn right to go to Tabor Hill Winery, tasting room and restaurant. Return to Hills Road and turn right.

15.8 Stop sign. Turn left on Snow Road.

16.0 Road curves to right and becomes Hills Road again.

17.1 Turn right on Singer Lake Road.

17.8 Ninety-degree curve to left.

18.4 Stop sign. Turn left on Lemon Creek Road. Bigger hills.

19.1 Baroda Township Park. Restrooms.

20.1 Stop sign/flashing red light. Turn right on First Street, which becomes Stevensville-Baroda Road. Bill's Tap and Restaurant just past intersection.

21.4 Stop sign/flashing light for Cleveland Avenue. Continue straight. Gas station.

24.2 Stevensville. Stevensville Station Restaurant and Lounge.

24.4 Stop sign/flashing light. Turn left onto John Beers Road. Immediate railroad tracks.

24.8 Traffic light for Red Arrow Highway. Continue straight. Use caution at exit/ on-ramps on I–94 overpass.

25.3 Turn left on Thornton Drive immediately after the I–94 overpass. For a rest-room, continue straight for another 0.3 mile and go to the park where the paved road ends. Turn around and turn right on Thornton.

25.8 Grand Mere State Park.

27.2 Left on Thornton Drive. Willow goes straight—no outlet.

28.5 Stop sign. T intersection. Turn left on Livingston Road.

29.0 Railroad tracks. Turn right on Gast Road after tracks.

32.3 Stop sign. Turn right on Snow Road.

33.5 Follow curve around to left, staying on Snow. Do not cross railroad tracks.

35.0 Stop sign. Turn right on Browntown Road.

36.4 Stop sign. Turn right on Red Arrow Highway, staying on shoulder.

36.5 Turn left into Warren Dunes State Park. Bikes enter free. Continue straight to beach in 1.1 miles. Restrooms.

(continued)

38.7 Turn right at stop sign onto Red Arrow Highway, and make an immediate left onto Browntown Road.

39.2 Rough pavement on overpass. Turn right onto Flynn Road (unmarked) immediately after overpass. Look for Backroads Bikeway sign, which you'll see after you begin to turn.

41.2 Turn right on Harbert Road.

43.3 Stop sign. Make wide left turn onto Red Arrow Highway.

43.8 Turn right on Lakeshore Drive.

46.7 Curve to the right. Watch for pedestrian traffic.

48.6 Turn right on Marquette Drive.

49.1 Enter Stevenson Beach.

51.1 Port of New Buffalo. Boat launch, marina, concessions.

51.2 Veer left on Whitaker.

51.5 Railroad tracks, followed by lots of restaurants.

52.1 Turn left on Jefferson Road. Jefferson becomes Maudlin Road. Nice scenic road here. (1.3 miles of bad pavement between Hoder and Lakeside Roads.)

57.0 Stop sign for Basswood Road. Continue straight, going onto Forest Lawn Road.

59.0 Stop sign. T intersection. Turn left on Three Oaks Road. In town, Three Oaks becomes Elm Street. A billboard tells about *Prancer*, the 1989 children's movie, which was filmed in and around here.

60.6 Turn right on Central to return to Bicycle Museum.

South of Warren Dunes State Park is where this route leaves the Backroads Bikeway's Grand Mere Trail and joins the Lake Michigan Trail. A 6-mile stretch north of New Buffalo along Lake Michigan is another nice section. Homes prevent you from seeing the lake all the time, but it's a low-traffic, pedestrian-friendly residential area. New Buffalo is a teeming tourist town, so use caution riding through it before turning back east to Three Oaks. Jefferson Road/Maudlin Road is another pleasant, quiet, shaded road on the way back to Three Oaks.

After crossing U.S. Highway 12, the road becomes Elm Street. Odd that a town named Three Oaks would name its main drag Elm, but perhaps you can ponder that while enjoying a meal and a beverage at one of several establishments in downtown Three Oaks. Or, think about what this ride would be like riding the boneshaker.

LOCAL INFORMATION

♦ Southwestern Michigan Tourist Council; (269) 925–6301; www.swmichigan.org.

Grapes ripen in a southwestern Michigan vineyard. Courtesy of Michael O. Henderson

♦ Harbor Country Chamber of Commerce; www.harborcountry.org. Represents several Lake Michigan communities, including New Buffalo, Union Pier, and Three Oaks.

LOCAL EVENTS/ATTRACTIONS

♦ Bicycle Museum, open daily from 9:00 A.M. to 4:30 P.M. or 5:00 P.M. Call ahead on weekdays. (269) 756–3361; www.applecidercentury.com.
♦ At the Sounds of Silence Film Festival, watch classic silent films and listen to live music. Held at Vickers Theatre in Three Oaks in mid-August. (800) 362–7251; www.vickerstheatre.com.
♦ The Tabor Hill Winery is on the route. (800) 283–3363; www.taborhill.com. For information on other southwest Michigan wineries, see www.mitrailwine .com.
♦ The Ship and Shore Festival features a parade, a 5K run/walk, arts and crafts, kids' event, and a beer tent. Held on the first weekend in August in New Buffalo. (269) 469–4934; www.shipnshore.org.

RESTAURANTS

♦ Froehlich's, 26 North Elm Street, Three Oaks; (269) 756–6002. Great preride stop. From-scratch bakery. Also lunch.

◆ Bill's Tap and Restaurant, 8906 First Street, Baroda; (269) 422–1141. Bar and restaurant on route.

◆ The Featherbone Restaurant, 6741 West US 12, Three Oaks; (269) 756–6821. Restaurant and lounge.

◆ Graziano's Pizza, 28 North Elm Street, Three Oaks; (269) 756–3385.

ACCOMMODATIONS

◆ Treasure House Bed & Breakfast, 210 South Elm Street, Three Oaks; (269) 756–2117. Advertises itself as "a unique lodge designed for the comfort and convenience of the serious cyclist." Two blocks from museum. Shared baths.

◆ Holiday Inn Express, 11500 Holiday Drive, New Buffalo; (269) 469–3436. Seven miles from Three Oaks.

◆ Garden Grove Bed & Breakfast, 9549 Union Pier Road, Union Pier; (269) 469–6346. One mile from Lake Michigan.

RESTROOMS

◆ Start/finish: Bicycle Museum.
◆ Mile 15.0: Tabor Hill Winery.
◆ Mile 19.1: Baroda Township Park.
◆ Mile 25.6 (0.3 mile off route): park.
◆ Mile 37.6: Warren Dunes State Park.
◆ Mile 51.5: various restaurants in New Buffalo.

29

Grand Ledge Ramble

Migrant Indian tribes led by Chief Okemos called this area *"Big Rocks." White settlers weren't much more original, naming the town for the ancient sandstone ledges along the Grand River. But the ledges don't need embellishment to be impressive. The ledges aren't accessible by bike, but a walk along the river trail in Fitzgerald County Park, the ride's departure point, makes an excellent pre- or postride excursion. The ride travels rural roads south of the small community, passing centennial farms. In the fall an extra 5-mile spur to a farm market/mill is a good option. This is an excellent ride for riders accustomed to bike trails who want to try road riding or for experienced road riders looking for a low-traffic, relaxed ride.*

One of Michigan's best-known attractions is the Pictured Rocks National Lakeshore, the sheer, striated rock cliffs along Lake Superior's southern shore, near Munising. I think the Grand Ledge ledges are a scaled-down but more accessible version of the Pictured Rocks. They're popular with rock climbers, but the climbing is concentrated at a different park. Fitzgerald Park offers a peaceful trail that wends its way between the ledges and the Grand River. I suggest visiting them before setting off on the ride.

From the parking area by the Fitzgerald County Park office and red barn, go down the stairs to the river. Turn right at the bottom of the staircase (the left trail dead-ends shortly), and then go straight over the small bridge. The River Path goes 1.5 miles to Island Park in downtown Grand Ledge, but in just a 15-minute walk you'll get a good look at a variety of ledge formations, from protrusions that create shallow caves to rough stacks to smooth sheer faces. On the

A tree clings to the ledges.

ride you'll notice that some of the homes and farms have adopted the ledge look in their yards, with boulders setting off driveways or otherwise used in landscaping.

After touring the ledges you'll get on your bike and leave the park heading toward downtown Grand Ledge. You'll also cruise through the River Ledge Historic District, a half-mile stretch of homes centered around Jefferson Street that are on the National Register of Historic Places. Built between 1850 and 1949, many of the homes show significant pride of ownership. All the front porches are particularly inviting.

Leaving Grand Ledge, you'll ride through the typical fringe development before entering farm country. Some farms display the Michigan centennial farm signs, indicating that they have been operated by the same family for at least one hundred years. In between these farms, however, you can see the encroaching residential development, and mini-estates now sit where corn grew less than ten years ago. Most of the ride is still open fields, though, largely flat but with the periodic pleasant roll. In summer, orange wild daylilies and hot pink and fuchsia sweet peas bring color to the uniform green of the corn and soybean fields.

After heading essentially south, you'll have the option to take an additional 5-mile spur to the Country Mill. It's best visited in the fall, when it has the most-extended hours. Besides the cider and doughnuts, there's the "Mighty Mac Goat Walk," a replica model of the Mackinac Bridge used in 4-H shows.

You'll head back north into Grand Ledge on a parallel road, through more of the same rural environment. In Grand Ledge turn right at Bridge Street to explore downtown. At River Street is the Opera House. Built in 1886 as a roller rink, it served as a theater and furniture store before becoming the chamber of commerce.

Turn left on River Street and go half a block to visit Island Park. It's a remnant of Seven Islands Resort, a recreation area centered on this island from 1870 to 1910. Thousands came by train to enjoy the ledges, steamboat rides, vaudeville theater, roller coaster, boat rides, and fishing. Today August brings the annual Island Art Fair.

If you're hungry, try the Log Jam or Cugino's for a bite to eat. Top it off with ice cream at the Corner Cone on Jefferson at Harrison, before heading back to Fitzgerald Park.

THE BASICS

Start: Fitzgerald County Park in Grand Ledge.

Length: 21.5-mile lariat, with an optional 5-mile sidetrip to Country Mill.

Terrain: Flat to gently rolling on the more southern roads.

Traffic and hazards: Traffic is heaviest on Michigan Highway 100 when leaving and returning to Grand Ledge. Outside town the route is very rural and lightly traveled.

Getting there: From the Interstate 69/96 bypass around Lansing, take exit 93A. Go west on Michigan Highway 43/Saginaw Highway. Cross MI 100 in 3.4 miles. At the flashing light in 5.5 miles, turn right onto Jefferson Street, after the brown Fitzgerald County Park sign. In a half mile, turn left onto Fitzgerald Park Road. Pay the $2.00 entry fee and park in the back lot, by the park office and red barn.

LOCAL INFORMATION

♦ Grand Ledge Area Chamber of Commerce, 121 Bridge Street, Grand Ledge; (517) 627–2383; www.grandledgemi.org.
♦ Greater Lansing Convention and Visitors Bureau; (517) 487–6800 or (888) 2–LANSING; www.lansing.org.

LOCAL EVENTS/ATTRACTIONS

♦ Yankee Doodle Days includes a parade, a craft show, a carnival, fireworks, and a musical review on Second Island (Island Park). End of June. (517) 627–2383.

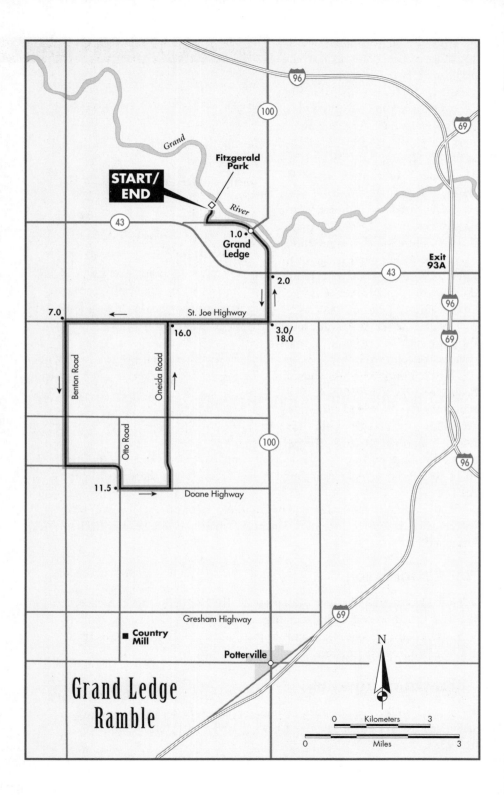

START/
END

Fitzgerald
Park

Grand

River

96

100

69

43

1.0
Grand
Ledge

2.0

43

Exit
93A

St. Joe Highway

7.0

16.0

3.0/
18.0

96

69

Benton Road

Oneida Road

Otto Road

100

11.5

Doane Highway

96

Gresham Highway

69

■ Country
Mill

Potterville

N

Grand Ledge
Ramble

0   Kilometers   3

0   Miles   3

0.0 From entrance to park, turn left on Jefferson Street.

1.0 Traffic light at Bridge Street in downtown Grand Ledge. Continue straight.

1.4 Veer to the right at curve.

1.7 Traffic light. Cross Edwards Street and continue straight on what is now Clinton Street.

2.0 Traffic light. Cross MI 43 and continue straight on what is now Hartel Road/MI 100.

3.0 Turn right on St. Joe Highway.

7.0 Turn left on Benton Road.

10.0 Stop sign. Turn left onto Needmore (unmarked).

11.0 Follow curve to right. Road becomes Otto Road.

11.5 Turn left on Doane Highway. **Sidetrip:** For a 5-mile spur, continue straight on Otto Road to the Country Mill, in 2.5 miles. Return the same way. Best in the fall, when the Country Mill is running full tilt.

12.5 Turn left on Oneida Road.

16.0 Stop sign. Turn right on St. Joe Highway.

18.0 Stop sign. Turn left on Hartel Road/MI 100.

19.0 Traffic light. Cross MI 43 and continue straight on what is now Clinton Street.

19.3 Traffic light. Cross Edwards and continue straight on what is now Jefferson Street.

19.5 Curve to left on Jefferson, using caution as you will be crossing in front of oncoming traffic. Willow Highway goes to the right.

20.0 Traffic light. Bridge Street. Turn right or left to explore downtown Grand Ledge. Corner Cone, Log Jam Restaurant. Return to this intersection and continue west on Jefferson Street.

21.5 Turn right onto Fitzgerald Park Drive. Railroad crossing immediately. Return to parking area.

♦ The Island Art Fair features arts-and-crafts exhibits, riverboat rides, food, and music on Second Island (Island Park). (517) 627–2383.

♦ The Country Mill is open 9:00 A.M. to 6:00 P.M. Thursday through Saturday and 11:00 A.M. to 6:00 P.M. Sunday. August to October; 11:00 A.M. to 3:00 P.M. Saturday other months of the year. (517) 543–1019.

RESTAURANTS

♦ Log Jam, 110 West Jefferson Street, Grand Ledge; (517) 627–4300. Exposed-log interior and taxidermy trophies give this place an up-north feel. Sandwiches, salads, steaks, pizza.

- Cugino's Italian Restaurant, 306 South Bridge Street, Grand Ledge; (517) 627–4048. Pasta, pizza, salads in your typical red-checked-tablecloth, dimly lit Italian place. Look for the Italian flag in front.

ACCOMMODATIONS

- Edwards Windcrest Bed and Breakfast, 11883 Oneida Road, Grand Ledge; (517) 627–2666.
- Best Western Midway Hotel, 7711 West Saginaw Highway, Lansing; (517) 627–8471 or (877) 772–6100.
- Holiday Inn West, 7501 West Saginaw Highway, Lansing; (517) 627–3211.

RESTROOMS

- Start/finish: Fitzgerald County Park.
- Mile 14.0 (on optional spur): Country Mill.

East Lansing Cruise

*I*t's fitting that this ride starts at Michigan State University's Livestock Pavilion, since MSU is the nation's first "Moo U," or land-grant institution. Opened in 1857 as the Agricultural College of the State of Michigan, it served as the prototype for seventy-two agricultural research colleges later chartered under federal legislation. These roots are evident on the beginning of the ride, as you pass by buildings dedicated to the research of swine, dairy cattle, and plant pathology, to name a few. The ride then meanders through the farm country of Ingham County and passes through two villages. The roads around Lansing, Michigan's state capital, are in ideal condition, and you'll enjoy smooth asphalt, light traffic, and the most well-marked roads in the state. You'll also see lots of local cyclists, as members of the Tri-County Bicycle Association use this route a lot.

Since its beginnings as the nation's pioneer land-grant institution, Michigan State University has certainly expanded. Its program offerings now include a school of osteopathic medicine, a respected journalism program, and a renowned hospitality program. In football and basketball the MSU Spartans have earned their way to the top, appearing in the Rose Bowl and the Final Four, respectively. But there's no doubt that Michigan State remains the heart and soul of agriculture in Michigan.

That's apparent from the departure point and first mile of this ride. From the Livestock Pavilion, you'll ride past at least half a dozen buildings in which animals and crops are researched. From dairy cattle to viticulture (grape

Start: MSU Livestock Pavilion.

Length: 41.3-mile lariat, with an optional, highly recommended, 2.4-mile sidetrip to the MSU Horticultural Demonstration Gardens.

Terrain: Flat to rolling. More hills in the southern part of the ride, around Dansville.

Traffic and hazards: In late summer, tall crops can make it difficult to see at intersections. You may need to inch past stop signs to be sure it's clear. The Lansing area can boast of some the most pleasant roads in the state, in terms of both pavement conditions and traffic volume. Busier roads have decent shoulders. All intersections are marked in advance.

Getting there: From Interstate 496 through Lansing/East Lansing, take exit 9, Trowbridge Road. Cross Harrison Road to enter the Michigan State University campus. Turn right on Farm Lane Road. The Livestock Pavilion is located on the right, just south of Mt. Hope Road. Turn right onto Pavilion Drive and park in the lot north of the building, if possible.

growing), it's studied here, and it's probably growing or grazing in the test plots and fields around East Lansing.

Farm country isn't often considered scenic. But the deep, rich green of a cornfield, contrasted with the golden color of ripe alfalfa planted across the road, can be as striking as the deep blue of the Great Lakes shoreline that you'll find on many other rides in this book. Farm scenery in Michigan is also more varied than in other, flatter Midwestern states, where the fields stretch to the horizon. Many field boundaries here are punctuated with trees. Walline Road, at mile 9.0, is a beautiful road, with trees on either side creating a shady arch over the pavement.

As you ride south, especially after you pass Michigan Highway 36 and are coming into Dansville, the terrain becomes more rolling. Diamond Road, at mile 16.0, is a fun stretch of small rollers. Dansville consists of a grocery store, a restaurant, a gas station, and a store. If you're riding on a Sunday, eat here at the Wooden Nickel Cafe, as several of the establishments in Mason, the other village on the route, are closed Sundays.

Dansville is the farthest point on the ride. Mason is less than 10 miles away, and the Livestock Pavilion is another 10. Mason is the Ingham County seat, and has a courthouse building that almost rivals the state capitol. It's on the National Register of Historic Places. The courthouse square is the center of commerce, with restaurants and shops scattered around it.

From Mason, there's one turn west and then it's a long straight shot north back into East Lansing. Before you load your bike back up, however, I highly recommend a side trip to MSU's Horticultural Demonstration Gardens. The round trip will add 2.4 miles, and biking in enables you to avoid the parking fee. Admission to the gardens themselves is free. Even if you're not a gardener, the showcases of MSU's horticulture department are well worth a visit. There are rose gardens; perennial gardens; a curved pergola loaded with huge, colorful hanging baskets of annuals; and a children's garden that will delight adults, too.

Combined, the East Lansing Cruise and the MSU garden finale will make for a capital day in the capitol area.

LOCAL INFORMATION

♦ Greater Lansing Convention and Visitors Bureau; (517) 487–6800 or (888) 2–LANSING; www.lansing.org.

LOCAL EVENTS/ATTRACTIONS

♦ During the East Lansing Art Festival, artists fill the downtown streets. In mid-May. (517) 337–1731, ext. 6804.

♦ The Ingham County Fair includes livestock exhibits, a midway, grandstand entertainment, and food. Held in late July/early August in Mason. (517) 676–2428.

♦ The Great Lakes Folk Festival features music, dance, food, and traditional crafts. Early August in East Lansing. (517) 335–0368.

♦ Michigan State University: For campus tours, call (517) 355–4458; for general information, (517) 355–1855; for the Horticultural Demonstration Gardens, (517) 355–0348; www.msu.edu.

RESTAURANTS

♦ Cayenne Grill, 402 South Jefferson, Mason; (517) 676–7113. At this former department store, you can eat at tables set up in the former display windows.

Cyclists take a break in the demonstration gardens on the Michigan State University campus.

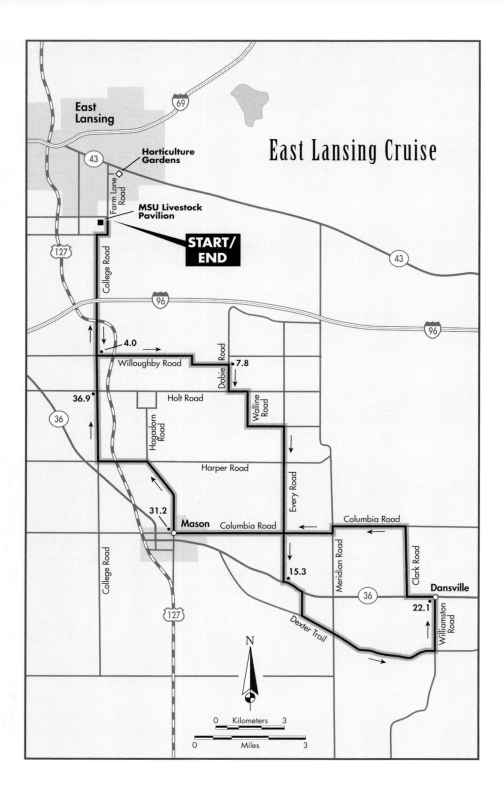

East Lansing Cruise

East Lansing

Horticulture Gardens

Farm Lane Road

MSU Livestock Pavilion

START/ END

College Road

Willoughby Road

4.0

Dobie Road

7.8

Walline Road

36.9

Holt Road

Hagadorn Road

Harper Road

Every Road

31.2

Mason

Columbia Road

Columbia Road

15.3

Meridian Road

Clark Road

Dansville

22.1

Williamston Road

College Road

Dexter Trail

N

0   Kilometers   3

0   Miles   3

0.0 From Pavilion Drive, turn right onto Farm Lane Road.

0.3 Stop sign. Turn right at T intersection onto Forest Road.

0.5 Turn left onto College Road.

4.0 Turn left on Willoughby Road.

6.5 Stop sign. T intersection. Turn right on Okemos Road, following arrow pointing to Willoughby Road.

6.8 Turn left on Willoughby Road.

7.8 Stop sign. T intersection. Turn right on Dobie Road.

8.5 Stop sign. T intersection. Turn left on Holt Road.

9.0 Turn right on Walline Road.

10.0 Stop sign. T intersection. Turn left on Lamb Road.

11.0 Stop sign. Turn right on Every Road.

13.0 Stop sign. Cross Howell Road and continue on Every. Intersection is just slightly offset. Sign for Vevay Township.

15.3 Stop sign. Turn left on MI 36.

15.9 Turn right on Diamond Road. More hills/rolling.

16.6 Stop sign. Turn left on Dexter Trail.

20.6 Stop sign/flashing red light. Turn left onto Williamston Road.

22.1 Stop sign at Mason Street/MI 36 in Dansville. Wooden Nickel Cafe on right, Dansville Grocery Store on left, Marathon gas station with restroom across street. To leave town, turn left (west) on MI 36.

22.7 Turn right on Clark Road.

24.8 Stop sign. Turn left on Columbia Road.

26.8 T stop. Turn left on Meridian Road, following sign for Columbia Road.

27.0 Turn right on Columbia Road.

30.3 Enter Mason.

31.1 Flashing yellow light. Cross Rogers and continue straight. (To visit Dairy Hill for ice cream, turn left on Rogers and left again on Ash in 3 blocks.)

31.2 Stop sign. Turn left (south) on Jefferson to go into town.

31.4 Traffic light at Maple. Go straight to tour courthouse square area. Cayenne Grill and Bookseller restaurants ahead. To reach the Depot, turn right on Maple, right on Lansing in 2 blocks, right on Columbia, and left on Mason. To leave town, ride back north on Jefferson and continue straight out of town, following MSU/EAST LANSING sign. Outside Mason, road becomes Hagadorn Road.

33.5 Turn left on Harper Road, which comes up suddenly; Hagadorn curves opposite this turn.

(continued)

33.9 Stop sign for railroad tracks, followed by yield for one-way bridge.

34.4 Rough pavement on overpass.

34.9 Stop sign. Right on College Road.

41.3 Stop sign. Continue straight, entering back entrance of Livestock Pavilion. Follow Pavilion Drive back to parking lot. To visit the MSU gardens, follow the sidetrip below.

Sidetrip:

0.0 Turn left from Pavilion Drive onto Farm Lane Road.

1.0 Traffic light. Turn right at Wilson Road.

1.2 Yield to enter traffic circle. Take first right onto Bogue Street. The Horticultural Demonstration Gardens are the third driveway on the right.

Cigar-store Indians, guns, and taxidermied trophies mounted on the walls create a western motif. Breakfast highly recommended. Closed Sunday.

♦ The Depot, 111 Mason, off Columbia, Mason. Follow the railroad tracks. (517) 676–3344. During recent construction, which cut the Depot off from traffic, a sign announced, THE DEPOT IS OPEN AND WORTH THE DETOUR TO GET THERE. You be the judge. Breakfast and lunch only in a former working train depot. Closes at noon Saturday, closed Sunday.

♦ El Azteco, 225 Ann Street, East Lansing; (517) 351–9111. Mexican food near campus. Great margaritas. Rooftop dining.

♦ Traveler's Club International Restaurant and Tuba Museum, 2138 Hamilton Road, Okemos; (517) 349–1701; www.tubacharlies.com. Not as convenient to the ride as the others, but an offbeat atmosphere (tubas hanging all over the walls), home-brewed beer (made one barrel at time), and not-quite-ordinary menu make it worth the trip.

ACCOMMODATIONS

♦ Kellogg Hotel and Conference Center, Harrison Road just south of Michigan Avenue, East Lansing; (517) 432–4000. The lab of sorts for MSU's hospitality program. On the East Lansing campus.

♦ Wild Goose Inn, 512 Albert Avenue, East Lansing; (517) 333–3334. Bed-and-breakfast just off campus.

♦ University Quality Inn, 3121 East Grand River Avenue, East Lansing; (517) 351–1440.

RESTROOMS

♦ Mile 22.1: restaurant, gas station in Dansville.

♦ Mile 31.4: various restaurants in Mason.

31

Hell Challenge

Wandering through the still-rural portions of four different southern Michigan counties, this ride through Hell is actually heavenly. This is one of the longer routes used by the Ann Arbor Bicycle Touring Society for its annual "One Helluva Ride," a popular one-day tour held in July. Lightly traveled roads cut through rolling terrain, a few hills, and several villages, including Hell. There you can take the requisite photo next to the Hell signs or the Hell Meterorological Station, which tells you what to expect for the next 65 miles: hotter than hell, colder than hell, raining like hell, or windier than hell. Whatever the weather, after a trip through Hell, you'll want to come back.

Cyclists, rejoice. This is one of those euphoric rides—a full day in the saddle (for most) spent touring scenic countryside relatively free from traffic, with small towns just about perfectly positioned for restroom breaks or a bite to eat. If you happen to get a nice day, it's hard to imagine life getting any better.

This is also one of those rides that gives you a sense of trepidation about the future. The specter of sprawl from both east and west lurks over this area, where the corners of Washtenaw, Livingston, Ingham, and Jackson Counties meet. It's not quite encroached-upon yet. You won't see the subdivisions filled with mini-mansions that are eating up the land and filling roads with congestion between metro Detroit and Ann Arbor and west of Ann Arbor. But Livingston County (home of Hell) was the fastest-growing county in the state in the last census, and Washtenaw's in the top five. The area is midway between the state capital and metro Detroit, and there's no doubt developers have an eye on it.

So while you still can, look hard at the views of centennial farm fields, at the open vistas, at the tall, old trees.

The ride starts at the Hudson Mills Metropark in Washtenaw County, where you can also get in an extra 3 miles on the paved path around the park. From the park entrance you'll head north into Livingston County. Hell is 7 miles up the road. It's all of three businesses, but they've built quite an enterprise out of their name. You can have your tax returns mailed from Hell, for instance. Or order a diploma from Damnation University (campus, of course, in Hell). Check out the weather in Hell at the side of the Screams Ice Cream from Hell and Halloween building, pick up a snack at the Hell Country Store, or have a meal at the Dam Site Inn. Once you've had it up to here with Hell, continue out of town on County Road D32, a narrow, winding, two-lane road.

After Hell you'll come to the community of Gregory in another 6 miles. Between Gregory and Stockbridge you'll find some larger hills. Stockbridge is also in Ingham County, and for 10 or so miles you'll enjoy the excellent road signage the state's capital county offers, with each intersection marked in advance. The terrain flattens out a bit between Stockbridge and Munith.

The Hell, Michigan, meteorological station.

Crossing into Jackson County you'll be riding south toward the Waterloo State Recreation Area. Between Portage Lake and Grass Lake, you'll also encounter more hills, especially along Race Road, a beautiful, wide road sheltered by the tall trees that line both sides. You'll go under Interstate 94 on Race Road and then turn back east to parallel it for a while. This section warrants the greatest caution of the ride; for a half mile you'll be riding on Ann Arbor Road, which merges onto I–94. You'll turn off just before the highway, but it is still a fast road.

You'll be on a frontage road along I–94 for another mile before turning south again toward Grass Lake, a burg about the size of Gregory and the southernmost town on the ride. At mile 45.8, you've got about two-thirds of the miles behind you and some of the most interesting scenery ahead.

You'll ride east and then north out of Grass Lake, passing through more farm country, before turning east again on Clear Lake Road. Crossing into Washtenaw County, bound for Chelsea, you'll be on one of the most popular roads with local cyclists. It's rolling and winding and features the kind of wetland, marshy, cattail-filled scenery you don't see much of anymore in the Lower Peninsula. As you approach Chelsea, beyond the trees you'll also catch a glimpse of the Jiffy Mix milling towers that form the Chelsea "skyline."

At mile 61.3 is downtown Chelsea. Its thriving Main Street offers many restaurants, coffee shops, and retailers. So does downtown Dexter in another 7 miles, so divide your appetite. From Dexter it's an easy 3 miles along Huron River Drive, another popular cycling route, back to Hudson Mills, where the 3-mile bike path is again an option. Since you've already been to Hell and back, what's another 3 miles?

THE BASICS

Start: Hudson Mills Metropark north of Dexter.

Length: 72.7-mile loop, with a 3-mile optional trail around the metropark.

Terrain: Rolling, a few hillier stretches.

Traffic and hazards: The ride generally follows two-lane back roads, most without shoulders. Many are winding, which keeps car speeds down somewhat, but riders should be comfortable in traffic. Use caution at the 41-mile point, after the Interstate 94 underpass, where you will turn onto a frontage road just before merging onto the highway.

Getting there: Hudson Mills Metropark is northwest of both Ann Arbor and Dexter. From either, follow Huron River Drive to North Territorial Road. Turn left. The park is 0.3 mile ahead on your left. There is a $4.00 vehicle entry fee. Turn to the right to park after the payment booth.

LOCAL INFORMATION

♦ Ann Arbor Convention and Visitors Bureau; (800) 888–9487; www.annarbor.org. Serves all of Washtenaw County, including Dexter and Chelsea.

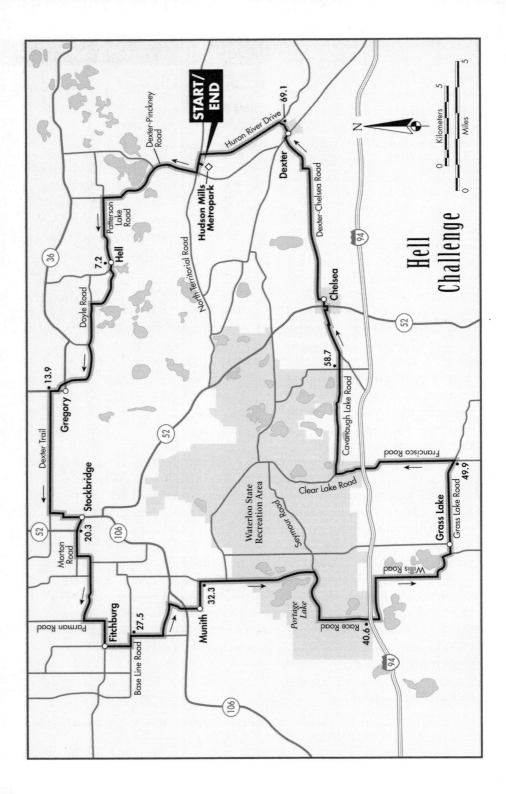

START/END

Dexter-Pinckney Road

Huron River Drive • 69.1

Dexter

Hudson Mills Metropark

North Territorial Road

Dexter-Chelsea Road

Patterson Lake Road

36

Hell • 7.2

Doyle Road

Chelsea

• 58.7

52

Cavanaugh Lake Road

Gregory • 13.9

Dexter Trail

Stockbridge

52

Francisco Road

Grass Lake • 49.9

Grass Lake Road

Morton Road

20.3

106

Clear Lake Road

Waterloo State Recreation Area

Seymour Road

Willis Road

Parman Road

Fitchburg • 27.5

Base Line Road

Munith • 32.3

Portage Lake

Race Road

• 40.6

94

106

94

52

N

Hell
Challenge

Kilometers 0   5   5
Miles   0   5

0.0 From the entrance to Hudson Mills Metropark, turn left onto North Territorial Road. **Option:** At either the beginning or the end of the ride, you can add 3 miles by cycling the path around the park.

04 Traffic light. Turn right on Dexter-Pinckney Road.

4.6 Turn left on Darwin Road (D32).

7.2 Hell, Michigan.

9.3 Veer to the left on Doyle Road, staying on D32.

11.6 Unadilla Road. Continue straight here.

12.4 Curve to the right. Road becomes Unadilla Road.

13.4 Gregory. Road becomes Church. Follow through town and leave on Michigan Highway 36, following road sign for Dansville and Mason.

13.9 Turn left on Dexter Trail. Hills. Narrow with no shoulder, better pavement than through Hell.

18.5 Turn left on Main Street.

19.9 Flashing red light. Turn right onto Main Street/Michigan Highway 52 (unmarked) in Stockbridge.

20.3 Yield sign. Turn left onto Morton Road. Use caution.

21.4 Turn left on Heeney Road.

24.4 Stop sign. T intersection. Turn left on Parman Road.

25.2 Turn right on Fitchburg Road.

26.2 Turn left on Friermuth Road.

27.1 Stop sign. T intersection. Turn left on Baseline Road.

27.5 Turn right on Fitchburg Road.

28.7 Turn left on Territorial Road.

29.9 Turn right on Mesbach Road.

30.7 Stop sign at Plum Orchard Road/Michigan Highway 106. Continue straight. Becomes Main Street through Munith.

(continued)

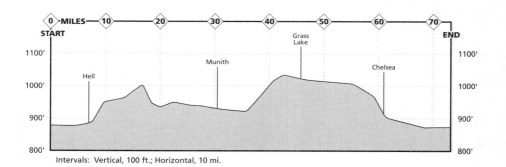

Intervals: Vertical, 100 ft.; Horizontal, 10 mi.

31.2 Turn left on Waterloo-Munith Road.

32.3 Turn right on Huttenlocker Road.

34.4 Stop sign. Continue straight onto Portage Lake Road, using caution.

35.6 Park and pit toilet.

36.6 Stop sign. Turn right on Seymour Road. Country Corner Store/Deli. Rico's Grill.

38.6 Turn left on Race Road.

40.6 I–94 underpass. Use caution at on- and exit ramps.

40.8 Stop sign. Turn left on Ann Arbor Road, watching for more traffic that will merge onto I–94 ahead.

41.3 Turn right on Stull Road, just before merging onto I–94. Follow sign to All Seasons Resort in Grass Lake. Road becomes Knight Road and is a frontage road to I–94 until next turn.

42.5 Turn right on Willis Road.

44.9 Turn left on Winegar Road.

45.8 Stop sign. Turn right on Lake Street in Grass Lake.

45.9 Railroad tracks. Cross and turn left on Michigan Avenue at the light.

46.4 Traffic light. Turn right on Union.

46.5 Stop sign. Continue straight across Church. Road curves left out of town, passing football field.

46.9 Stop sign. Continue straight. Road becomes Grass Lake Road.

49.9 Turn left on Francisco Road.

52.7 Curve to the left to stay on Francisco Road/Clear Lake Road. Unpaved road ahead.

53.4 I–94 overpass. Caution.

54.5 Turn right on Harvey Road.

55.4 Enter Washtenaw County. Road becomes Cavanaugh Lake Road.

57.0 Park, pit toilets.

57.3 Curve around to right. Glazier/Kalmbach Road roads merge in. Then stay to left as Kalmbach veers off right.

60.6 Curve to the right. Road becomes Cleveland. Cross railroad tracks, then curve left. Road becomes Middle.

61.3 Traffic light at Main Street. Explore Chelsea in either direction. Return to this intersection and continue straight (east).

61.5 Turn left on McKinley Road, following sign to Dexter. Cross railroad tracks.

61.6 Turn right onto Railroad, following sign to Dexter. Road becomes Dexter-Chelsea.

68.3 Right at yield sign onto Dexter-Pinckney Road/Main Street in Dexter.

(continued)

68.5 Turn left on Central Street.
69.1 Turn left on Huron River Drive.
72.4 Flashing red light/stop sign. Turn left on North Territorial Road.
72.7 Hudson Mills Metropark.

♦ Livingston County Convention and Visitors Bureau; (800) 686–8474; www.lccvb.org.
♦ Jackson County Convention and Visitors Bureau; (800) 245–5282; www.jackson-mich.org.

LOCAL EVENTS/ATTRACTIONS

♦ Fleas of Hell is a flea and farmers' market held every Saturday from May to October in Hell.
♦ At Chelsea Summer Fest, you'll find entertainment, arts and crafts, a beer garden, and food. Held in July. (734) 433–0354.
♦ The Dexter Daze includes entertainment, a parade, and children's activities. Held in Dexter in August. (734) 426–0887.
♦ The Dexter Cider Mill is the oldest continuously operated cider mill in Michigan. 3685 Central Street, Dexter; (734) 426–8531.

RESTAURANTS

♦ Hell Country Store & Spirits (sandwiches, pizza, salads), Screams Ice Cream from Hell and Halloween, and the Dam Site Inn (the local watering hole—and you can bet they need one in Hell; get it?) are all in a row along Patterson Lake Road in Hell.
♦ Cleary's Pub, 113 South Main Street, Chelsea; (734) 475–1922. Just like it sounds, an Irish pub.
♦ Clock Works Coffee House, 8074 Main Street, Dexter; (734) 426–8002. Coffee, natch, as well as pastries, yummy sandwiches, ice cream, and art for sale.
♦ Lighthouse Cafe, 8124 Main Street, Dexter; (734) 426–2255. Great locals spot. Good for breakfast if you stop en route to the starting point.

ACCOMMODATIONS

♦ Chelsea Comfort Inn, 1645 Commerce Park Drive, Chelsea; (734) 433–9565. Stay here, start the ride in Chelsea, and hit the Lighthouse Cafe in Dexter for breakfast on the bike.
♦ Best Western Executive Plaza, 2900 Jackson Road, Ann Arbor; (734) 665–4444. Twenty to thirty minutes from the start of the ride.

RESTROOMS

- Start/finish: Hudson Mills Metropark.
- Mile 7.2: establishments in Hell.
- Mile 13.4: establishments in Gregory (Gregory, Stockbridge, and Grass Lake all have at least a gas station on the route; also try restaurants you patronize).
- Mile 19.9: establishments in Stockbridge.
- Mile 35.7: Portage Lake park (seasonal pit toilet).
- Mile 45.8: establishments in Grass Lake.
- Mile 57.0: roadside park.
- Mile 61.3: establishments in Chelsea.
- Mile 68.4: establishments in Dexter.

32

Ann Arbor Ramble

As the home of the University of Michigan, city blends with campus in Ann Arbor, resulting in a one-of-a-kind community. This is probably the most pedestrian- and bike-friendly city in the state, with many dedicated bike paths and even bike lanes. It has all the trappings of a liberal college town: food co-ops and used bookstores, trendy restaurants and cafes, and lots of pizza joints and bars. Ann Arbor's been likened to other places—the Berkeley of the Midwest for its leftward tendencies, the Harvard of the Midwest for its academic reputation. Perhaps true. But in Michigan, Ann Arbor is unique. On this ride you'll enjoy all of her highlights—campus, downtown, residential neighborhoods, and parks.

The ride starts in Gallup Park, a wonderful multiuse park along the Huron River. Consisting of 83 acres of land, 153 acres of water and 4.6 miles of trails, it also offers paddleboat and canoe rentals. You can fish, inline skate, bike, or stroll. You can read a good book, picnic, or take a nap. It's also a place with abundant parking, a rarity in A-squared. You'll ride south out of the park into a gracious old residential neighborhood. The streets are winding and sometimes hilly. While you'll need to follow the directions pretty closely to navigate much of this ride, in this neighborhood, for the most part, you can follow the BIKE ROUTE signs.

When you turn onto Packard Street at mile 2.1, you're leaving residential Ann Arbor and heading for collegiate Ann Arbor. Packard is busy but has a dedicated bike lane, and you'll pass student houses and apartment buildings

Start: Gallup Park.

Length: 9.5-mile loop, with a 3-mile optional ride around Gallup Park.

Terrain: Flat to hilly—shorter and steeper hills rather than long and gradual.

Traffic and hazards: While this ride is categorized as a ramble, riders should be comfortable in traffic. Many one-way streets and frequent traffic controls make for lots of stops, starts, and turns. The longest stretches are about a half mile; in the downtown and campus area, directions change as often as every block. On the plus side, bikes are common and drivers are typically courteous. The ride is best ridden on weekends and in the summer. Weekday traffic, both vehicular and pedestrian, will be very heavy, especially through the campus when school is in session.

Getting there: Exit U.S. Highway 23 at Geddes Road and go west past Huron Parkway. The entrance to Gallup Park is on your left just past the parkway.

and businesses catering to students. At this point you're mostly skirting Central Campus and its academic buildings, however.

You'll turn off Packard onto Main Street, transitioning to the city's downtown. Restaurants and shops line Main and are especially vivid in summer, when the outdoor cafes are filled. Turning west on Washington Street, you'll ride through another residential neighborhood. While much smaller than the stately custom homes of the Devonshire neighborhood south of Gallup Park, many of the homes here show pride of ownership, with creative landscaping and porch furniture.

You'll turn north again on Seventh Street and pass West Park, with its noticeable band shell. At Seventh Street and Miller Avenue, turn back east toward downtown. You'll have a downhill ride back to the business district. Miller becomes Catherine Street, which is the southern boundary of Kerrytown. Turn left on Detroit Street to go to the farmers' market or Zingerman's Deli, one of Ann Arbor's best-loved restaurants.

After the Kerrytown neighborhood, you'll start zigzagging south and east toward campus. State Street is where townies and students blend most, and you'll turn off State to cut through the U-M Diag, nearly a half mile that cuts through the heart of campus. In the middle of the Diag is the bronze "M" seal. Campus lore says that if students step on it before they take their first exam, they'll fail the exam. I'm not sure if there are repercussions for riding over it, but you might want to avoid it just in case.

You'll exit the Diag through the engineering arch and turn left on South University Avenue. Student bars, restaurants, and ice-cream shops (try Stucchi's) line South U. You'll turn on Church Street, then Geddes Avenue, and then Observatory. You'll be climbing up a hill on Observatory, going behind some U-M dorms. You'll be behind the University of Michigan Hospitals.

Free parking in Ann Arbor is like ice in the Sahara—take advantage of it. Courtesy of Michael O. Henderson

Watch for more traffic as you turn onto Glen Avenue and circle the medical complex. At the intersection of Medical Campus Drive, get on the bike path paralleling Fuller Street. You'll have your longest straight stretch here, 0.7 mile, before following the path to the right after Mitchell Field to reenter Gallup Park. The path will take you back to the one-lane car bridge. You can add a few miles circling Gallup Park, enjoy one of the other recreational pastimes, or just loll along the Huron, people-watching.

LOCAL INFORMATION

♦ Ann Arbor Convention and Visitors Bureau; (800) 888–9487; www.ann arbor.org.

♦ The city of Ann Arbor put out a great bicycle map of the city and Washtenaw County, color-coded to indicate bike lanes, paved shared-use bike paths, and low traffic volumes. Supplies were limited, however. Contact the department of parks and recreation at (734) 994–2780 or www.a2gov.org. May also be available at area bike shops.

♦ University of Michigan; (734) 764–INFO; www.umich.edu. Whether you want to watch the maize and blue at the Big House or the performing arts at Hill Auditorium, there's something going on on campus.

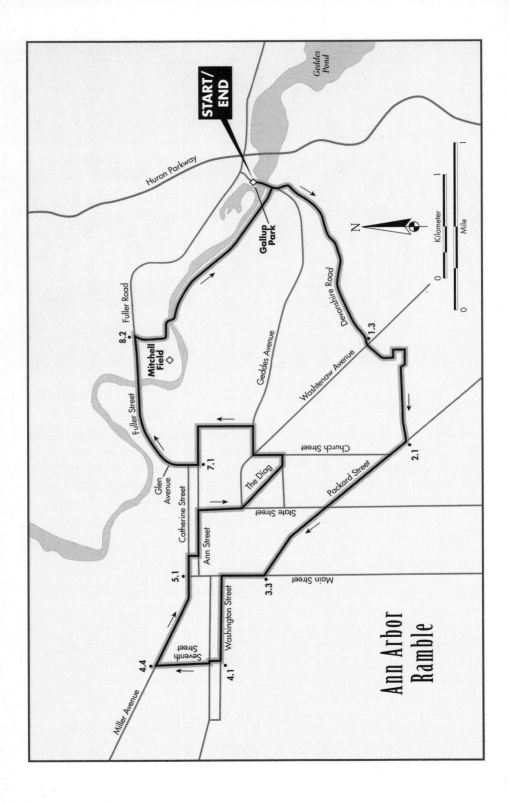

Ann Arbor
Ramble

0.0 Gallup Park, just south of the one-lane bridge, get on the bike path paralleling the fence with stone pillars, riding due south toward the railroad tracks. Cross tracks and crosswalk across Geddes Avenue. Veer right on trail. **Option:** At either the beginning or the end of the ride, you can add 3 miles by riding the double loop around the park.

0.1 Turn right on Devonshire Road. Residential neighborhood. Follow bike route signs for next 1.5 miles.

0.6 Stop sign for Arlington. 5-way intersection. Continue straight on Devonshire.

1.3 Traffic light for Washtenaw Avenue. Cross and continue on Austin.

1.5 Turn right on Wallingford, then veer at the first right onto Hermitage. Street sign is cockeyed.

1.6 Turn right on Ives.

1.7 Stop sign. Cross Ferndon Road. Road becomes Granger Avenue on the other side.

2.1 Traffic light. Turn right on Packard Street, riding in bike lane.

3.3 Turn right at Main Street at the light.

3.6 Turn left at the light on Washington Street.

4.1 Flashing light. Turn right on Seventh Street, staying in right lane to follow Seventh through the traffic light at Huron Street and slight jog left.

4.4 Traffic light. Turn right on Miller Avenue, which will become Catherine Street.

5.1 Traffic light for Main Street. Continue straight. To go to Kerrytown neighborhood, continue straight less than 0.1 mile through the next stop sign, at Fourth Street, and turn left on Detroit Street, at Argiero's Restaurant. Farmers' market on Saturdays, shops, restaurants. Zingerman's Deli, located across Fifth Street. You'll have to walk your bike as the street is one-way the wrong way here. Return to intersection of Detroit and Catherine Streets and continue east on Catherine.

5.2 Traffic light. Turn right on Fifth Street. Get in the left lane of this one-way street.

5.3 Traffic light. Turn left on Ann Street.

5.4 Turn left on Division Street and turn right immediately, at the unmarked street, which is Ann Street.

5.5 Stop sign. Turn right off Ann Street on State Street.

5.8 Traffic light. Turn left on University Avenue and down the Diag, heading southeast through campus.

6.2 Exit the Diag at the corner of East University and South University Avenues. Turn left on South University.

6.3 Turn left on Church Street.

(continued)

6.4 Turn right on Geddes Avenue.

6.6 Traffic light. Turn left on Observatory Street.

6.9 Traffic light at East Medical Center Drive. Continue on Observatory, going around a roundabout to make a left turn on East Ann Street.

7.1 Traffic light on Glen Avenue. Turn right. Watch for more traffic.

7.5 Traffic light at East Medical Campus Drive/Maiden Lane. Go through light and get on bike path paralleling Fuller Street here.

8.2 Turn right on the path after Mitchell Field and before the intersection of Fuller Court/Bonisteel. Entering Gallup Park.

9.5 Veer to the left as you approach the one-lane bridge, reentering Gallup Park.

LOCAL EVENTS/ATTRACTIONS

♦ Ann Arbor Art Fairs is a huge event—really three fairs in one—that turns the city into an outdoor art galley in mid-July. Avoid trying to ride at this time, as the fairs take over much of downtown and create lots of traffic. (734) 995–7281.

♦ You'll ride right by the farmers' market in the business district. Get there early for the best pickings. 315 Detroit Street, in Kerrytown. Open 7:00 A.M. to 3:00 P.M. Wednesday and Saturday May to December. 8:00 A.M. to 3:00 P.M. Saturday January to April.

♦ Taste of Ann Arbor and the Rest of the World: At Ann Arbor's many ethnic restaurants, you really can get a sampling of the cuisines outside southeast Michigan. June. (734) 668–7112, ext. 32.

RESTAURANTS

Ann Arbor has it all, from Asian to Zingerman's. You'll pass many restaurants on the ride—if one looks interesting, give it a try. The fierce competition tends to winnow out the losers, so it's hard to go wrong.

♦ Zingerman's Deli, 422 Detroit Street, Ann Arbor; (734) 663–DELI. If there is a quintessential Ann Arbor restaurant, this Jewish deli is it. Named "best deli" in the *Detroit Free Press* "Best of Detroit" list. Sandwiches, baked goods, coffee. It also offers free bike parking on the porch. Outdoor dining available.

♦ Prickly Pear Southwest Cafe, 328 South Main Street, Ann Arbor; (734) 930–0047. Unusual southwestern dishes, including seafood. Outdoor dining available. Downtown.

♦ Brown Jug, 1204 South University Avenue, Ann Arbor; (734) 761–3355. A campus favorite. Bar and restaurant.

ACCOMMODATIONS

◆ Bed & Breakfast on Campus, 921 East Huron Street, Ann Arbor; (734) 994–9100. Contemporary building with atrium dining and deck overlooking Central Campus.
◆ Embassy Hotel, 200 East Huron Street, Ann Arbor; (734) 662–7100. Downtown Ann Arbor.
◆ Quality Inn and Suites, 3750 Washtenaw Avenue, Ann Arbor; (734) 971–2000.

RESTROOMS

◆ Start/finish: Gallup Park.

Oakland Lakes Challenge

T his route was designed by the local cyclists to be a tour offered specifically on Memorial Day, as the holiday reduces traffic. Even then, however, cyclists should be comfortable sharing the road with cars to take on this meandering ride through western Oakland County's lake country. A 3.4-mile bike-path shortcut allows riders who want a shorter distance to take off 8.3 miles, as well as to bypass the heaviest traffic. A paved trail around Indian Springs Metropark gives you the option to add back 8 miles, so you can still get pretty close to the metric century mark.

If you're not already familiar with it, you'll get a good sense of Oakland County on the ride to the departure point. You'll pass lots of new subdivisions filled with new condos and huge new homes, and tons of shopping malls to serve the typically well-heeled Oakland County residents. (Depending on what source you check, Oakland is the second- or third-wealthiest county in the nation in terms of per-capita income.) The modest Richardson Community Center is across the street from the huge new Walled Lake High School, built thanks to the healthy tax base.

One of the things that makes Oakland County an attractive place to live is that it's chock full of little lakes (some 1,400, according to the chamber of commerce), including Walled, Proud, White, Pontiac, Oxbow, Round, and Carroll. However there isn't a lot of actual shoreline riding on this route, since many of these lakes are developed around the shore. There are several state recreation areas where the natural resources are open to the public. The Highland State Recreation Area and Pontiac Lake Recreation Area/Indian Springs Metropark are along the route, while Proud Lake State Recreation Area and the Kensington Metropark are nearby.

A shoreline exception is Walled Lake, which at 4.3 miles is the first highlight of the road ride. There's a nice bike lane for more than a mile along East Lake Drive, and you can observe the evolution of the small cottage to the waterfront mini-estate.

If you choose to take the bike trail, which goes through some older neighborhoods with what now look like small houses, you'll miss Walled Lake. But the bike path has its own appeal. It has two bridge crossings, which you'll approach on a down-hill. The second one is especially steep. Go slowly, as the trail is not flush with the bridge, creating quite a lip that you don't want to hit going downhill. The trail goes through a couple of parks with a restroom at about the 2-mile point. You'll come to a Commerce Township municipal complex with a fire station and a sheriff's substation. Continue 0.4 mile to the trail turnout on Glengary/Wixom Road, and turn left onto the road. You'll rejoin the road route at mile 12.5, where the ride heads west, forming the first stair-step of Wixom Road. Wixom will turn north again in another mile and then west again in another mile and a half, forming the second stair-step.

THE BASICS

Start: Richardson Community Center, across from Walled Lake High School, on Oakley Park Road.

Length: 54.5-mile loop with an optional 8.3-mile shortcut and an optional 8-mile ride in Indian Springs Metropark.

Terrain: Flat to rolling.

Traffic and hazards: This route is best ridden early on weekend mornings, or on a holiday (try the Fourth of July or Labor Day, when I scouted it) when there's less of the suburban traffic. Due to two-lane roads with narrow shoulders where shoulders exist, riders should be experienced and comfortable with traffic. There are lots of subdivisions, many of which seem to have bike paths along the perimeter. These are intermittent and start and stop abruptly but may be a good option for some riders. The trail from Richardson Center to Glengary/Wixom Road near Proud Lake Recreation Area cuts off worst road traffic.

Getting there: Exit Interstate 96/275 onto Haggerty Road at either Six, Seven, or Eight Mile Road. Continue north on Haggerty to Oakley Park Road (3 miles past Fourteen Mile Road.) The Richardson Community Center is on the right, across from Walled Lake High School.

Approaching Milford, you'll ride through a more residential area. Colasanti's Market, in Highland, is a good place to pick up picnic supplies. Located at 468 South Milford Road, just south of the Michigan Highway 59 intersection, it boasts a deli, bakery, and produce and meat market. Shopping at Colasanti's is also a unique experience, since the store is surrounded by a kind of private park, complete with birds, including waterfowl, and animals.

The northernmost 15 miles along Harvey Lake Road, Davisburg Road, and

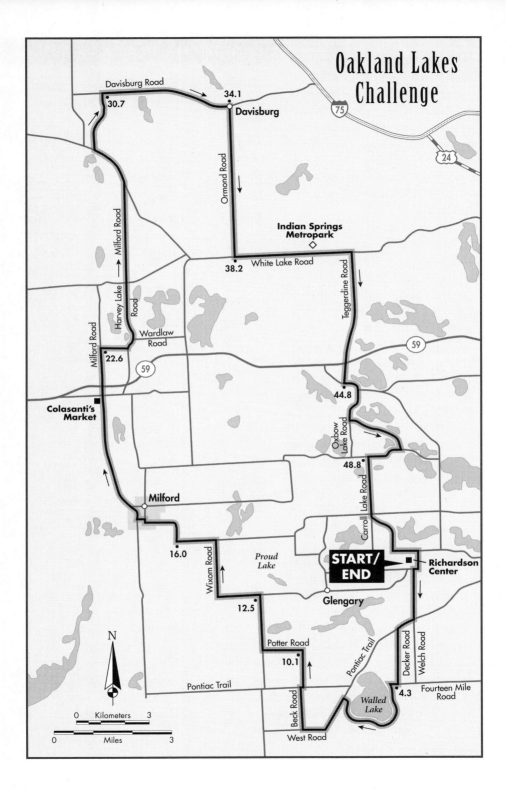

Oakland Lakes Challenge

Davisburg Road

34.1

30.7

Davisburg

Ormond Road

Indian Springs
Metropark

Milford Road

Harvey Lake
Road

38.2 White Lake Road

Teggerdine Road

Wardlaw
Road

Milford Road

22.6

59

59

Colasanti's
Market

44.8

Oxbow
Lake Road

48.8

Milford

Carroll Lake Road

16.0

Proud
Lake

Wixom Road

START/
END

Richardson
Center

12.5

Glengary

Potter Road

Pontiac Trail

Decker Road

Welch Road

10.1

N

Beck Road

Walled
Lake

4.3

Fourteen Mile
Road

Pontiac Trail

West Road

0   Kilometers   3

0   Miles   3

0.0 From the entrance to the Richardson Community Center, turn left onto Oakley Park Road. Or, to cut 8.3 miles off the route and avoid the worst traffic, follow the option below.

Option: Turn right from the entrance onto the bike path paralleling Oakley Park Road, heading westbound. Use caution at the two bridges, as you'll be coming down inclines and the trail is not flush with the bridge, creating a lip. Just past the fire station, follow the trail to the right to its turnout on Glengary/Wixom Road. Turn left onto the road. Go straight through the light at Wixom Road, rejoining the road route at mile 12.5.

0.6 Traffic light at Welch Road. Turn right.

2.0 Traffic light. Turn right onto Pontiac Trail. Shoulder.

2.5 Traffic light. Turn left on Decker Road.

4.0 Traffic light. Turn right on Fourteen Mile Road.

4.3 Stop sign. Turn left onto East Lake Drive, riding along Walled Lake. Bike lane.

5.4 Stop sign. Turn left onto unnamed road (South Lake Drive).

5.5 Stop sign. Turn right on Thirteen Mile Road.

5.6 Traffic light. Turn right on South Lake Drive. Still along lake. Hill, no shoulder.

6.0 Park on left—restrooms.

6.9 Turn left onto West Park Drive.

7.4 Traffic light. Turn right onto West Road, before I–96 sign.

7.9 Traffic light. Turn right on Beck Road—unmarked.

10.1 Traffic light for Potter Road. Turn left.

11.0 Traffic light. Turn right on Wixom Road, going northbound.

12.0 Traffic light for Loon Lake Road. Continue straight. (For restroom, turn right for 0.7 mile and then left on Chickasaw, going uphill, to enter Gilbert Willis Park Pavilion.)

12.5 T intersection. Turn left on Wixom/Glengary Road.

13.5 Turn right on Wixom Road.

15.0 Turn left on Wixom Road.

16.0 Turn right, continuing on Wixom Road.

16.5 Turn left, continuing on Wixom Road/Atlantic Street.

16.9 Turn right onto Crystal Street (becomes Commerce).

17.3 Turn left onto Summitt Street.

18.1 Turn right onto Milford Road. Use caution at railroad and MI 59 crossing.

22.6 Turn right onto Wardlow Road. Use caution at railroad crossing.

23.3 Turn left onto Harvey Lake Road.

(continued)

25.2 Harvey Lake Road becomes Milford Road. Use caution at two intersections.

30.7 Turn right onto Davisburg Road.

34.1 Turn right onto Ormond Road.

38.2 Turn left onto White Lake Road.

40.1 Entrance to Indian Springs Metropark. **Option:** Enter for 8-mile loop around bike path.

41.3 Turn right onto Teggerdine Road. Use caution at MI 59 intersection.

44.8 Turn left onto Elizabeth Lake Road.

45.1 Turn right onto Oxbow Lake Road.

46.2 Turn left onto Cedar Island Road.

47.6 Turn right onto Round Lake Road.

47.9 Turn right onto Cooley Lake Road.

48.8 Turn left onto Carroll Lake Road.

50.3 Turn left onto Commerce Road.

50.8 Turn right onto Newton Road.

51.8 Turn left onto Richardson Road.

52.8 Turn right onto Martin Road.

53.3 Turn right onto Oakley Park Road.

54.5 Turn right into Richardson Community Center.

Ormond Road is one of the prettiest parts of the ride, with some hills and less development.

Turning east off Ormond onto White Lake Road, you'll come to Indian Springs Metropark, which offers an 8-mile paved trail. If you didn't take the bike-trail cutoff, you can do this loop and make your ride a metric century. There's also a nature center, restrooms, and food service.

Leaving the park you'll turn right onto Teggerdine Road in just over a mile. From here it's pretty much a straight—OK, slightly wiggly—shot south back to the Richardson Center.

LOCAL INFORMATION

♦ Lakes Area Chamber of Commerce; (248) 624–2826; www.lakesarea chamber.com. Serving Commerce, White Lake, and Waterford Townships, including cities of Walled Lake and Wixom.

LOCAL EVENTS/ATTRACTIONS

♦ Meadow Brook Theatre, on the campus of Oakland University: visit www.oakland.edu/mbt for performance schedules and ticket information, or call (248) 377–3300.

♦ Meadow Brook Music Festival is an outdoor music festival dating back to 1964. The venue is also the summer home of the Detroit Symphony Orchestra. On the campus of Oakland University, 3554 Walton Boulevard, Rochester Hills; www.palacenet.com; (248) 377–0100.

♦ At the Woodward Dream Cruise, a singular Motor City event, classic cars cruise Woodward Avenue from downtown Detroit to Pontiac in Oakland County. Third Saturday of August. (248) 625–2826.

RESTAURANTS

♦ Bogey's Bar and Grille, 142 East Walled Lake Drive, Walled Lake; (248) 669–1441. Big deck on the lake, let-loose atmosphere, typical bar-and-grill fare.

♦ Duke's West, 1200 South Milford Road, Highland; (248) 887–8230. On the route. Italian and American food.

♦ Beans and Cornbread, 29508 Northwestern Highway, Southfield; (248) 208–1680. It's in the opposite corner of Oakland County, but it was named "best soul food" in metro Detroit by readers of the *Detroit Free Press.*

ACCOMMODATIONS

♦ Hampton Inn, 20600 Haggerty Road, Northville; (734) 462–1119.

♦ Courtyard by Marriott, 42700 Eleven Mile Road, Novi; (800) 359–4827.

RESTROOMS

♦ Mile 2.0: bike trail.

♦ Mile 6.0: roadside park; also at various gas stations and fast food restaurants in first 12.5 miles of the road route.

♦ Mile 12.8: Gilbert Willis Park Pavilion (off route).

♦ Mile 40.1: Indian Springs Metropark.

34

Tour de Wayne and Washtenaw Classic

M etro Detroit doesn't spring to mind as the best training turf for competitive cycling, but it worked for Frankie Andreu, who submitted this ride. A nine-time finisher of the Tour de France, former U.S. Postal Service teammate of Lance Armstrong, and native of the Detroit suburb of Dearborn, Andreu says it takes him four and a half to five hours to do this ride through mostly suburban and exurban areas. If you're more accustomed to a leisurely pace, there are plenty of places to linger along the route, including Northville, Dexter, Ann Arbor, and Plymouth.

The ride starts out on Hines Drive, one of the most popular cycling routes in the metro area. Hines is a linear park that wends its way through western Wayne County and offers wide paved shoulders as well as a bike path. It's a fairly easy 16 miles out to Northville, with a couple of grade changes over a mostly flat course. At the Northville Downs Racetrack, you can turn right to visit downtown Northville, a spick-and-span version of Our Town, packed with restaurants, cafes, and shops. Ride back down to the racetrack intersection and continue west on Seven Mile Road.

For those who are used to the commercially clogged Mile Roads as they exist in eastern Wayne County, Seven Mile out here is a pleasant surprise. You'll stay on this for 15 miles, till it dead-ends at Whitmore Lake. Another nice thing about this route: it follows relatively long straight stretches that free you from reading directions and allow you to enjoy the ride.

At mile 31, with a little more than a third of the miles behind you, you'll hit Whitmore Lake. To go into the town of Whitmore Lake, turn left. Stores and restaurants are about a mile down the road. Otherwise, turn right to do a half lap of the lake. Use caution at the underpass under US 23, and then enjoy 3 miles of shoulder into the burg of Hamburg.

After Hamburg, when you turn right on Strawberry Lake Road, you'll notice the surroundings turning more rural and traffic getting a little lighter. The exurban pressure is no doubt on, but for now, development is sporadic, with cornfields still holding their own against Bigfoot homes, and signs warning of farm equipment on the roads.

You'll enter Washtenaw County and turn south on Mast Road. At the intersection of Huron River Drive, you can continue straight into Dexter, another small town offering a friendly downtown with several shops and eateries. You'll pass the Dexter Cider Mill, the oldest continuously operated cider mill in Michigan. Leave Dexter the way you entered and turn east on Huron River Drive. Immediately you'll notice the welcome SHARE THE ROAD SIGNS with the bicycle logo. The winding, scenic road is very popular with Ann Arbor–area cyclists. There's no shoulder, but the vehicle speed limit is 35 miles per hour. There are a few hills and open views of the Huron River along the 9 miles of the drive.

THE BASICS

Start: Helms Haven recreation area along Hines Drive.

Length: 85.6-mile lariat with an optional 0.8-mile sidetrip to Northville.

Terrain: Flat to rolling. Two steep hills on Glazier Way heading out of Ann Arbor.

Traffic and hazards: Use caution at the U.S. Highway 23 underpass at mile 32.9, after circling Whitmore Lake. Exercise greatest caution coming into Ann Arbor at mile 55.5, as you turn off Huron River Drive onto Main Street, where you'll be merging with traffic coming off Michigan Highway 14. Also use caution on Fuller Road past the University of Michigan Hospitals and VA Hospital.

Getting there: *From the west:* Take the Hines Drive exit off westbound Ford Road (Michigan Highway 153), which is between the Southfield Freeway (Michigan Highway 39) and Telegraph Road (U.S. Highway 24). Cross the light at Outer Drive. Helms Haven is about a quarter mile down on your left.
From the east: Go east on Ford Road to Outer Drive. Turn left on Outer Drive (a "Michigan left," which means going through the intersection, making a U-turn to head back westbound on Ford Road, and then turning right onto Outer Drive). Pass St. Anselm Church on your left. Hines Drive is the second light. Turn left. Helms Haven is about a quarter mile down on your left.

The entrance to the University of Michigan's Diag through campus. If you take a break in Ann Arbor, stop for a stroll. Courtesy of Michael O. Henderson

Huron River Drive ends rather abruptly at the edge of Ann Arbor. You'll be turning right onto Main Street. A state highway, MI 14, is also merging onto Main at this point, so use caution, as the two lanes of traffic are moving fast as they come into town.

After following the curve to the right, you'll need to get in the left lane soon to turn onto Depot Street. After the railroad trestle bridge, watch for buckled sections in the brick street. Straight ahead is the University of Michigan Hospitals, which you'll essentially circle as you turn left on Glen Avenue and then ride onto Fuller Street. At the VA Hospital, turn left onto Glazier Way. The worst traffic is now behind you. I've revised the last 27 miles from the route Frankie originally suggested to stay on prettier, less trafficked roads.

Cross the boulevard on Huron Parkway to stay on Glazier Way. Two steep hills are ahead. At the T intersection with Earhart Road, turn left. You'll cross over US 23, then turn right on Plymouth–Ann Arbor Road, staying in the shoulder of the four-lane road. It will narrow to two lanes in about 2 miles, after going through the tiny burg of Dixboro. Stop in the general store for a snack and a saddle break.

Like Seven Mile Road, Plymouth–Ann Arbor Road is a congested commercial strip farther east, but out here it's practically rural. You'll stay on it for about 8.5 miles after Dixboro before turning onto Ann Arbor Trail. When riding this direction, however, the road takes you into bucolic downtown Plymouth, a town akin to Northville. It's a good place to fuel up for the homestretch.

A few miles out of Plymouth, the shoulder on Ann Arbor Trail deteriorates, but you've only got 2 more miles to go before returning to Hines Drive. The last 7 miles repeat the first 7.

Back at Helms Haven, congratulate yourself on completing a ride that prepared a rider for the Alps, the Pyrenees, and the Champs-Elysées.

LOCAL INFORMATION

♦ Dearborn Chamber of Commerce; (313) 584–6100; www.dearbornchamber .org/visitor.
♦ Northville Community Chamber of Commerce, 195 South Main Street, Northville; (248) 349–8730; www.northville.org.
♦ Ann Arbor Convention and Visitors Bureau; (800) 888–9487; www.ann arbor.org. Serves all of Washtenaw County, including Dexter and Chelsea.

LOCAL EVENTS/ATTRACTIONS

♦ The Henry Ford is an indoor museum and outdoor village depicting nineteenth-century American life. Founded by Henry Ford as a tribute to his friend, Thomas Edison. IMAX theater. 20900 Oakwood Boulevard, Dearborn; (313) 982–6100; www.thehenryford.org.

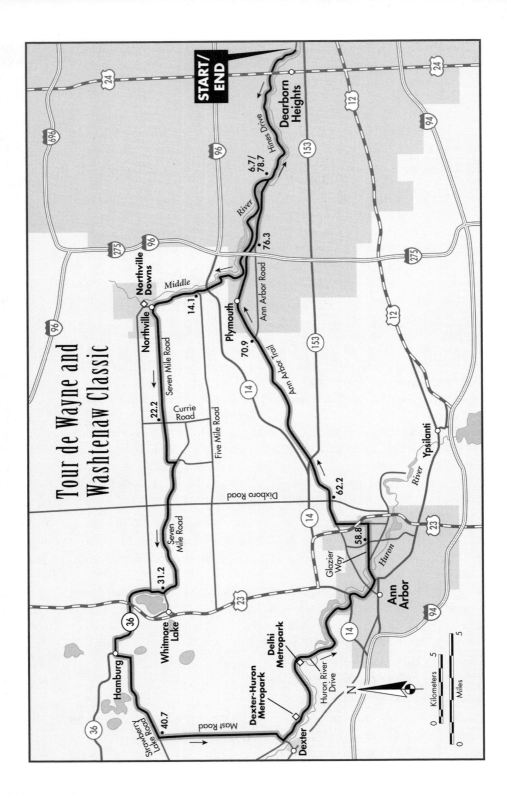

Tour de Wayne and Washtenaw Classic

START/END

Dearborn Heights

6.7/78.7
Hines Drive
River

76.3

Northville Downs
Middle

Northville

14.1

Plymouth
70.9
Ann Arbor Road

22.2
Currie Road
Seven Mile Road

Five Mile Road

Ann Arbor Trail

62.2

Dixboro Road

Seven Mile Road

31.2

58.8

Whitmore Lake

Glazier Way
Huron

Hamburg

Ann Arbor

Delhi Metropark

Dexter-Huron Metropark
Huron River Drive

River
Ypsilanti

40.7
Strawberry Lake Road
Mast Road

Dexter

N

0 Kilometers 5

0 Miles 5

0.0 Turn left out of Helms Haven playground/parking area onto Hines Drive. Restrooms.

2.8 Watch for traffic merging onto Hines Drive on the right.

6.3 Nankin Mills Interpretive Area. Nature Center open Tuesdays to Saturdays 9:00 A.M. to 4:00 P.M. Restrooms across road.

13.7 Stop sign. Turn left on Northville Road (T intersection). Watch for more traffic. No shoulder here.

14.1 Traffic light at intersection with Five Mile Road. Continue straight, then turn sharply left to continue on Hines Drive. Shoulder resumes.

16.2 Stop sign. Bear left on Seven Mile Road West. Caution: Oncoming traffic does not stop.

16.3 Traffic light. Continue straight. **Sidetrip:** To visit downtown Northville, turn right onto Center Street. Northville Downs Racetrack on your right. Main Street is in 0.4 mile. Retrace your route and turn right on Seven Mile Road.

20.2 Cross Napier Road and enter Washtenaw County. Shoulder stops.

24.4 Stop sign/flashing red light. Turn right, staying on Seven Mile Road.

31.2 Stop sign. Turn right on East Shore Road at the T intersection. (To go into Whitmore Lake, turn left. Turn right on Main Street in 0.8 mile. Pizza places, Whitmore Lake Tavern, Dee's Ice Cream Store in 1.4 miles. Retrace your route.)

32.5 Stop sign. Turn left on Nine Mile Road, watching for traffic coming around the semiblind curve on the right.

32.9 Underpass under US 23.

36.1 Hamburg. Hamburg Food Center, Hamburg Pub. Shoulder ends.

36.3 Rough railroad tracks.

36.6 Turn right on Strawberry Lake Road.

40.7 Turn left on Mast Road, before pavement ends on Strawberry Lake Road.

46.4 Turn left on Huron River Drive, just after Dexter Party Store. (To go into Dexter, continue straight for a half mile. Mast becomes Central Street. Turn right at the stop sign on Main Street. Cookie shop, bakery, pub, and shops.)

47.5 Dexter-Huron Metropark. Restrooms.

48.8 Flashing yellow light at Zeeb Road. Watch for fast traffic.

50.5 Delhi Metropark. Restrooms.

53.7 Ann Arbor city limits.

55.5 Stop sign. Turn right on North Main Street. Watch for two lanes of heavy traffic merging from the left/behind you, coming off MI 14.

56.2 Turn left at traffic light on Depot Street.

(continued)

56.5 Amtrak Station. Restrooms inside. Go underneath trestle bridge, and watch for buckled sections of brick street.

56.9 Traffic light. Turn left on Glen Avenue. You are right behind the U-M Hospitals. Watch for more traffic. Can also ride along sidewalk bike path.

57.1 Traffic light at East Medical Center Drive/Maiden Lane. Continue straight onto Fuller Street. (Can also ride on bike path parallel to Fuller.)

58.4 Traffic light at Fuller Court/Glazier Way. Turn left on Glazier Way.

58.8 Intersection with Huron Parkway. Cross boulevard to stay on Glazier Way. Two hills ahead.

59.9 Stop sign/T intersection at Earhart Road. Turn left.

61.4 Turn right at traffic light onto Plymouth–Ann Arbor Road. Stay on shoulder.

62.5 Flashing yellow light for Cherry Hill Road. Dixboro General Store on right.

68.3 Plymouth Orchards and Cider Mill.

70.9 Flashing yellow light. Turn left on Ann Arbor Trail.

71.9 Plymouth Township Park on left. Restrooms.

73.5 Traffic light at Main Street in downtown Plymouth. Shops and restaurants in both directions. Continue straight from this intersection.

78.7 Traffic light. Turn right on Hines Drive.

85.6 Helms Haven Recreation Area.

♦ Held on Warren Avenue in East Dearborn, the Dearborn Arab International Festival is the epicenter of not only Michigan's but America's Arab community. Three days of food, music, dance, and cultural celebrations outside. (313) 945–1700; www.americanarab.com.

RESTAURANTS

♦ La Shish, East, 12918 Michigan Avenue, Dearborn; (313) 584–4477. La Shish West, 22039 Michigan Avenue, Dearborn; (313) 562–7200. A Middle Eastern meal is a must in Dearborn, the start of the ride and the home of the largest concentration of Middle Eastern citizens in the U.S.

♦ Rebecca's Restaurant, 134 North Center Street, Northville; (248) 348–2660. Breakfast, lunch, and ice cream daily. Dinner weekdays only.

♦ The Gandy Dancer, 401 Depot Street, Ann Arbor; (734) 769–0592. You won't want to go in your bike clothes. But if you're making this a two-day ride, Ann Arbor is a good overnight stop and will give you a chance to clean up. Reservations recommended.

♦ Dexter Pub, 8114 Main Street, Dexter; (734) 426–1234. Burgers, sandwiches in a cozy family atmosphere.

ACCOMMODATIONS

♦ Holiday Inn Fairlane-Dearborn, 5801 Southfield Service Drive, Detroit; (313) 336–3340. Five minutes from the start, Ford Road at the Southfield Freeway.

♦ Campus Inn, 615 East Huron Street, Ann Arbor; (734) 769–2200. If you make this a two-day ride with the overnight in Ann Arbor, go a few blocks farther on Main Street, hang a left on Huron Street, and you're there. Pricey.

♦ Embassy Hotel, 200 East Huron Street, Ann Arbor; (734) 662–7100. Farther east on Huron Street. Less expensive, much smaller.

RESTROOMS

♦ Start/finish: Helms Haven, also at regular intervals for the first 16 miles along Hines Drive (never more than 2 miles in between).

♦ Mile 31.5: establishments in Whitmore Lake (off route).

♦ Mile 36.1: Hamburg Pub.

♦ Mile 47.0: Dexter (off route).

♦ Mile 47.5: Dexter-Huron Metropark.

♦ Mile 50.5: Delhi Metropark.

♦ Mile 56.5: Amtrak station.

♦ Mile 71.9: Plymouth Township Park.

♦ Mile 73.5: establishments in Plymouth.

♦ Mile 78.7 and afterward at frequent intervals along Hines Drive.

Chelsea Ramble

Mix cool restaurants and shops, a vintage Main Street surrounded by well-preserved neighborhoods, and industry from food processing to automotive, surround it with lakes, trails, and public land, and you've got Chelsea. Located west of Ann Arbor, Chelsea combines college-town hipness with small-town flavor. Downtown is a wonderful place to sit with a cup of coffee and a paper or to people-watch. You'll earn it on the ride. Looping west of Chelsea through the Waterloo State Recreation Area—at 20,000 acres the largest park in the Lower Peninsula—this is one of the more difficult rambles in the book. While there are no big climbs, the ride is consistently rolling, and the winding roads are also narrow. This is a popular route with Ann Arbor–area cyclists, however, so drivers are used to cyclists.

A ride through the Waterloo State Recreation Area is a like reading a good book, one that makes you want to keep turning pages. You want to keep riding to see what's around the next bend or over the next rise. Dotted with lakes, bogs, marshes, woods, and farms, the area has an untamed feel that reminds me a bit of the Upper Peninsula. It's hard to believe that you're in southeastern Michigan.

Leaving Chelsea, you'll ride through a pleasant neighborhood of older homes, many with well-tended, colorful yards. After crossing a rough set of railroad tracks, you'll embark on the body of the route. While you'll see farms, it's not what you think of as typical farm country. Trees are thick and plentiful, but it's not a forest environment, either. The swampland that fills in between the dozen or so lakes allows vegetation to grow, but not to forest heights. As a result, it seems like you overlook the top of the cattails and other plants that thrive in wet conditions, to the forests or fields or lakes beyond. It's a variegated view that is most enjoyable from a bike seat.

Facilities are a bit scarce on this ride. If you don't want to go all the way to Portage Lake (and I'd recommend the option only if you want a few extra miles, not because Portage Lake is anything spectacular) but don't think you can wait until Waterloo at mile 17.6, then you should pedal the extra 0.7 mile or so to the corner store and restaurant intersection of Seymour and Portage Lake Roads. You'll have crossed the county line from Washtenaw to Jackson County at this point. The ride turns north briefly and then back east. Just before crossing back into Washtenaw, you'll reach the community of Waterloo. Consisting of Frank's Mill Pond Pizza, Grill and Dairy Bar (all in one place) and the Village Market, it's a good place to get a snack to fuel up for the hilliest part of the ride, which is just ahead. Check out the mural map painted on the Village Market wall and see if you can find your location without looking for the "you are here" arrow.

While in the homestretch, you'll no doubt notice the fence topped with rolled wire off Waterloo Road—it belongs to an alternative state corrections facility. It's a bit foreboding but also gives you an appreciation for the freedom you have to savor an afternoon of bike riding—followed, perhaps, by a slice of quiche at Zou Zou's or dessert at the Common Grill.

LOCAL INFORMATION

♦ Chelsea Area Chamber of Commerce; (734) 475–1145; www.chelseaweb.com.

LOCAL EVENTS/ATTRACTIONS

♦ Actor Jeff Daniels founded the Purple Rose Theatre in his hometown. Features performances of original and Broadway productions, plus educational programming. Even if you don't go to a show, wander down to take a look at

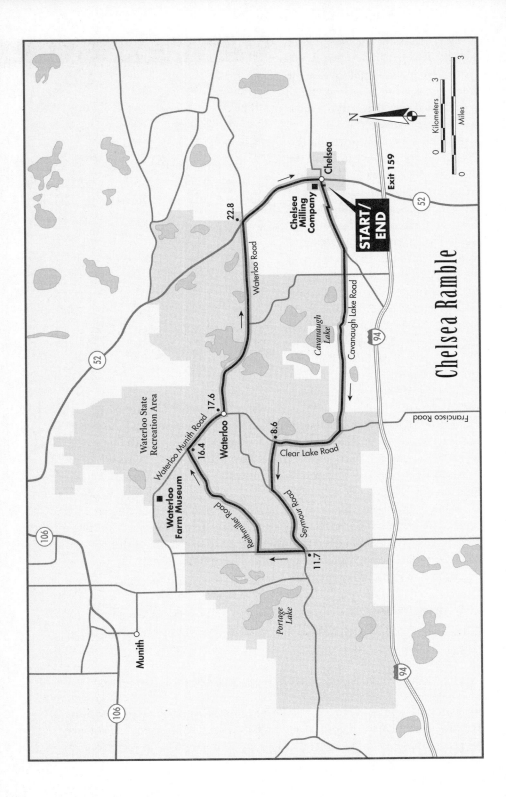

Chelsea Ramble

0.0 From the village parking lot, head out of town on Middle Street, going southwesterly. From the recommended parking lot, this is a left turn.

0.6 Yield and follow road curve to right. Cross rough railroad tracks. Road curves to left and becomes Cavanaugh Lake Road.

3.8 Sharp curve to the right. Road becomes Kalmbach Road. Chelsea Greenhouse. Road then curves to left and goes back to Cavanaugh Lake, and will later become Harvey Road.

6.8 Stop sign. Turn right onto Clear Lake Road.

8.4 Clear Lake Jackson County Park.

8.6 Turn left on Trist Road, which comes up quickly. **Option:** For 17.5-mile ride, continue straight on Clear Lake Road for 1.5 miles to Waterloo and continue from mile 17.6 below.

9.8 Follow curve to the left. Stay on the upper road, following signs to Portage Lake and Jackson. Road becomes Seymour Road.

11.7 Turn right on Mt. Hope Road. **Sidetrip:** For the 4-mile spur to Portage Lake, continue straight for 0.7 mile, then turn right on Portage Lake Road. Country Corner Store and Rico's Grill at intersection of Seymour and Portage Lake Roads. Portage Lake is 1 mile ahead. Retrace route.

12.8 Right on Reithmiller Road.

16.4 Stop sign. Turn right on Waterloo-Munith Road.

17.6 Waterloo. Frank's Mill Pond Pizza, Grill and Dairy Bar (restrooms for customers), Village Market. Cross Clear Lake Road and continue on Waterloo Road.

19.7 Curve to left, staying on Waterloo Road.

22.8 Stop sign. Turn right onto MI 52 and stay on shoulder.

25.1 Cross railroad tracks, then turn right on Middle Street and left into parking lot.

the building and, if it's open, the lobby. 137 Park Street, Chelsea. Box office: (734) 433–ROSE; www.purplerosetheatre.org.

♦ The Waterloo Area Farm Museum features a restored nineteenth-century home and other buildings, including a barn, one-room schoolhouse, and windmill. 9998 Waterloo-Munith Road, Waterloo Township; (517) 596–2254 or (734) 426–9135.

♦ Jiffy Mix is made in Chelsea, and Chelsea Milling's giant warehouse towers give Chelsea a distinctive skyline. Tours of the plant may be arranged in advance weekdays from 9:00 A.M. to 1:30 P.M. Call (734) 475–1361 to make reservations. www.jiffymix.com.

♦ Waterloo State Recreation Area: At almost 20,000 acres, the park boasts 11 lakes, 47 miles of hiking trails, 13 rustic cabins, and numerous equestrian trails. The Gerald E. Eddy Geology Center features year-round exhibits and nature programs on Michigan's geologic history. 16345 McClure Road, Chelsea; (313) 475–8307.

RESTAURANTS

♦ Common Grill, 112 South Main Street, Chelsea; (734) 475–0470. Anything but common. Chef Craig Common was solicited by Jeff Daniels' father to open a restaurant in Chelsea for Purple Rose Theatre patrons. Serving what it calls "upscale American bistro" cuisine, it's been a hit for more than a decade.
♦ Zou Zou's, 101 North Main Street, Chelsea; (734) 433–4226. Coffee, edibles, and art. Have a cup of coffee and sit and read awhile.
♦ Rico's Grill, 1227 Seymour Road, Grass Lake; (517) 522–3400. Located on the spur to Portage Lake. Outdoor dining. Sandwiches, pasta, steaks, seafood.

ACCOMMODATIONS

♦ South House Bed and Breakfast, 120 South Street, Chelsea; (734) 475–9300. Victorian home 1 block from downtown.
♦ Chelsea House Victorian Inn, 118 East Middle Street, Chelsea; (734) 433–HOME; http://chelseaweb.com/directory/chelseahouse.html. Another downtown B&B.
♦ Holiday Inn Express, 1540 Commerce Park Road, Chelsea; (734) 433–1600. Just off the interstate.

RESTROOMS

♦ Mile 12.4: store/restaurant (optional spur).
♦ Mile 13.5: Portage Lake (optional spur).
♦ Mile 17.6: Frank's (sign says customers only, so buy an ice-cream cone or something).

36

Hines Drive Ramble

The Hines Drive Ramble follows the path of the Middle Rouge River through western Wayne County and some of the older, inner-ring Detroit suburbs. This is the same Rouge River along which Henry Ford built his famous Rouge plant, one of the wonders of the industrial age. But though you're just minutes from the Motor City, it won't feel like it. Lined with playgrounds and picnic areas, ball fields and golf courses, Hines Drive cuts a welcome swath of green through the concrete. The ramble is an out-and-back ride, so riders can customize the distance to their liking and ability. The shops, restaurants, and cafes in pedestrian-friendly downtown Northville, an upscale community that hasn't forgotten its heritage, await at the end of the ride.

Hines Drive is a linear park that winds its way through the western half of Wayne County. For city riding, it's hard to beat. On the 6-mile stretch closed to cars on summer Saturdays, you'll have plenty of company including other riders, both serious and recreational, in-line skaters, parents pushing strollers, and the occasional walk-for-a-cause group event. Besides the wide shoulder, there is also a bike path/sidewalk paralleling Hines. However, it's not as smooth or wide as the road. You'll be more comfortable and have a better view from the road.

There's a playground or ball field about every mile on Hines Drive, with restrooms almost as frequently, making it a great one to do with kids. One of the places you'll likely linger longest is Nankin Mills Interpretive Center at mile 6.3. Two gristmills built in the mid-nineteenth century occupied this site, which Henry Ford purchased as part of a plan to develop village mill industries along the Rouge, producing engravings, carburetor parts, rivets, and bearings.

Start: Helms Haven playground area, on Hines Drive just west of Outer Drive in Dearborn. (*Alternate start for those who want a shorter ride:* Nankin Mills Interpretive Center, at mile 6.3.)

Length: 33.3-mile out and back.

Terrain: Mostly flat. A couple small changes in grade.

Traffic and hazards: There is some rough pavement on this route. Two-lane Hines Road can be busy but has a shoulder on both sides wide enough for two to easily ride abreast. The ramble is best ridden Saturdays from the first of May through the end of September, when a 6-mile stretch of Hines Drive (Warrendale parking area to Nankin Mills) is closed to vehicular traffic from 9:00 A.M. to 3:00 P.M. Use caution between mile 13.7 and 14.1, when you'll turn left onto busier Northville road in order to continue on Hines Drive. This route is not recommended for early spring, as the Rouge frequently floods its banks, putting portions of the road under water.

Getting there: *From the west:* Take the Hines Drive exit, located between the Southfield Freeway (Michigan Highway 39) and Telegraph Road (U.S. Highway 24) off westbound Ford Road (Michigan Highway 153). Cross the light at Outer Drive. Helms Haven is about a quarter mile down on your left. *From the east:* Go east on Ford Road to Outer Drive. Turn left on Outer Drive (a "Michigan left," which means going through the intersection, making a U-turn to head back westbound on Ford Road, and then turning right onto Outer Drive). Pass St. Anselm Church on your

(continued)

Ford, who had strong ideas about people and society, believed farmers working in an atmosphere of cleanliness and tranquility would restore balance between industrial cities and rural areas.

The mills were unprofitable, however, and closed after World War II. Wayne County Parks then acquired Nankin Mills, and it opened as a nature center in 1956. Nankin Mills often hosts special events that require advance registration and a small fee. See the "Local Information" section for more details.

For the first half of the ride, the Rouge runs a narrow course through high banks and is largely hidden by trees drooping over it. At about 9 miles, however, the river finds a wider, more open path. Sumac Pointe Recreation Area at mile 9.4 is a nice spot to pull over and admire it.

At mile 12.7 you'll have the option to go to "Historic Old Village," a 4-square-block area with cafes, antiques shops, and a bookstore. It's similar to but on a smaller scale than Northville at the end of the ride.

Just outside downtown Northville is the Northville Downs Racetrack. It offers live harness racing from October through the beginning of April, but if you're taking an early spring or late fall ride, you might want to check it out.

Up the hill from the racetrack is downtown Northville. The town's Victorian-era buildings give the pedestrian-friendly downtown much of its charm. From Center Street, turn right on Main Street. A drinking fountain by the clock tower is a place to refill your water bottles. Farther down on Main is the Water Wheel Center, formerly the Ford valve plant. The waterwheel that provided power to the plant still works.

While on that end of town, stroll down Griswold Street to visit Mill Race Village, an 11-acre collection of nineteenth-century buildings, including a blacksmith shop, an inn, several homes, a church, and an interurban rail station. It's operated by the Northville Historical Society.

Coming back to the central business district, choose from coffeehouses, cafes, ice-cream shops, and restaurants galore.

THE BASICS (continued)

left. Hines Drive is the second light. Turn left. Helms Haven is about a quarter mile down on your left.

The alternate start, Nankin Mills Interpretive Center, is 6 miles farther west on Hines Drive on the right. It can also be accessed off Merriman Road, a major north-south road that intersects Interstates 94 and 96. Take the Hines Drive exit off Merriman and go about 1 mile west.

Part of Hines Drive is closed to cars on summer Saturdays, making it one of the most popular places to ride in metro Detroit. Courtesy of Michael O. Henderson

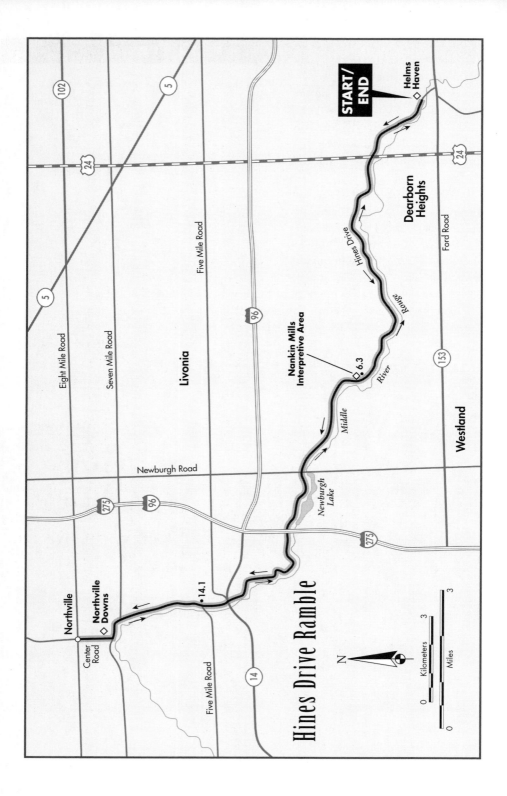

Hines Drive Ramble

START/
END

◇ Helms
Haven

Dearborn
Heights

Hines Drive

◇ 6.3
Nankin Mills
Interpretive Area

Middle

Rouge

River

Livonia

Westland

Eight Mile Road

Seven Mile Road

Five Mile Road

Newburgh Road

Newburgh
Lake

102

5

24

5

96

24

153

Ford Road

275

96

275

14

Northville

Northville
Downs ◇

Center
Road

• 14.1

Five Mile Road

N

0 — Kilometers — 3

0 — Miles — 3

0.0 Turn left out of Helms Haven playground/parking area onto Hines Drive. Restrooms.

0.5 Warrendale parking area.

0.9 Parr Recreation Area. Restrooms.

2.0 Bridge. Road narrows, shoulder disappears but resumes afterward.

2.7 Nolar Bend Recreation Area. Restrooms.

2.8 Watch for traffic merging onto Hines Drive on the right.

3.1 Perrin Recreation Area. Restrooms.

5.3 Merriman Hollow Recreation Area. Restrooms, picnic pavilion.

5.5 Hawthorne Ridge Recreation Area. Restrooms.

6.3 Nankin Mills Interpretive Area. Nature Center open Tuesdays to Saturdays 9:00 A.M. to 4:00 P.M. Restrooms across road. **Option:** Start here to shorten the ride to 20.7 miles.

8.4 Levan Knoll Recreation Area. Restrooms.

9.9 Newburgh Pointe Recreation Area. Restrooms.

12.8 Traffic light at Wilcox Road. Continue straight or turn left to visit "Historic Old Village." Go a quarter mile to Mill Street. Turn left at the fork. Take Mill Street to Liberty and turn right. Turn right on Starkweather, which merges with Mill and takes you back to Hines Drive. Turn left at the traffic light onto Hines.

12.9 Wilcox Lake Recreation Area. Restrooms.

13.8 Stop sign. Turn left on Northville Road (T intersection). Watch for more traffic. No shoulder here.

14.1 Traffic light at intersection with Five Mile Road, after railroad trestle. Go through light, then turn sharply left to continue on Hines Drive. Shoulder resumes.

15.5 Benton Hills Disc Golf Course.

16.0 Northville West Recreation Area. Restrooms.

16.4 Stop sign. Bear left on Seven Mile Road West. Caution, oncoming traffic does not stop.

16.5 Traffic light. Turn right onto Center Street. Northville Downs Racetrack on your right. Follow Center into downtown Northville.

16.7 Main Street. To leave town, return to this intersection and turn left on Center Road.

17.1 Turn left at the light onto Seven Mile Road after passing Northville Downs, and veer right onto Hines Drive.

19.2 Stop sign. Turn right on Northville Road. Go through light at Five Mile Road, then underneath railroad trestle.

(continued)

19.6 Turn right on Hines Drive, turning opposite large yellow sign with arrow pointing left for Northville Road.

27.0 Nankin Mills.

33.3 Helms Haven Recreation Area on the right.

LOCAL INFORMATION

♦ Wayne County Parks: For special events at Nankin Mills Interpretive Center, (734) 261–1990 or go to www.waynecounty.com/parks/events.htm and click on "Nankin Mills."

♦ Northville Community Chamber of Commerce, 195 South Main Street, Northville; (248) 349–8730; www.northville.org.

LOCAL EVENTS/ATTRACTIONS

♦ A flower sale is held on Saturday and Sunday of Memorial Day weekend in downtown Northville.

♦ Parmenter's Cider Mill is open from the end of August through the end of November. 714 Baseline Road, east of Novi Road, south of Eight Mile Road, Northville; (248) 349–3181.

♦ Northville Downs runs harness racing from October through early April. Located at Seven Mile and Sheldon Roads, Northville. (248) 349–1000.

♦ Maybury State Park contains 1,000 acres and miles of trails for hiking, mountain biking, horseback riding, and cross-country skiing; (248) 349–8390. Also Living Farm, a 40-acre replica of a 1900s Wayne County farm with a hands-on livestock exhibit. Beck Road at Seven Mile Road, Northville.

RESTAURANTS

♦ Tuscan Cafe, 150 Center Street, Northville; (248) 305–8629. Funky coffeehouse atmosphere. Serving bread from the dean of Detroit-area delis, Ann Arbor's Zingerman's. Recommended by staff at D & D Bicycles across the street.

♦ Rebecca's Restaurant, 134 North Center Street, Northville; (248) 348–2660. Also recommended by the folks at D & D Bicycles. Breakfast, lunch, and ice cream daily. Dinner weekdays only.

♦ Starting Gate Saloon, 135 Center Street, Northville; (248) 349–5660. Bar-and-grill fare.

♦ American Spoon Foods, 105 Center Street, Northville; (248) 347–1643.

◆ Genetti's Hole in the Wall, 108 East Main Street, Northville; (248) 349–0522. Dinner theater.

ACCOMMODATIONS

◆ Fraser Inn, 501 West Dunlap, Northville; (248) 349–8809. Bed-and-breakfast.
◆ Hampton Inn, 20600 Haggerty Road, Northville; (734) 462–1119.
◆ Country Inn & Suites, 2165 Haggerty Road, Novi; (248) 596–9800.

RESTROOMS

◆ There are many restrooms along the route; you won't ride more than 3 miles without coming across one.

Downriver Ramble

The historically working-class communities along the Detroit River, south of the city, are collectively known as the "downriver" area. While the area's reputation is industrial, and eyebrows may rise when you say you're going to ride downriver, this ramble follows the river to an urban oasis—Grosse Ile. The largest island in the Detroit River, Grosse Ile is now an upscale suburban community with quiet, mostly well-paved roads and a bike path bisecting the island. Homes are built across the road from the shoreline, so you'll have a water view along the perimeter roads. There's a small business district with restaurants to relax in before you return to the mainland.

The downriver suburbs grew up as the bedroom communities for the working class who spent their days on Detroit's assembly lines. These days, Wyandotte, the starting point for the ramble, is experiencing gentrification. Upscale condos now line the river, and the downtown, where a well-regarded art fair is held in mid-July, is resurging. You'll ride through downtown on your way to Grosse Ile, crossing over a short bridge. The bike toll is 25 cents.

After crossing the bridge, you'll see the bike path that bisects Grosse Ile north to south. For the moment, however, stick to the roads and continue east, over to the opposite shore.

Once on the northeast side of the island, as you look upriver on a clear day, you'll be able to see the skyline of Detroit, notably the triple towers of the Renaissance Center. On a cloudy or foggy day, it looks more ghostly, like a mirage. That's also how it feels. You might spot one of the local bumper stickers: SLOW DOWN. THIS AIN'T THE MAINLAND. In a car or on a bike, Grosse Ile is

10 square miles of sanctuary from the Motor City.

Across the river lie the shores of Ontario, Canada. To most people, Canada is America's northern neighbor. The peninsula that pokes between Lake St. Clair and Lake Erie, however, is Canada's southernmost point. The city of Detroit is in fact north of Windsor, its Canadian sister.

The Detroit River connects those two lakes, and Grosse Ile is the largest of some twenty-one islands scattered along its 32-mile course. Both the Potawatomi Indians and the French explorers used its size to name it. The Potawatomi called it *Kitche-min-ishen.* French explorers called it *La Grosse Ile,* from which the present-day Grosse Ile was derived.

Its strategic location on a major waterway between two nations has given Grosse Ile a rich history, which you'll learn about riding along East River Road. At mile 7.1 you'll see St. James Episcopal Chapel, a site on the National Register of Historic Places. It was built in 1867 with the willed savings of a freed slave. A military outpost maintained by the U.S. Army after the War of 1812 is noted farther south. Some of the island's earliest homes, built prior to the Civil War, are also along East River Road.

You'll take East River Road until Groh Road. Turn right and you'll come to Knapp's Island Alpacas, right next to the municipal airport. There's a place for the public to watch the alpacas graze. The airport, at mile 9.0, now servicing primarily private planes, was a U.S. Naval Air Station during World War II. According to the Grosse Ile Historical Society, the first President George Bush was stationed there for a couple months shortly before the war ended.

Rounding the southern tip of the island, you'll come up West River Road. There's some rough pavement here, and the view of the smokestacks on the other side of the river here contrasts sharply with the open views from East River Road. The Famous American Grill restaurant is located at the Water's Edge Country Club at mile 10.0. It's open to the public. Stop here for lunch or

THE BASICS

Start: Wyandotte city parking lot #1.

Length: 18.1-mile lariat.

Terrain: Flat. Some rougher pavement on West River Road between miles 10 and 11.

Traffic and hazards: Use caution on Biddle Avenue/Jefferson Avenue through downtown Wyandotte, especially at the Y intersection where you'll veer off to Grosse Ile, as you will cross in front of both lanes of traffic. The bridge across the Detroit River to the island is a grate surface for less than 0.1 mile; ride with caution here. You'll also need two bits for the bike toll.

Getting there: From southbound Interstate 75, exit at Southfield Road. Take Southfield east until it dead-ends into the river. Turn right onto Jefferson Avenue, which later becomes Biddle Avenue. Follow this 2.6 miles into downtown Wyandotte, passing Henry Ford Wyandotte Hospital, and turn left on Oak Street. Park in the city parking lot along the river.

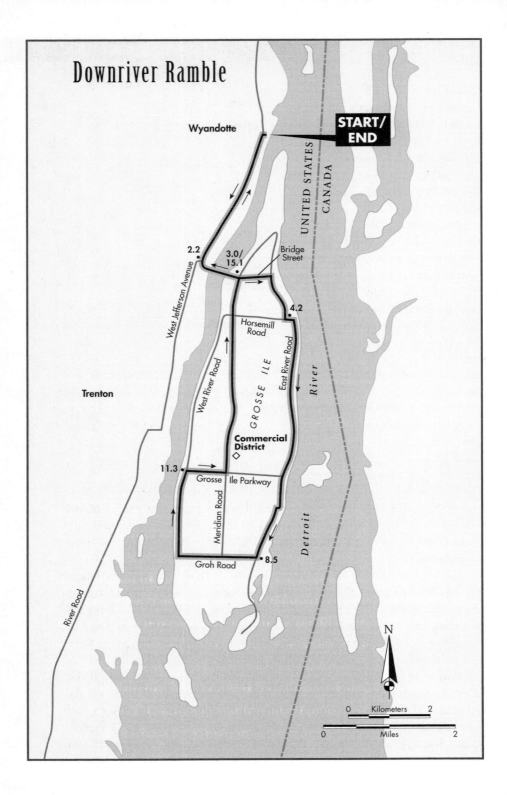

Downriver Ramble

Wyandotte

START/ END

UNITED STATES

CANADA

2.2

3.0/ 15.1

Bridge Street

West Jefferson Avenue

4.2

Horsemill Road

GROSSE ILE

West River Road

East River Road

Trenton

Commercial District

11.3

Grosse Ile Parkway

Meridian Road

Detroit

Groh Road

8.5

River

River Road

N

0 Kilometers 2

0 Miles 2

0.0 From the parking lot, turn left onto Oak Street.

0.1 Traffic light. Turn left onto Biddle Avenue.

0.4 Traffic light at Eureka Road. Continue straight to ride on road, or turn left and get on sidewalk paralleling street, which becomes a bike path in 0.3 mile.

1.5 Traffic light at Pennsylvania. Biddle becomes Jefferson. Continue straight.

1.9 Two sets of rough railroad tracks.

2.2 Bear left at Y intersection, following sign for bridge. Use caution, as you will be crossing in front of upcoming and oncoming traffic.

2.5 Cross bridge. Less than 0.1-mile section of grate surface in the middle, by the toll booth. Bike toll is 25 cents.

3.0 Traffic light at Meridian Road. Cross and continue on Bridge Street. Corner by bike path is where signs for community events and festivals are often placed.

3.5 Stop sign at T intersection. Turn right on Parke Lane.

4.2 Stop sign. Turn left on Horse Mill Road. Follow around curve; becomes East River Road.

7.5 Stop sign. East River Road jogs to the right, then left.

8.5 Turn right on Groh Road. Ride on road or on bike path on opposite side of road.

9.1 Flashing red light/stop sign. Cross Meridian Road. Bike path switches sides of street here.

9.5 Bike path switches sides again.

9.7 Stop sign. Cross South Point Drive and follow Groh around to the right; it becomes West River Road. Bike path ends; if riding on it, turn left onto Groh and follow around to West River. Some rough pavement ahead.

11.1 Turn right on unmarked road, back inland.

11.3 Stop sign. Turn right on Grosse Ile Parkway.

11.8 Traffic light at Meridian Road. Turn left, riding on road or along bike path.

12.1 Traffic light at Macomb Street. Turn right to visit Grosse Ile's commercial district, including shops and restaurants.

12.6 Flashing light at Ferry Street. Continue straight. Bike path switches to other side of street. It will switch back and forth along Meridian.

15.1 Traffic light. Turn left on Bridge Street to cross bridge. Pay 25-cent toll.

15.8 Traffic light. Turn right on Jefferson Avenue.

16.1 Two sets of rough railroad tracks.

16.5 Traffic light at Pennsylvania. Jefferson becomes Biddle. Continue straight.

16.7 Bike path parallels Jefferson Avenue.

17.4 Bike path ends, becomes sidewalk.

18.0 Turn right at light on Oak Street.

18.1 Turn right to return to parking lot.

St. James Episcopal Church on Grosse Isle was built with the willed savings of a freed slave.
Courtesy of Michael O. Henderson

hang on for the few miles to the island's commercial district and more choices.

At the Grosse Ile Parkway, the "free" bridge connecting the island with the mainland, turn right. Turn left on Meridian Road and take either the road or the bike path that bisects the island to Macomb Street and Grosse Ile's commercial district.

After exploring the shops and restaurants along Macomb, continue north on Meridian or on the bike path paralleling it. Turn left on Bridge Street at mile 15.1 to return to the mainland. Remember the bumper sticker, and be prepared for more traffic as you pedal back to Wyandotte.

LOCAL INFORMATION

♦ City of Wyandotte; www.wyandotte.net, click on "Local Business" and then "Dining Out" for a thorough restaurant guide.
♦ Grosse Ile Township; www.grosseile.com (calendar of events and historical society link).
♦ Grosse Ile information: Tune radio to 1700 AM.
♦ Downriver Council for the Arts; www.downriverarts.org (an online calendar of events).

LOCAL EVENTS/ATTRACTIONS

♦ IslandFest: Held at the end of May/beginning of June, Grosse Ile's community festival includes a parade, pancake breakfast, fireworks, and guided historical tours. (734) 675–2364.
♦ The Wyandotte Street Art Fair is a juried art fair on Biddle Street in downtown Wyandotte. Mid-July. Call (734) 324–4506 or see the Wyandotte Web site listed above.
♦ The Detroit International Freedom Festival is a joint American-Canadian patriotic festival celebrated with Windsor, Ontario. Held in late June. (313) 923–7400.

RESTAURANTS

♦ Airport Inn, 9264 Groh Road, Grosse Ile; (734) 675–4200. By the airport, of course. Pizza, sandwiches, burgers.
♦ Kathy's Café, 9105 Macomb Street, Grosse Ile; (734) 671–0059. Cheap and hearty. They serve waffle-cut fries! Smoking in main dining area, but points for allowing non-patrons in bike shorts to use restroom. First restaurant on the Macomb strip; go a little farther for more restaurants, including a bakery and coffee shop.
♦ Famous American Grill, 25555 West River Road, Grosse Ile; (734) 362–1099. At Grosse Ile's Water's Edge Country Club, but open to the public.

◆ Portofino on the River, 3455 Biddle Avenue, Wyandotte; (734) 281–6700. Change out of your bike shorts before you go.
◆ Sport's Brew Pub, 166 Maple Street, Wyandotte; (734) 285–5060. Watch the Wings, Wolverines, Lions, or Tigers here. Probably not the Tour de France, though. Outdoor dining available.

ACCOMMODATIONS

◆ Holiday Inn Express, 21500 West Road, Woodhaven; (800) 359–5672. About ten minutes from start.
◆ Grosse Ile Pilot House, 9645 Groh Road, Grosse Ile; (734) 671–2295.
◆ Bishop Cottage Bed and Breakfast, Grosse Ile; (734) 671–9191.
◆ Dearborn Inn, 20301 Oakwood Boulevard, Dearborn; (313) 271–2700. Historic hotel built in 1931. Dining also available. About fifteen minutes from start.

RESTROOMS

◆ Mile 12.1: restaurants on Macomb Street.

Belle Isle Ramble

B elle Isle is a microcosm of the city of Detroit. Potential for destination-city status abounds, but there's much to overcome to achieve it. When and if that happens, though, Belle Isle will no doubt be part of the reason why. Designed by the same man who planned New York's Central Park, it's an oasis of green. It has a great view. It has some wonderful facilities, including an aquarium, a conservatory, and a beautiful, huge marble fountain. It's home to the Detroit Yacht Club. Belle Isle also has a closed zoo, restrooms in poor condition, and eyesores like a dilapidated nature center oddly juxtaposed opposite a new, beautifully landscaped golf course. Though this ride is classified as a ramble, riders should be experienced and game for an adventure.

There's no doubt that you're in the Motor City on this ride. On the way to the start, you'll pass the headquarters of the United Auto Workers, Solidarity House. GM's logo is emblazoned atop the Renaissance Center, better known as the RenCen, the most prominent building on the city skyline. If you do the extra miles into Detroit, you'll cross over the Chrysler Freeway.

But Belle Isle is truly a world removed. "A jewel in the hearts of Detroiters," proclaims the historical marker on the island, named for then-Gov. Lewis Cass's daughter Isabella in 1845 and purchased by the city of Detroit in 1879. Today the jewel shows tarnish here and there, with some facilities closed and others whose maintenance is mediocre. But it still provides a huge chunk of accessible, recreational green space to residents of this otherwise paved-over city. City officials dream of a revived riverfront, with parks and paths connecting the Belle Isle bridge to the RenCen and downtown. That's years away. But

Start: Riverside parking lot across from Scott Fountain.

Length: 10.8-mile double loop, with an optional 6.6-mile sidetrip to downtown Detroit's Greektown entertainment neighborhood.

Terrain: Flat.

Traffic and hazards: Watch for glass on roads. This ramble best ridden in morning or early afternoon. Belle Isle attracts a young, party-minded crowd in the evenings, especially at the east end. While the extra 6.6 miles to downtown Detroit and back is pleasant for urban riding, it *is* urban riding and is not recommended for kids due to frequent lights and one very busy crossing (Jefferson Avenue). For ultimate peace of mind, scout the route in your car first. Bring a bike lock. Greektown is, however, one of the most bustling, safe neighborhoods in the city, with real big-city flavor that sets this ride apart from others in this book.

Getting there: From Interstate 94, take exit 218 to Van Dyke Avenue, which is north of Interstate 75. Turn right at the light at the top of the exit ramp. Kettering High School will be on your right. Go about 2 miles south to Jefferson Avenue (be aware that the neighborhood you'll ride in does improve significantly) and turn right at the light. At the fourth light, turn right on Grand Boulevard to make a "Michigan left." You'll turn around immediately, at the sign that says TO BELLE ISLE crossing Jefferson Avenue onto the Douglas MacArthur Bridge. The entrance/exit to the island is a traffic circle. Follow the one-way road to the right. Park in the lot on the right at the intersection of Sunset and Fountain Drives, across from the fountain.

it's something to think about as you circle the 981-acre park, planned by Frederick Law Olmsted, who also designed Central Park in New York City.

The ride starts from a parking lot on the island's western end and consists of two counterclockwise loops. On the exterior loop, car traffic is one-way. From the parking lot, which offers a view of Detroit's skyline, you'll quickly round Belle Isle's narrow, pointed west end. As you ride along the Strand, which runs the length of the island, you'll have a view of Windsor, Ontario, on the south bank of the Detroit River. South? It's true. The river wraps around a Canadian peninsula, giving Detroit the geographical distinction of being north of Canada. The Detroit-Windsor border is the busiest crossing between the two countries, connected by both the Ambassador Bridge (visible back at the parking lot) and a tunnel under the river. The river is a busy transportation route, too, and freighters are a common sight.

Most attractions are easily accessible from either loop of this ride. Since what's open and closed can change with some frequency, visit the White House (park office) for a map and the most current information on what's open.

To get there, turn left at Inselruhe, 1 mile down on The Strand. You'll see the Whitcomb Conservatory and aquarium on your left. Public facilities are concentrated on the western end of the island, while the eastern end has

The Detroit River is a major commercial thoroughfare, and freighters glide by Belle Isle daily.
Courtesy of Travel Michigan

more open space. The Strand becomes Lakeside Drive after the Coast Guard station at the southeastern end. Well-kept golf facilities are on the right, and in one of those odd juxtapositions, a dilapidated nature center building is on the left. Rounding the eastern end you'll pass Lake Muskoday, the third of three inland lakes, on the left and the Detroit Yacht Club on the right. The road becomes Riverbank Road. The most consistently open restrooms are on your left at mile 4.7. You'll pass them again on the inner loop.

Approaching the traffic circle that controls traffic entering and exiting Belle Isle, move into the left lane so you're not routed off the island. You'll come to the parking area, where you'll turn left on Fountain Drive to ride the inner loop.

Scott Memorial Fountain is one place where Belle Isle shines. James Scott, an eccentric city benefactor, bequeathed his fortune to build the huge white marble fountain, erected in 1933. "From the good deed of one comes benefit to many," reads the inscription on the bronze armchair in which Scott's figure is ensconced, looking over his fountain out to the city skyline.

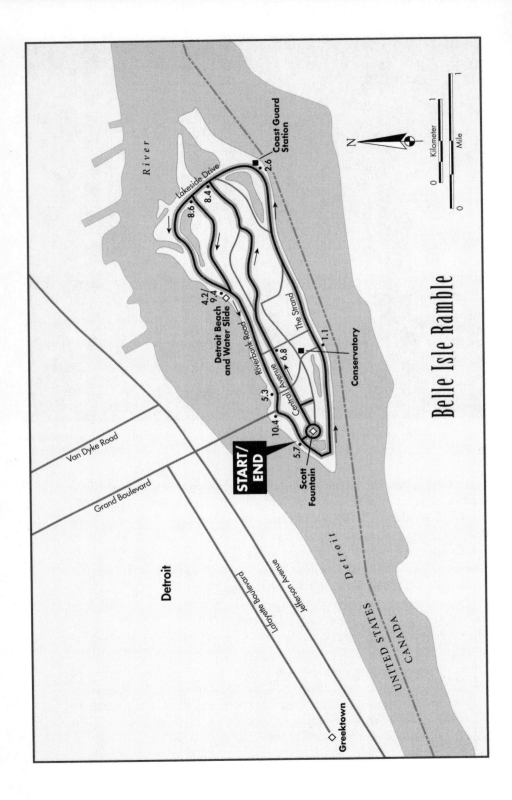

Belle Isle Ramble

0.0 From the parking lot opposite the fountain, turn right onto Sunset Drive.

0.5 Road becomes The Strand. The shore across the river is Windsor, Ontario.

1.1 Intersection with Picnic Way. Turn left for Whitcomb Conservatory and aquarium.

1.2 Intersection with Inselruhe. Turn left here to go to the White House (park office) for a map of the island. Conservatory and aquarium on left.

2.1 Fork in the road. Continue straight on The Strand.

2.6 Coast Guard station. Road becomes Lakeside Drive. Rougher pavement here.

4.2 City of Detroit beach and water slide. Restrooms open when water slide is open. Road becomes Riverbank Road.

4.7 Bath/Lunch pavilion on left. Restrooms.

5.4 Merge into left lane to go around entrance/exit traffic circle. Turn left at flagpole. Right-lane traffic is routed over Douglas MacArthur Bridge off island.

5.6 Veer to right at Belle Isle Park welcome sign. Left will take you back around traffic circle.

5.7 Turn left on Fountain Drive to continue on inner loop. Follow road around Scott Fountain.

6.0 Turn right on Central Avenue.

6.2 Turn right on Casino Way for restrooms at Casino building and historical marker. Return to Central Avenue.

6.8 Intersection with Inselruhe. Turn right to visit Whitcomb Conservatory and aquarium, or follow Central around the statue on the right. Giant slide on right, Bath/Lunch pavilion and restrooms on left.

7.1 Belle Isle Zoo—closed.

7.5 Cross bridge and veer to right.

7.7 Veer to right.

8.4 Stop sign. Turn left on Lakeside Drive.

8.6 Turn left on Oakway Trail.

9.4 Golf course. Refreshments and restrooms. Stop sign immediately afterward, merge onto Riverbank Road. Water slide.

9.9 Bath/Lunch pavilion. Restrooms.

10.4 Merge into left lane to go around entrance/exit traffic circle. Turn left at flagpole.

10.6 Veer to right at Belle Isle Park welcome sign. Left will take you back around traffic circle.

10.8 Parking lot on right.

(continued)

0.0 **Sidetrip:** To visit Detroit's Greektown entertainment neighborhood, begin at mile 10.4, above. Stay in the right lane and cross the Douglas MacArthur Bridge.

0.6 Cross the traffic light at Jefferson Avenue.

0.8 Traffic light at Lafayette Boulevard. Turn left.

1.7 Traffic light at Robert Brady Drive. Road widens to six lanes and center median begins. Continue straight.

3.1 Lafayette intersects Beaubien Street. Greektown Casino on right. Detroit People Mover (elevated light rail train) above. Lock bikes to bench or sign post. Explore Greektown on foot, or board the People Mover at the station on Beaubien south of Lafayette for a loop tour of downtown Detroit. To return to Belle Isle, return to the intersection of Lafayette and Beaubien and ride east on Lafayette.

4.5 Traffic light at Robert Brady Drive. Continue straight. Road narrows to two lanes.

5.4 Traffic light at East Grand Boulevard. Turn right.

5.5 Straight through light for turning traffic.

5.6 Traffic light at East Jefferson Avenue. Cross Jefferson onto Douglas MacArthur Bridge.

6.2 Veer to right off bridge and again at Belle Isle welcome sign, onto Sunset Drive.

6.6 Parking lot on right.

From Fountain Drive, you'll ride down Central Avenue, which bisects the island. If you didn't before, turn right on Inselruhe to visit the conservatory and aquarium. Beyond the "dry" slide, there's the Belle Isle Zoo, now closed due to city budget constraints. A nice wooded section takes you back out to the golf course, then cuts back inland again before intersecting Riverbank Road at the water slide. Return to the parking lot through the traffic circle, unless you choose to do the extra 6.6 miles into downtown Detroit and Greektown. To do that, stay in the right lane as you approach the circle, which will split off into the Douglas MacArthur Bridge, a half-mile span over the Detroit River.

After crossing busy Jefferson Avenue, you'll make a left turn on Lafayette Boulevard and ride a straight shot into Greektown. Two lanes at first, Lafayette becomes a divided six-lane road with a grassy median down the middle for the last mile and a half. The outer lane in which you'll ride is also a parking lane, so you'll be separated from moving traffic, but watch for opening doors. When you get to the Greektown Casino, at Lafayette and Beaubien Street, I recommend locking your bike to a bench or street sign and exploring the neighborhood on foot. There are lots of sidewalk cafes, shops, and a Detroit People Mover station. For 50 cents you can ride the 3-mile elevated loop around the downtown area. The station entrance is actually in the west entrance to the Greektown Casino, above Beaubien. The stations, which all feature public art, are one of the coolest parts of the People Mover, and the Greektown station is one of the best.

After you've had your fill of feta and saganaki, return to Belle Isle the way you came, going out of the traffic circle at the first opportunity to return to the parking lot.

LOCAL INFORMATION

♦ Detroit Metro Convention and Visitors Bureau; (800) DETROIT; www.visit detroit.com.
♦ www.detroit.com (Web site unaffiliated with the city but a useful guide, especially to hotels).
♦ Belle Isle Park; (313) 852–4075.

LOCAL EVENTS/ATTRACTIONS

♦ Monroe Street, 1 block north of Lafayette Boulevard, is the hub of the Greektown shopping and entertainment district. For information call the Greektown Merchants Association at (877) GREEKTOWN.
♦ Charles H. Wright Museum of African-American History: As the nation's largest city with a black majority population, Detroit has played a key role in this history and is a fitting host. Closed Mondays and Tuesdays. 315 East Warren Avenue, Detroit; (313) 494–5800; www.maah-detroit.org.
♦ Eastern Market, the nation's oldest and largest outdoor market, has been running since 1841. Flower Day, the Saturday before Memorial Day, is a popular annual event. Open Monday to Saturday. Located at 2934 Russell Street, between Mack and Gratiot Avenues. (313) 833–1560; www.easternmarket.org.
♦ Take a self-guided tour of a Pewabic Pottery, working, century-old studio and a National Historic Landmark. On Jefferson Avenue north of Belle Isle. (313) 822–0954; www.pewabic.com.

RESTAURANTS

♦ The Mini Restaurant, 475 University West, Windsor; (519) 254–2221. Add a little international flavor to your trip. Located across the Detroit River in Windsor, Ontario, the Mini (and it really is) specializes in Vietnamese cuisine.
♦ Xochimilco Restaurant, 3409 Bagley, Detroit; (313) 843–0179. In Mexicantown, near the Ambassador Bridge.
♦ In Greektown, try any of the following, all on Monroe Street: Pegasus Taverna, Cyprus Taverna, Laikon Cafe, New Hellas Cafe, New Parthenon.
♦ The Whitney, 4421 Woodward Avenue, Detroit; (313) 832–5700. Voted "best place for a special occasion" by the *Detroit Free Press*. You'll get a meal and surroundings equally elegant here. Pricey.

ACCOMMODATIONS

♦ Hotel Pontchartrain, 2 Washington Boulevard, Detroit; (313) 965–0200. The Pontch, as it's known locally, is located on the site of a French fort of the same name. Upscale prices.

♦ Omni Detroit Hotel Riverplace, 1000 Riverplace, Detroit; (313) 259–9500 or (800) 843–6664. On the Detroit River, very convenient to Belle Isle. Upscale prices.

♦ Courtyard by Marriott, Downtown Detroit, 333 East Jefferson Avenue, Detroit; (313) 222–7700. Connected to the Renaissance Center. Moderate prices.

RESTROOMS

♦ Mile 4.2: city beach and water slide (when water slide is open).
♦ Mile 4.7: Bath/Lunch pavilion.
♦ Mile 6.2: Casino building.

Grosse Pointe Ramble

The Pointes, as the five suburbs north of Detroit are known collectively, are old-money, exclusive residential communities. On Lake Shore Drive, the highlight of the Grosse Pointe Ramble, you'll ride by old homes built by barons of the auto and other industries. Stunning in terms of size and extravagance, they are outdone only by their view of Lake St. Clair. On this ride you'll get to enjoy that view, too. Though PRIVATE PROPERTY signs seem to be everywhere in the Pointes, there's a 3-mile stretch along Lakeshore where the view is free for the looking. The pavement is smooth, and a plethora of choices for after-ride refreshment await on the "Nautical Mile" in St. Clair Shores.

To many, the five Grosse Pointes—Shores, Farms, Park, Woods and city of—epitomize the demographic and economic divide between the suburbs of Detroit and the city itself. Indeed, driving north along Jefferson Avenue, it's impossible not to notice a difference once you cross Maryland Avenue, the border between Detroit and Grosse Pointe Park. Maryland is the southern limit of the Grosse Pointe Ramble, which will take you through all five of the Pointes. As you make the loop, you'll see that stratification exists within the Pointes, too. From your bike seat you can observe and appreciate those differences, from the charm of a front porch on a Grosse Pointe Park duplex to the estate lawns of a lakefront mansion in Grosse Pointe Shores.

The ride starts in St. Clair Shores but goes directly into Grosse Pointe Woods, the only one of the five without frontage on Lake St. Clair. You'll pass two country clubs, however, Lochmoor and the Country Club of Detroit. You'll briefly ride on Lake Shore Drive in order to get around the latter, before a long stretch on Kercheval Avenue, highlighted by two pleasant shopping neighborhoods. First is the Hill, about 6 miles into the ride. In terms of its slope, it's not really a hill at all. On the 2-block strip you'll find Freezing Point Ice Cream and Candy Shop at 92 Kercheval and the Coffee Grinder at 98 Kercheval. You probably won't have worked up an appetite for a full meal yet, but check out the menus at Lucy's on the Hill, a moderately priced tavern/restaurant whose menu mixes surprises with the standard, as well as the Hill, a pricier establishment specializing seafood and chops.

Less than a mile down Kercheval, you'll enter the Village, a larger shopping district, with chain as well as local stores and restaurants. You'll find stiff competition for your coffee/bagel dollar in the Village, with Einstein Brothers, Caribou Coffee, Starbucks, Brueggers, and Panera Bread Co. all located along Kercheval Avenue, plus a cafe inside Borders Books. Kressbach Place, a small plaza with a fountain, benches, and flowers, is a nice place to sit at the corner of St. Clair and Kercheval.

The shopping neighborhoods grow progressively funkier as you ride south on Kercheval, getting closer to Detroit. The neighborhood at Maryland and Kercheval Avenue, with places like Buscemi's Pizza, Janet's Lunch, and M'Dears

Lake St. Clair makes for a beautiful view on the Grosse Pointe Ramble. Courtesy of Michael O. Henderson

Creole Cooking, has quite a different vibe than the more reserved neighborhoods farther north. You'll turn east on Maryland, riding through Grosse Pointe Park, then head back north along Jefferson Avenue, which later becomes Lake Shore Drive.

There's no shoulder along Lake Shore, but cyclists are common around here, and the vehicle speed limit is a relatively low 35 miles per hour. Still, some experience riding in traffic is recommended before riding this route. You'll pass the lakefront home of Edsel and Eleanor Ford, the only son of Henry Ford and his wife, north of the Grosse Pointe Yacht Club.

You'll return to the parking area and continue north for another mile and a half in order to ride the Nautical Mile. Six marinas between Nine and Ten Mile Roads, plus many restaurants and entertainment establishments, make this a great place to end the ride.

Whichever restaurant you patronize, use the facilities while you're there, as there are no public restrooms along the route. All of the parks along the lake are for residents of the Pointes only, and they do check at the entrances. The Grosse Pointe Yacht Club is also private. The Grosse Pointe War Memorial, at about mile 11, hosts special events that are open to the public, but it is not available as a public pit stop.

LOCAL INFORMATION

♦ www.grossepointe.com; (313) 884–0106.

LOCAL EVENTS/ATTRACTIONS

♦ Edsel and Eleanor Ford House: Tour the lakefront home of Henry Ford's son. Tours of house and grounds are available daily except Mondays. Tickets $6.00 for adults. 1100 Lake Shore Drive, Grosse Pointe Shores; (313) 884–4222; www.fordhouse.org.

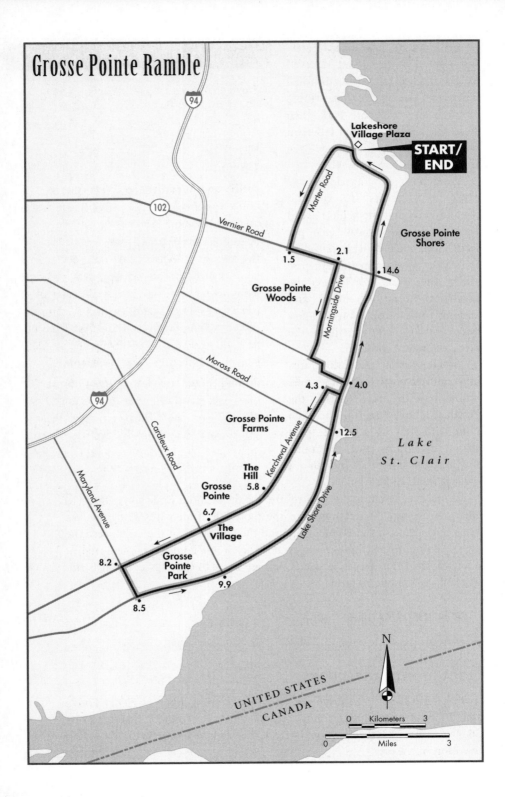

Grosse Pointe Ramble

94

102

Vernier Road

Marter Road

Lakeshore Village Plaza

START/ END

Grosse Pointe Shores

1.5   2.1   •14.6

Grosse Pointe Woods

Morningside Drive

Moross Road

4.3• •4.0

Grosse Pointe Farms

Kercheval Avenue

•12.5

Lake St. Clair

94

Cadieux Road

The Hill
5.8•

Grosse Pointe
6.7•

Maryland Avenue

The Village

8.2•

Grosse Pointe Park

9.9•

Lake Shore Drive

8.5

N

UNITED STATES

CANADA

0 Kilometers 3

0 Miles 3

0.0 From shopping plaza, turn right onto Marter Road.

1.5 Traffic light. Turn left on Vernier Road.

2.1 Turn right on Morningside Drive, after Grosse Pointe North High School.

2.5 Four-way stop. Turn right, then make a quick left through intersection.

2.6 Veer left at next intersection, cross Lochmoor Boulevard, staying on Morningside.

3.4 Stop sign. Turn left on Cook.

3.5 Stop sign. Turn right on Ballantyne.

4.0 Stop sign. Turn right on Lake Shore Drive.

4.1 Turn right on Provencal.

4.3 Flashing light. Turn left onto Kercheval Avenue.

5.8 Traffic light. Cross Muir Road and enter the Hill, a shopping area, which is not really a hill. Local shops and restaurants.

6.7 Traffic light at St. Clair. Enter the Village, a shopping area that is larger than the Hill. Chain as well as local establishments, including five coffee/bagel places.

8.2 Turn left at traffic light on Maryland Avenue. Another shopping neighborhood.

8.5 Turn left on Jefferson Avenue at traffic light.

10.8 Traffic light at Fisher. Continue straight. Grosse Pointe War Memorial on right.

11.2 Jefferson becomes Lake Shore Drive.

14.6 Traffic light at Vernier Road. Continue straight. Grosse Pointe Yacht Club on right.

16.5 Traffic light on Marter Road. Turn left to return to Lakeshore Village parking lot, or continue straight into St. Clair Shores Nautical Mile district.

17.0 Traffic light. Cross Nine Mile Road and enter Nautical Mile district. Lake Shore Drive becomes Jefferson Avenue again.

17.5 Light at Fresard. Continue straight. Wahby Waterfront Park on the right.

18.0 Traffic light at Ten Mile Road. Go through light and make a "Michigan left," riding back south on Jefferson.

19.6 Turn right on Marter Road to return to Lakeshore Village parking lot.

♦ The Grosse Pointe War Memorial is a community center hosting programs and special events for veterans and the general community. Summer concert series features jazz and classical music Monday nights, pop music Wednesday nights. Doors open at 6:30 P.M., concerts begin at 8:00 P.M. Hosts annual "Battle of the Bands," once won by Bob Seger. 32 Lake Shore Drive, Grosse Pointe Farms; (313) 881–7511.

RESTAURANTS

♦ Fishbone's Rhythm Kitchen Café, 23722 Jefferson Avenue, St. Clair Shores; (586) 498–3000. Soul/Cajun/Creole food. One of three in Detroit area.

♦ Andiamo on the Water, 24026 Jefferson Avenue, St. Clair Shores; (586) 773–7770. On Lake St. Clair. Pricier.

♦ Steve's Back Room, 24935 Jefferson Avenue, St. Clair Shores; (586) 774–4545. Middle Eastern food. Though removed from the epicenter of the Detroit area's Middle Eastern community, here you'll find fatoush and babaganouj. Also a few American dishes.

♦ Lucy's on the Hill, 115 Kercheval Avenue, Grosse Pointe Farms; (313) 640–2020. Tavern/restaurant. More menu variety than you'd expect.

♦ The Hill, 123 Kercheval Avenue, Grosse Pointe Farms; (313) 886–8101. Seafood and chophouse. Pricey. Famous for its hill (pile) of perch.

ACCOMMODATIONS

Hotels are scarce in the immediate area.

♦ Detroit Days Inn, 3250 East Jefferson Avenue, Detroit; (313) 568–2000. South of start.

♦ Red Roof Inn, 31800 Little Mack Road, Roseville; (586) 296–0310. North of start.

RESTROOMS

♦ There are no public restrooms, only those at restaurants along the route.

St. Clair River Cruise

O n the St. Clair River Cruise, you'll ride along waterfront, to historical sites, through farmland and coast hills—all in less than 50 miles. The varied scenery, terrain, and range of things to do in Port Huron make the St. Clair River Cruise appealing for lots of different riders. Groups with riders of varying ability can reconnoiter easily in Port Huron, Ruby, or Wadhams along the route. Depending on your taste, you can stroll shops, docks, or museums in Port Huron or take a break in one of the restaurants. The Blue Water Bridge, a double span connecting Port Huron with Sarnia, Ontario, is another highlight of the ride.

Using your left hand as a convenient map of Michigan, St. Clair and Port Huron are located at about the knuckle of your thumb. Despite this, the communities aren't considered part of the Thumb, the rural, halfway-up-north communities along Lake Huron north of Port Huron.

They're also beyond the reaches of the metro Detroit area to the south, though the industry along the banks of the St. Clair River is a fact in common with Detroit, and both gaze across at Canadian shores.

Like the communities it passes, this ride consists of many different parts that make it difficult to categorize. It's on the longer side for a cruise. On the other hand, there's a good-sized town to break it up and smaller places to rest on the second half. The terrain is slightly rolling at first, then flattens out, then turns into hills midride. However, this is one of those rare rides where you seem to get more downhill than uphill. There are waterfront and farmland, historical attractions, and modern fast-food restaurants.

In short, the St. Clair Cruise is best experienced. You'll leave from St. Clair High School and follow the course of the river—sometimes in sight of it, sometimes not—for the 10 miles up to Port Huron. The St. Clair is a key waterway within the Great Lakes system, connecting Lake Huron to Lake St. Clair, which in turn connects with the Detroit River and then Lakes Erie and Ontario. Weekends or weekdays, you're likely to see freighters moving all manner of goods out on the river.

Once in Port Huron, you'll pass through several distinct neighborhoods. Coming in from the south, you'll ride through a modest residential area, across from the industrial plants of Port Huron's eastern neighbor, Sarnia, Ontario.

After the drawbridge over the Black River comes the downtown area, which shows signs of both struggle (empty storefronts) and vitality, like the weekend of the Port Huron to Mackinac sailing race, when thousands throng downtown and the restaurants and bars on Quay and Huron Streets.

The third neighborhood is the north end of town, starting at the Blue Water Bridge area. Several historical attractions are clustered here, including the *Huron Lightship*. Assigned in 1935 to the Corsica Shoals, shallow waters 6 miles north of Port Huron that were the site of frequent groundings, the *Huron* was the last lightship on Great Lakes. She was retired in 1970.

Just down the Thomas Edison Parkway from the lightship is the Thomas Edison Depot and Museum, a tribute to the inventor who spent his boyhood in Port Huron before leaving to invent the electric light, the phonograph, and the motion picture.

Beyond the bridge is open Lake Huron, and prosperous homes fill the north side of town. You'll ride through the neighborhood on your way to Keewahdin Road, which you'll take west. First you'll encounter flat farm country, but that gives way to the forested Beards Hills region. When you look at a St. Clair County map, Beards Hills/Port Huron State Game Area stand out as

No helmets, but this statue along St. Clair's riverfront is an inspiring send-off.

the biggest chunk of green. It's a pretty stretch of 6 miles or so, from past the Dorsey House Restaurant through Ruby, including a beautiful, newly paved stretch of Abbotsford Road outside Ruby.

The last leg of the route, through Wadhams, requires riders to use the most caution. It's a two-lane road without a shoulder, and it can get busy, especially at mileage points 33.7, just outside the community of Wadhams, and about 43, where there are on- and off-ramps to major freeways. You'll be on Wadhams Road for 10 miles and will turn back to St. Clair on Rattle Run Road.

LOCAL INFORMATION

♦ Blue Water Area Convention and Visitors Bureau; (800) 852–4242; www.bluewater.org.
♦ Main Street Port Huron Visitors' Center, 223 Huron Avenue, Port Huron; (888) 305–8696; www.mainstreetph.com.
♦ St. Clair Chamber of Commerce; (810) 329–2962.

LOCAL EVENTS/ATTRACTIONS

♦ Even if you don't sail, you can partake in the party the weekend of the Port Huron–to–Mackinac Island Race, held the second or third weekend in July. (888) 305–8696.

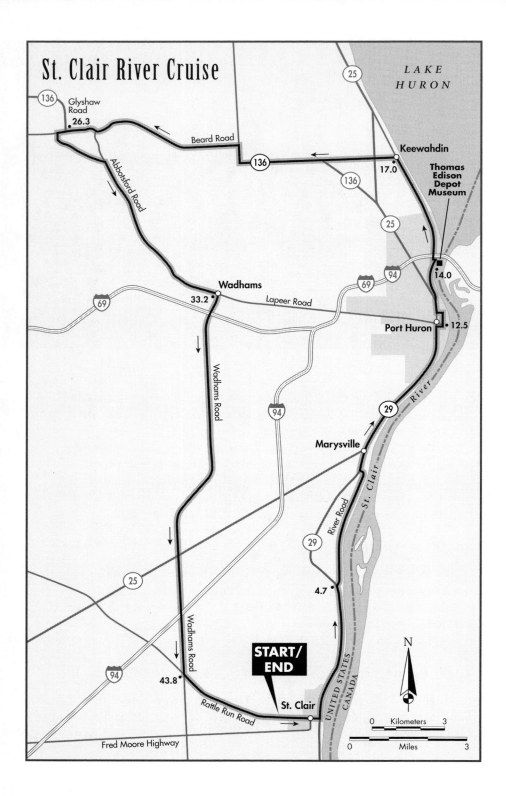

St. Clair River Cruise

LAKE HURON

136 Glyshaw Road
● 26.3

Beard Road

136

Keewahdin

136

Thomas Edison Depot Museum

25

Abbotsford Road

69

Wadhams
33.2 ●

Lapeer Road

69

94

Port Huron
● 12.5

■ 14.0

94

River

29

Wadhams Road

94

Marysville

River Road

St. Clair River

25

29

4.7 ●

Wadhams Road

START/ END

43.8 ●

Rattle Run Road

St. Clair

UNITED STATES
CANADA

Fred Moore Highway

N

0   Kilometers   3

0   Miles   3

0.0 From St. Clair High School, turn left onto Clinton Avenue.

1.3 Turn left at light onto Riverside Avenue.

2.4 Riverside narrows to two lanes. Shoulder begins.

4.7 Turn right on River Road.

5.0 Northbound lane narrows to a half lane for about a half mile. Vehicular traffic limited to local traffic.

7.1 Huron Boulevard. Restrooms. Marysville City Park ahead.

7.8 Railroad tracks, then stop sign. Turn right on Michigan Highway 29/Busha Highway.

8.5 Traffic light, followed by railroad tracks at an extreme angle. Use caution and cross perpendicular. Shoulder/parking lane begins.

9.5 Enter city of Port Huron. MI 29 becomes Military Street. Road becomes one-way.

12.4 Traffic light at Water Street, followed immediately by light on bridge over Black River.

12.5 Traffic light at Quay Street. Restaurants down Quay. Restrooms ahead at Port Huron Welcome Center, on the left.

12.6 Turn right at light on Grand River Avenue. Go through light at unmarked street (Michigan Street) and turn left at the next stop sign onto Fort Street.

12.9 Yield sign. Turn left on Glenwood Avenue.

13.0 Traffic light. Turn right onto Huron Avenue, and then make an immediate right to stay on Huron.

13.2 Stop sign for Lincoln Avenue. Veer to the left/ahead, staying on Huron. Small parking area on right, Blue Water Bridge ahead. You'll pass the Coast Guard moorings and go through Pine Grove Park. Portable toilet.

13.5 Stop sign. Turn right onto unnamed street, and follow it immediately around to the left, alongside the river. *Huron Lightship* at corner. Road becomes Thomas Edison Parkway.

14.0 Thomas Edison Depot Museum. Go under the bridge and turn left on State Street, before reaching the giant U.S. and Canadian flags ahead.

14.1 Turn right on Gratiot Avenue.

14.5 Traffic light at Garfield Street. Hank's Corner Store on the right, Palmer Park. Restrooms open in park administration building during weekday business hours. Continue straight.

15.4 Lakeside Park. Restrooms.

17.0 Traffic light at Keewahdin Road. Turn left.

19.0 Stop sign. Turn right on Michigan Highway 136 west and ride on shoulder.

(continued)

21.0 Follow curve in road *before* traffic light to stay on MI 136.

21.5 Turn left on Beard Road/MI 136.

24.2 Dorsey House Restaurant and Lounge. Curving downhill follow.

26.3 Continue straight on Beard Road, watching as you cross against oncoming traffic, instead of following MI 136 to right. Pass sign for Glyshaw Road right away.

26.5 Turn left on Abbotsford Road. A 7 percent short downhill grade follows.

27.3 Yield sign. Follow road curve to right onto Brott.

27.8 Ruby General Store.

28.7 Pick up Abbottsford Road again, heading out of Ruby. Newly paved road.

32.1 Stop sign. T intersection. Turn left on unmarked road (Lapeer).

32.5 Enter Wadhams. Pizza joints, ice cream, fast food.

33.2 Turn right on Wadhams Road.

33.7 Light for freeway exit and on-ramps. Continue south on Wadhams.

34.0 Traffic light for freeway exit and on-ramps.

43.8 Flashing red light. Turn left on Rattle Run Road, following sign to St. Clair.

46.2 Rough pavement for 0.1 mile.

46.4 St. Clair High School.

♦ Farmers' markets are held in Port Huron on the 200 block of Huron Avenue/Main Street, from 8:00 A.M. to 2:00 P.M. Saturdays from May to October (810–985–8843) and in St. Clair at St. Clair Riverview Plaza, from 7:30 A.M. to 1:00 P.M. Wednesdays.

♦ Juried art fairs are held in late August in downtown Port Huron and on the last weekend in June at Riverview Plaza in St. Clair.

♦ The Thomas Edison Museum is dedicated to the father of American ingenuity, who spent his boyhood in Port Huron. Beneath Blue Water Bridge. (810) 982–0891; www.phmuseum.org.

RESTAURANTS

♦ Mike's Voyageur Sports Bar, 525 Riverside Avenue, St. Clair; (810) 329–3331. Riverview dining and bowling, too, on the river in St. Clair.

♦ Quay Street Brewing Company, 330 Quay Street, Port Huron; (810) 982–4100; www.quaybrew.com. House microbrews and standard pub menu plus a few unusual items, like New Orleans muffuletta sandwiches. Outdoor deck.

♦ The Pita Restaurant, 402 Quay Street, Port Huron; (810) 984–3122. Mediterranean cuisine.

ACCOMMODATIONS

♦ St. Clair Inn, 500 North Riverside Avenue, St. Clair; (810) 329–2222. Cozy and elegant Tudor-style inn on the St. Clair River, dating to 1925 and on the National Register of Historic Places. Dining on premises.

♦ Thomas Edison Inn, 500 Thomas Edison Parkway, Port Huron; (810) 984–8000. Dining on premises.

♦ Davidson House Bed and Breakfast, 1707 Military Street, Port Huron; (810) 987–3922; www.davidsonhouse.com. Historic Victorian home.

RESTROOMS

♦ Mile 7.1: Marysville City Park.

♦ Mile 12.5: Port Huron Welcome Center, 223 Main Street, just north of Quay Street.

♦ Mile 14.5: Port Huron Parks Department office in Palmer Park; open regular weekday business hours only.

♦ Mile 15.4: Lakeside Park.

♦ Mile 32.5: restaurants in Wadhams.

RIDES AT A GLANCE
(Listed in order of distance)

CHALLENGES

47.6 miles	Copper Harbor Challenge, ride 1
52.7 miles	Torch Lake Challenge, ride 9
54.5 miles	Oakland Lakes Challenge, ride 33
56.1 miles	White Lake Challenge, ride 19
60.6 miles	Three Oaks Challenge, ride 28
72.7 miles	Hell Challenge, ride 31

CLASSICS

62.0 miles	Keweenaw Classic, ride 2
75.4 miles	Tip of the Mitt Classic, ride 6
85.6 miles	Tour de Wayne and Washtenaw Classic, ride 34

COMBINED RIDES

36.8 miles **11 & 13. Leland Ramble & Leelanau South Ramble.** Start with Ride 13. At mile 22.2 continue straight on MI 204 instead of turning left onto County Road 643. Pick up Ride 11 directions at mile 9.0 and follow to end, then from the start to mile 9.0. Return to Ride 13 directions at mile 22.2.

63.6 miles **11 & 12. Leland Ramble & Leelanau North Cruise.** Start with Ride 12. Follow directions from start to mile 34.7, then stay on MI 204 instead of turning left onto County Road 643. Pick up Ride 11 directions at mile 9.0 and follow to end, then from the start to mile 9.0. Return to Ride 12 directions at mile 34.7.

71.2 miles **12 & 13. Leelanau North Cruise & Leelanau South Ramble.** These rides have the same starting point, so after you complete one ride, follow the directions for the second ride.

79.1 miles **25 & 26. Saugatuck Ramble & Southwest Shore Cruise.** Start with Ride 26 and follow Option B. At mile 27.3 turn left onto Butler Street. Pick up Ride 25 directions at mile 0.2. Follow Ride 25 to the finish. Return to Ride 26 directions at mile 27.5.

85.8 miles **11, 12, & 13. Leland Ramble, Leelanau North Cruise, & Leelanau South Ramble.** Start with Ride 12. Follow directions from start to mile 34.7, then stay on MI 204 instead of turning left onto County Road 643. Pick up Ride 11 directions at mile 9.0 and follow to the end, then from the start back to mile 9.0. Cross MI 204 to go to the boat launch and pick up Ride 13 directions at mile 0.4. Follow Ride 13 to the finish.

91 miles

1 & 2. Copper Harbor Challenge & Keweenaw Classic. Start with Ride 2. Follow directions to mile 33.4, then stay on MI–26 instead of turning onto Eagle Harbor Road. Follow Ride 1 directions from mile 33.3 to the end, then from the start to mile 22.6. Return to Ride 2 directions and follow from mile 41.3 to the end.

95.1 miles

32 & 34. Ann Arbor Ramble & Tour de Wayne and Washtenaw Classic. Start with Ride 34. Follow the directions to mile 57.1 then pick up Ride 32 directions at mile 8.2. Complete Ride 32 to the end, then from the start to mile 8.2. Return to Ride 34 directions at mile 57.7 and complete the ride.

127.6 miles

6 & 8. Tip of the Mitt Classic & Tunnel of Trees Cruise. Start with Ride 6. Follow directions to mile 54.9, then turn left onto Lakeshore instead of right. You will be at the farthest possible point on the sidetrip of Ride 8: Cross Village/Legs Inn. Pick up Ride 8 directions at mile 19.4 and follow to the end, then from the start to mile 19.4, continuing on to Cross Village. Return to Ride 6 directions at mile 54.9 and ride to the finish.

Appendix:
Selected Bicycling Organizations

League of Michigan Bicyclists
Statewide bicycling advocacy organization. Sponsors several multiday state tours each year. Contact information for more than forty local bike clubs available on its Web site. Publishes annual calendar of bicycling events statewide.

P.O. Box 16201
Lansing, MI 48901-6201
(888) MI–BIKES (in Michigan only)
(517) 334–9100
www.lmb.org

Three Oaks Spokes
Publishes a map of the Backroads Bikeways, twelve cycling routes in southwest Michigan.

P.O. Box 366
Three Oaks, MI 49128
(888) 877–2068
(616) 756–3361

Cherry Capital Cycling Club
Publishes a durable, weather-resistant bicycling map of Grand Traverse (northwest) region. Includes sixteen road tours from Mackinaw City to Benzie County. $6.00.

P.O. Box 1807
Traverse City, MI 49685-1807
(231) 941–BIKE (rideline and to leave messages)
http://cherry-capital.com/cccc (click on "Forms" to get order information for map.)

Ann Arbor Bicycle Touring Society
One of the few clubs that puts maps of its routes on its Web site.

P.O. Box 1585
Ann Arbor, MI 48106
(734) 913–9851
www.aabts.org (Click on "Maps.")

Michigander
Annual cross-state mountain bike trip using rail trails.

Rails to Trails Conservancy (Michigan field office)
416 South Cedar Street, Suite C
Lansing, MI 48912
(517) 485–6022
www.railtrails.org/field/michigan

Travel Michigan
Official state tourism office. On the Web site, click on "Outdoors" and then "Biking" for more information.

(888) 78–GREAT (888–784–7328)
www.travel.michigan.org

About the Author

Cari Noga is an award-winning newspaper reporter and veteran cyclist. She worked seasonally as a tour leader for Michigan Bicycle Touring and lives in Traverse City, Michigan, with her husband, Mike Henderson.